ARG Fraser
31st June 2010

Re-Humanising Shakespeare

For Katie Mousley, 1923–2006

Re-Humanising Shakespeare
Literary Humanism, Wisdom and Modernity

Andy Mousley

Edinburgh University Press

Edinburgh University Press Ltd
22 George Square, Edinburgh

Typeset in Sabon and Futura
by Servis Filmsetting Ltd, Manchester, and
printed and bound in Great Britain by
Biddles Ltd, King's Lynn, Norfolk

A CIP record for this book is available from the British Library

ISBN 978 0 7486 2318 1 (hardback)

Contents

Acknowledgements

I am grateful to De Montfort University, Leicester, for granting me research leave to complete this book. I would also like to thank Tom Olsen for his wise as well as witty comments on an entire draft, Jane Dowson and Martin Halliwell for their support and comments on individual chapters, Jane again for finding the cover image, Jackie Jones at Edinburgh University Press for her unswerving efficiency and sound advice, Dan because he is a good egg, Debbie for her proofreading, and Debbie and Dan both for their care of me. The book is dedicated to my mother.

Introduction: Literary Humanism, Wisdom and Modernity

Can Shakespeare help us with the question of how to live? If Philip Yancey's *What's So Amazing about Grace?* (1997) is at all representative of its type, then the answer from today's spiritual self-help genre is 'yes'. This is how Yancey concludes his exegesis of Jesus' parable of the unforgiving servant:

> God has granted us a terrible agency: by denying forgiveness to others, we are in effect determining them unworthy of God's forgiveness, and thus so are we. In some mysterious way, divine forgiveness depends on us.
>
> Shakespeare put it succinctly in *Merchant of Venice*: 'How shalt thou hope for mercy, rendering none?'[1]

It is to Shakespeare as sage that Yancey quite naturally turns here, on the assumption that great writers are 'great' on account of their eloquent encapsulation of durable truths. Turning to the world of professional literary criticism, it might be reasonable to suppose that the answer to my opening question is altogether otherwise. Surely the combined forces of scepticism, historicism and specialisation have put paid to the faith in the universally valid wisdom of sages? 'Criticism for the past two generations', writes Margreta de Grazia in 'The Ideology of Superfluous Things: *King Lear* as Period Piece' (1996), 'has tended to situate Shakespeare in history rather than assume his universality'.[2] Although de Grazia wrote this some time ago, universals are still distrusted, still equated with what Simon Barker in *New Casebooks: Shakespeare's Problem Plays* (2005) refers to as the 'traditional criticism' which 'modern theory' has superseded.[3] There is another story to tell, however, and one which does not come only from die-hard traditionalists.

Sages, Specialists and Sceptics

Taking his cue from *King Lear*, Terry Eagleton in *After Theory* (2003) himself dons the role of sage when he offers the following insights:

> To perceive accurately, we must feel; and to feel we need to free the body from the anaesthesia which too much property imposes on it. The rich are insulated from fellow feeling by an excess of property, whereas what impoverishes the bodies of the poor is too little of it. For the rich to repair their own sensory deprivation would be for them to feel for the privations of others. And the result of this would be a radical social change, not just a change of heart. In Shakespeare's imagination, communism and corporeality are closely allied.[4]

It is difficult to disentangle the voices of Eagleton and Shakespeare in this passage. Possibly this is for the reason given by Robert Watson in 'Teaching "Shakespeare": Theory versus Practice' (1988). 'Few modern Shakespeareans', writes Watson, 'would dare to say explicitly that our courses will teach "what Shakespeare had to say about life" ',[5] but, he continues, further on in his argument:

> Though we are not in a position to claim that what we want is what God or nature dictates (as racists, sexists, and imperialists like to claim), we have something almost as good: we can recommend a philosophy, a theology, or a mode of conduct under the pretext that Shakespeare recommends it.[6]

According to Watson, teachers of literature are closet Romantics whose belief in the 'enhanced enlightenment' that authors can bring complicates their unbelief in the 'author-as-oracle'.[7] This duality applies to Eagleton in *After Theory*, for there he writes not just as a historically minded, materialist critic setting himself the task of contextualising literature and recent literary/cultural theory, but as a sage in the tradition of what might be called 'sage discourse' within literary criticism. The discourse of the sage partly basks in the reflected glory of the perceived wisdom of literature itself, but also extrapolates its own wisdom (socialist wisdom, in the case of Eagleton). Sages in literary criticism are still around, and perhaps even on the increase, but they are still not as prominent or dominant as they were in the Arnold-influenced days of F. R. Leavis, for example. The idea that great books 'matter' because they have the capacity to guide and nurture may survive in the self-help genre, where texts from the past are unequivocally revered as repositories of wisdom, but it is somewhat surprising to witness the staunchly materialist and debunking critic that Eagleton has often been so openly avow the wisdom of old books. Eagleton in *After Theory* is joining up traditions within literary criticism – those represented by the historical critic and sceptic on the one hand and the sage on the other – which in recent years have gone their separate ways: either into ever more specialised historical work that supports through its distrust of universals a hermeneutics of suspicion or into ever more urgent attempts at the level of popular culture to provide existential meaning, sustenance and guidance for a seemingly beleaguered humanity.

This division is not new.[8] As recent histories of literary criticism before, during and after its establishment as an academic discipline have shown, tensions between generalists and specialists have always been intrinsic to it. It is to these histories that I want briefly to turn, beginning with Eagleton's own in *The Function of Criticism* (1984). Of the prehistory of academic literary criticism in the eighteenth century, Eagleton writes:

> Literary criticism as a whole, at this point, is not yet an autonomous specialist discourse, even though more technical forms of it exist; it is rather one sector of a general ethical humanism, indissociable from moral, cultural and religious reflection.[9]

However, even when literary criticism did emerge as an autonomous discourse in the last quarter of the nineteenth century in the form of a separate academic discipline, the tension between specialisation and a 'general ethical humanism' still persisted. As Gerald Graff in *Professing Literature* (1987) argues:

> The union of Arnoldian humanism and scientific research which gave birth to academic literary studies was never free from strain. Traditional humanists argued that the compartmentalization of literature in narrowly specialized 'fields' and the glorification of quantitative 'production' in research tended to undermine Arnold's ideal of a broad general culture and his view of literature as a coherent criticism of life.[10]

Graff focuses mainly on American criticism, while taking into account the influence of critics such as Arnold on the American scene. But the story told of Anglophone criticism in general by Chris Baldick in *Criticism and Literary Theory: 1890 to the Present* (1996) is similar. Arnold's influence is again evident in Baldick's account. 'Most of the twentieth century', he writes, 'could safely be said to belong to the "Arnoldian age" in English-language criticism'.[11] And the nature of his influence is similarly regarded. In F. R. Leavis and his followers, Arnold's continuing presence is evident in the construction of a ' "central" position' for literary criticism as 'the keeper of living human values, regarding all other intellectual pursuits and disciplines as merely fragmentary specialisms'.[12] Baldick's account also makes clear that Arnoldian humanism has not one but two antagonists: specialisation and 'modern scepticism'. The opposition of humanism to scepticism emerges in Baldick's discussion of I. A. Richards, the early twentieth-century Cambridge critic:

> Like Arnold, Richards believed that values needed to be safeguarded from the corrosions to which factual beliefs were exposed in the modern world, and that literature was a vitally important means of navigating through the rough seas of modern scepticism, in that it gave us values detached from positive beliefs.[13]

The conclusions that we can reach from these histories of the institution of literary criticism are threefold:[14] first, specialists and generalists have been long-standing bedfellows within literary criticism; second, they have not always been very companionable bedfellows; third, literary criticism and modern scepticism, sages and doubters, have also been antagonists. There is a connection to be drawn between doubting and specialising: both can have a similar, shrinking effect, for doubt can entail withdrawing from the large existential concerns and 'general ethical humanism' of the sage into the particularity of perspective that specialisation also entails. *Pace* Jean-François Lyotard, we might say that scepticism and specialisation both spawn 'little' rather than 'big' narratives such as the sage tends to generate about the human condition and human well-being.[15]

I want, now, to update and then backdate the tensions between the critic-as-sage and the critic-as-sceptic, in order to locate the kind of humanism in which I am mainly interested in a timescale which is broadly speaking (and as Baldick's reference to 'modern scepticism' implies) that of modernity itself. The most recent manifestation of scepticism within literary studies is arguably historicism, the several differences between which will be discussed in detail in Chapter 4. But for the moment I shall homogenise all forms of historicism and say that it is a form of scepticism on the basis that, as the earlier quotation from de Grazia indicates, contemporary cultural historians tend to distrust universals. In the place of identification and recognition, they therefore put distance, doubt and detachment. Instead of asking us, as does Eagleton in his role as sage, to recognise such existential 'truths' as 'To perceive accurately, we must feel', we are encouraged through historicism's appeal to historical and cultural difference to suspect the existence of existential truths. Backdating this current manifestation of 'modern scepticism' to at least the Renaissance, we could say that the critical detachment which present-day historicism involves can be taken as an instance of the disenchantment, disengagement and detraditionalisation which are central to the accounts of modernity given by such thinkers as Max Weber, Theodor Adorno and Max Horkheimer, Jürgen Habermas, and more recently Charles Taylor.[16] To anticipate a subsequent phase of my argument, in

Sources of the Self (1989) Taylor suggests that the disengagement entailed by various forms of rationality from Descartes to the present day 'demands that we stop simply living in the body or within our traditions or habits and, by making them objects for us, subject them to radical scrutiny and remaking'.[17] Taylor's account is comparable with Weber's disenchantment thesis and Habermas's notion of rationalised lifeworlds (discussed below), for these are both variations on the idea that modernity involves disengagement from the perceived immediacy of 'worldviews'. Applied to literature, disengagement would involve jettisoning an immediate engagement with the texts of literary wise men and women in the name of a 'cooler', more critical approach, orientated towards the historicisation of such concepts as 'literariness' and 'humanity', or such institutions as literary criticism. In each case, immediate involvement is substituted for critical detachment.

The accounts given by Eagleton, Graff and Baldick of the history of literary criticism are both fascinating and illuminating, but because their subject matter is literature as viewed by 'humanist' critics, many of whom are obviously enchanted by literature's existential wisdom and depth, I find myself naively wondering whether literature enchants them in any comparable way. Eagleton's *Lear*-inspired aperçu from his later book *After Theory* – 'To perceive accurately we must feel' – suggests that the 'moral seriousness' of the sage is always liable to resurface because, as the histories of criticism show, it is intrinsic to the very discipline. If, as John Joughin suggests in *Philosophical Shakespeares* (2003), 'disenchantment only ever serves to usher in new forms of re-enchantment as its necessary accomplice',[18] then literary criticism has been especially susceptible to this process, by virtue of the fact that literature has often been perceived as less of a disengaged 'object' of analysis than as a source of human engagement and enrichment which supplies a counter-experience to objectification and instrumentalisation. As Horkheimer and Adorno put it in *Dialectic of Enlightenment* (1944): 'The work of art still has something in common with enchantment: it posits its own, self-enclosed area, which is withdrawn from the context of profane existence, and in which special laws apply'.[19]

Eagleton and Watson are not isolated examples of the resurgence of sage discourse within literary criticism. Drawing on 'poststructuralist ethics and the proliferation of new historicist work in early modern studies', Ewan Fernie's *Shame in Shakespeare* (2002) also sounds at times like a self-help manual in its use of traditionally revered books as sources of quasi-folkloristic wisdom. Described as one of the 'most intense and painful of our human passions', shame according to Fernie can nevertheless lead 'to a better and more fulfilling life' – it can be a 'spiritual opportunity' – and it is Shakespeare who reveals to us this redemptive possibility.[20] The emphasis on 'personal growth' is not at the expense of historical perspective – the first three chapters of the book are entitled 'Shame before Shakespeare', 'Shame in the Renaissance' and 'Shame in Shakespeare' – but historical issues are treated as though they are inseparable from existential ones. Their inseparability seems to me to be of paramount importance, for if history were to be totally deprived of a 'human interest' element, then why should it matter to us? Paul Hamilton in *Historicism* (1996) comments that for the eighteenth-century philosophers Giambattista Vico and J. G. Herder, history 'had to be understood as something we are actively engaged in, like purposeful living, not external to, like the phenomena rationalized by scientific investigation'.[21] A form of historicism from which appeals to the human had been totally expunged would be in danger of turning history into just such an externalised, alienated object, voided of any existential significance. Dehumanised history, history denied any kind of human face and scale, would cease to hold any significance for who we are. I shall further explore the relationship between the historical and the human in Chapter 4.

Fernie and Eagleton not only integrate existential with historical insights, but emotion with intellect. Fernie's appeal to the 'better and more fulfilling life' to which Shakespeare's understanding of shame can lead addresses us as human beings with emotional lives rather than as disembodied minds. Through such (occasional) appeals, Fernie asks us to engage with shame on a personal as well as intellectual level. Shakespeare himself, it is implied, appeals to us in this holistic way. Literature, according to this kind of 'whole-person engagement', as Valentine Cunningham puts it in *Reading after Theory* (2002), either recombines human faculties that have been split apart, or restores to health faculties that have been diminished as a result of the prioritising of other faculties.[22] Thus when literary critics are in danger of becoming too 'coldly' sceptical, by putting texts in their ideological and historical places or by subjecting the literary to deconstructive analysis, literary critical sages will often come to the rescue of faculties, such as the emotions, that literature is also seen as nurturing. A literary education, in short, is seen as being an education of the whole person – heart, soul and intellect – rather than an education of one or another disconnected part of a person. 'Being able', writes Robert Eaglestone in 'Critical Knowledge, Scientific Knowledge and the Truth of Literature' (2003), to 'taxonomise Shakespeare's prosody or discuss his historical context is not the same as being moved by his plays'. While Eaglestone distances himself from the evangelical view of the government-commissioned

Newbolt Report on the teaching of English of 1921, that 'literature is not just a subject for academic study, but one of the chief temples of the Human Spirit', he nevertheless takes seriously the notion that literature is more than an object of dispassionate professional or antiquarian enquiry.[23]

Arguments about literature's ability to restore human beings to wholeness have taken different forms. It is not only that emotional engagement balances critical disengagement, but that, depending on the critic, literary education is seen as an antidote to instrumentalism, technology, capitalism and/or organised culture, or it is perceived as straddling such otherwise deepening rifts as those between professionalism and amateurism, the specialised and the non-specialised, intellectualism and anti-intellectualism, work and play, the particular and the general, rationality and sensibility. For example, in *Defending Literature in Early Modern England* (2000) Robert Matz, using sixteenth-century poetics as his model, concludes by suggesting that a vision of utopian reconciliation between work and play, labour and pleasure, is 'what most nearly concerns us when we defend literary study for ourselves and our students' against the 'drive to make higher education more "productive" '.[24] In a similar-but-different vein, Thomas Docherty in 'Aesthetic Education and the Demise of Experience' (2003) sees aesthetic education as an antidote to the current skills-based model of education which in merely preparing 'the individual for the taking of her or his place in an uncritical workforce' exemplifies 'the instrumentalism of a reason that has been abstracted from our personal being or development'.[25] However, whereas for Matz it is the idea of non-alienated labour that literature saves from oblivion, for Docherty 'experience' is the category redeemed by the aesthetic. Experience, which is associated amongst other things by Docherty with profundity and depth, is seen as countering the unbearable postmodern lightness of being whereby everything is sampled but nothing is properly engaged:

> Things may 'happen', but they no longer acquire the *authority* of experience . . . This is akin to the situation in which we suspect that 'modern man' may spend the day reading books, hearing music, seeing pictures; but that it is all so vacuous, productive either of ignorance or of trite rehearsals of orthodox 'criticisms'. This is one direct consequence of the age of 'information': the information/aesthetic overload allows no time to engage properly with any of it.[26]

The pronouncements of Docherty and some of the other critics discussed in this Introduction, such as Eagleton, Fernie, Matz and Eaglestone, suggest that defences of the human against its diminution or degradation are once again making their presence felt in literary studies.

Such pronouncements challenge the axiomatic wisdom of sceptically inclined historicisms that the universality upon which such appeals often rest is, at best, 'wishful thinking' based on the assumption that our own 'historically limited experience represents a transhistorical truth of some kind', and, at worst, an expression of western colonial arrogance.[27] The accusation of arrogance, however, can be overturned by suggesting that universalism can just as often be an attempt to place some kind of *limit* on the human, a limit which counteracts the hubristic late capitalist belief in the infinite plasticity of human beings and their infinitely mouldable and remouldable desires. The further problem with anti-universalism is that it has discredited the language of human feeling and engagement which we might want to use to describe the experience of literature.[28] Some literary critics and theorists, however, are currently breathing new life into this language and returning to the notion that literature can act as an antidote to dehumanisation, alienation and instrumentalism and help us to lead a 'better and more fulfilling life', to recall Fernie's phrase. The name I give to the resurgence of sage discourse in literary criticism and theory is 'literary humanism'. In the sections which follow, I shall spell out what I mean by literary humanism, differentiate literary humanism from the humanism that anti-humanists have often loved to hate, and make connections between literary humanism and Renaissance humanism.

Literary Humanism

At the heart of literary humanism is the question: 'how to live'. The phrase is used by Matthew Arnold himself, in connection with his claim that poetry 'is at bottom a criticism of life; that the greatness of a poet lies in his powerful and beautiful application of ideas to life, – to the question: How to live'.[29] The phrase as used here by Arnold is nothing if not light and airy, so, extrapolating from the work of the 'modern Arnoldians' discussed earlier and preparing the phrase for the work I want it to perform in this book, I shall to try to weigh it down a little.

Of course, the question is a long-standing one and certainly not restricted to 'literature' as we have come to know it. It is central to the moral and political philosophy of classical writers, such as Aristotle, and central also, therefore, to the humanists of the Renaissance.[30] But it is the 'special' relevance of the question to literature and literary criticism upon which I want to focus. This is not to say that there is no significant overlap between the way in which the question is addressed within different discourses, but only to try to specify its relevance to 'literary humanism'.

First, the phrase 'how to live' has an obvious ethical orientation (how we *should* live). Ethics, including the turn or return in recent years of literary criticism to ethics, will be the particular focus of Chapter 5 (on *Macbeth*), but insofar as the entire book (but especially Part II) is preoccupied, as Shakespeare himself is, with the question of 'how to live', ethical concerns are central.

The *way* in which ethical concerns are omnipresent in Shakespeare leads to the second point, namely, that the phrase 'how to live' has a strong practical component. The kind of ethics which is relevant to literature and literary humanism is therefore a practical ethics. Practical ethics can generate two kinds of book: a simplified 'how-to' book (popular in the Renaissance, as now), offering unequivocal *sententiae*, such as Yancey gleans from *The Merchant of Venice* – 'How shalt thou hope for mercy, rendering none?' – or a more complex, because 'literary', version of the same. The complexity is due to literature's impulsion towards what has been variously referred to (though not always in direct reference to literature and not always sympathetically) as 'true lively knowledge' (Philip Sidney),[31] 'realization' (F. R. Leavis),[32] 'concreteness' (Leavis),[33] 'subjective experience' (Adorno),[34] 'sensuous empiricism' (Eagleton),[35] 'the texture of lived experience' (Eagleton),[36] 'embeddedness' (Lars Engle),[37] the 'un-nailable fluidity of experience' (Jane Adamson).[38] These phrases are variations on the notion that literature overflows with 'life' in all its concrete particularity and diversity, thereby making the question of 'how to live' a difficult and complex one. For some – for the Eagleton of *Criticism and Ideology* (1976), for example – the mimetic ability of literature is an illusion: 'literature appropriates the real as it is given in ideological forms, but does so in a way which produces an illusion of the spontaneous, unmediatedly real'.[39] For others, however, such as Leavis in *Education and the University* (1943), literature, epitomised by Shakespeare, actually captures the richly diverse reality of human life: the genius of Shakespeare, writes Leavis, is 'awe-inspiring' because of the 'inwardness and completeness of its humanity'.[40]

Stephen Toulmin in *Cosmopolis* (1990) lies somewhere between these historical (Eagleton) and ahistorical (Leavis) perspectives.[41] His argument is also important because it takes us closer to *Renaissance* humanism. For Toulmin, diversity appears to have always existed, but it has not always been considered significant:

> In modern times, novelists and poets find their grist in the very diversity of human affairs; but, for medieval scholars, this variety had little significance. Human beings were sinful and fallible in ways that later readers found fascinating; but medieval clerics and teachers saw these failings as making humans *less*, not *more*, interesting to write about.[42]

Toulmin traces the origins of literary interest in diversity and complexity to the recovery by Renaissance humanists of a fuller range of classical texts (including poetry and drama) than was available to medieval scholars.[43] Shakespeare can be seen as the beneficiary of this, but transforms what he receives into the rich, densely textured mimesis of human life so admired by the likes of Leavis, but treated with historicist suspicion by more sceptically inclined critics.

My own approach to this particular issue will be to talk about Shakespeare's inordinate ability to intensify the 'existential significance' of otherwise abstract ideas and precepts through human embodiment. Ideas are made to 'live' because they are incarnated in the sensate lives of entities we recognise as human beings. To give an example which I will revisit in Chapter 1: Hamlet's intuition in the last act of the play that there is a 'divinity that shapes our ends' is not just an abstract piece of religious doctrine but is embodied in Hamlet as an emerging attribute of character which eases his restlessness and agitation.[44] Where a fully secularised, anti-religious humanism might claim that human beings can only realise themselves independently of a religious framework, Shakespeare, by intensifying the existential significance of religion, gives us cause to wonder whether the secular self is a freedom or restriction. He gives us cause to question which way of living might be a more or less authentic expression of what it is to be human. By being so adept at embodiment, at putting flesh on the bones of ideas, Shakespeare presents us with vividly 'realised' (to use a Leavisite term) forms of life, ways of living. The conflicts between these forms of life create complexity. The question of 'how to live' is itself therefore a complex question. However, I shall argue in the case of Shakespeare that the complexity is not so great as to undermine totally the practical ethics which is also the goal of literary humanism. Kent Cartwright in *Theatre and Humanism* (1999) argues that sixteenth-century humanist drama 'derives productive tension from its mutual commitments to an enriched sense of human experience and to the possibility of knowable truths'.[45] In subsequent chapters, embodiment will be considered as the source of such 'knowable truths'. Embodiment is in other words not only a means to the end of lending existential substance to ideas and precepts, but is meaningful in itself in connection to the issue of how to live: human bodies are vulnerable and from this banal fact, certain conclusions follow.

Third, the 'how to live' of literary humanism involves ideas of authenticity and what it means to be fully or authentically human, as opposed to dehumanised. The concept of authenticity has often been associated with the attempt by twentieth-century German and French existentialist philosophers to combat 'the meaninglessness of modern technological civilization', as Paul Tillich put it in his essay on 'Existential Philosophy' of 1944.[46] Although it is a concept which has been subjected to harsh criticism, not least by Adorno in *The Jargon of Authenticity* (1964),[47] it is the necessary and important accomplice of literary humanism and can help to reorient literary criticism towards the question of what it might be to flourish as a human being and live a 'better and more fulfilling life', to recall Fernie's phrase once more. Fernie's appeal is not untypical, for old and new literary humanists, from Arnold to Docherty, Eagleton, Eaglestone, Fernie, Matz and Watson, look to literature for images of authentic human fulfilment or promise. The search for authenticity, however, should not rule out the need to acknowledge our *in*authenticity. This is the 'lesson' of Shakespearean comedy which I shall examine in more detail in Chapters 7 and 8.

Fourth, and closely connected to the previous point, to be able to contemplate living a 'fully human' life presupposes some concept of human nature. We must have some idea of what human nature is in order to judge when we have become alienated from it. This and the previous point about authenticity are minefields, because of the pervasive postmodern suspicion of essentialism. However, although I have used the word 'resurgence' to describe the kind of humanism which has returned to literary studies, in some quarters the question of how to live and the essentialist notions of authenticity which accompany it have never entirely vanished. In the various forms of overtly political criticism, such as feminism, Marxism, post-colonialism and gender studies, which have been influential within literary studies since the 1970s, ideas of authenticity and ethics have frequently been central. They are present, for example, in the hope of Marxists that class exploitation and the commodification of human life might one day end. They are also implicated in post-colonialism's critique of dehumanising ideologies of race, even when or especially when such ideologies are perpetrated in the name of humanity. And they are also evident in the feminist commitment to terminate the subjugation of women by men. Indeed, according to Andrew Hadfield, Dominic Rainsford and Tim Woods in *The Ethics in Literature* (1999), feminism has 'held the ethical high ground' during the 'vitriolic arguments between Marxists and poststructuralists'. They support this by suggesting that:

> The notion that women are more moral than men has been around for decades, based upon such patriarchal narratives of moral fantasy as an 'Angel in the House', or the 'Earth-Mother'. Nevertheless, much feminist argument continues to present the willingness to nurture and a ready capacity for emotional involvement as being essential to a humane moral stance in a world of injustice and alienation.[48]

Although many political critics and theorists since the 1970s have vociferously eschewed essentialist forms of thinking, on the basis that they naturalise what is unnatural and therefore changeable, they nevertheless implicitly share the common view that human beings ought not to be degraded or oppressed. They have, in other words, a concept of what a human being is and the conditions under which he or she might flourish or perish. Of course, the humanism which these forms of political criticism either imply or explicitly avow do not exclusively derive from literary criticism. However, insofar as literature has been regarded by literary humanists as a form of cultural criticism or 'criticism of life', to use Arnold's phrase, there is a natural alliance between the perceived counter-cultural power of literature and oppositional politics. This is not to say that literature has been the unalloyed friend of political criticism, for literature has often been viewed by political critics as complicit in oppressive ideologies of class, race and gender. However, it has also been the quasi-Romantic inspiration for imagining the unrealised possibilities of life thwarted by such ideologies. There are veins of political thought and cultural criticism, from Adorno to Kiernan Ryan in the case of Marxism, for example, which have regarded literature as a source of redemption, enrichment and utopian hope.[49] The other main 'tracks' of literary criticism – the specialist and sceptical tracks – may have at times submerged the 'literary humanist' orientation of political criticism, but it has never been entirely drowned.

The above points suggest that the literary humanist question of how to live (and the notions of authenticity and human nature which attend it) need not be set starkly against the critical trends associated with 'Theory'. Although I inevitably have questions to ask of some of these trends, and most notably of the anti-humanist conceptions of humanism which since the 1970s have done damage to the concept of 'the human', I do not want to recreate the humanism in which I am interested as the outright enemy of post-1970s criticism and theory. As the above outline of political criticism suggests, some of the developments associated with 'Theory' themselves lean towards a literary humanism, but even where they have been more sceptical about the human than affirmative of it, this scepticism demands attention. From the long perspective of modernity taken in this book, post-1970s critical theory is not a historical anomaly but part of the tradition of modern scepticism that cannot be easily dismissed, for without properly considering sceptical standpoints, the case I want to make for literary humanism will be weaker. The problem with the anti-humanist and humanist orientations of literary criticism in recent years is that they can become self-perpetuating enclaves, the one (anti-humanism, discussed below) by caricaturing humanism as being naive and uncritical, the other (humanism) by failing to deal adequately with the sceptical challenge and by ignoring the albeit covert humanism of at least some of their antagonists. For all of their illuminating insights, two recent books reclaiming different versions of a humanist Shakespeare re-enact the usual hostilities: Harold Bloom's influential *Shakespeare: The Invention of the Human* (1998) and Robin Headlam Wells's *Shakespeare's Humanism* (2005). While both share with my book the aim of restoring the term 'human' to critical vocabulary, their virtually unmitigated antagonism towards what Headlam Wells calls 'postmodern Shakespeare criticism'[50] and Bloom refers to as 'Parisian "theory" '[51] puts them at odds with both this book's engagements with scepticism and its affirmation that Arnoldian principles never entirely evacuated at least some of the forms of criticism associated with the umbrella term 'Theory'.

Fifth, and finally, the question 'how to live' assumes an intimate connection between 'literature' and 'life', thereby resisting the tendencies within certain strands of formalism, modernism and theory to remove literature from any intimate contact with 'life'. Notwithstanding their differences, including the different reflections of human experience they find in Shakespeare, the relevance of literature to life is affirmed throughout the work of twentieth-century humanist Shakespearean critics: from the notion informing A. C. Bradley's *Shakespearean Tragedy* (1904) that Shakespeare's larger-than-life tragic heroes reflect 'the possibilities of human nature';[52] to the Christian universals attributed to Shakespeare by G. Wilson Knight in such books of his as *The Wheel of Fire* (1930) and *The Crown of Life* (1947);[53] to the claim made by H. C. Goddard in *The Meaning of Shakespeare* (1951) that *King Lear*, the 'culmination of Shakespeare', can be 'regarded from almost as many angles as life itself';[54] to the 'great perennial truths' to which Shakespeare according to L. C. Knights in 'Historical Scholarship and the Interpretation of Shakespeare' (1955) gives us access.[55]

While there are dangers in an approach to literary texts which fails to take a 'whole-text' perspective, ignoring issues of form, structure, genre and technique, there are equally shortcomings in approaches which entirely sever the connection between text and world, literature and life, thereby denying the mimetic power of stories and texts. In the chapters which follow, I shall be devoting some attention to the dynamics of form and genre, particularly in connection to Shakespearean comedy, but genre will itself be read in terms of the kinds of existential statement that it makes.

Humanism in the Eyes of Anti-Humanism

Literary humanism, so defined, has little to do with the humanism which was attacked on various grounds by anti-humanists in the 1970s and 1980s, but ever since then the humanism of the anti-humanists has been routinely invoked as though it encompassed the whole of the humanist tradition. In 1980, at the high point of the popularised version of critical theory, Catherine Belsey in her influential and provocative *Critical Practice* located the essence of humanism in its inflated assumption that ' "man" is the origin and source of meaning, of action, and of history'.[56] Within this version of humanism, the individual is considered sovereign, his or her subjectivity autonomous, and the human nature, of which the individual is simultaneously representative, transcendent of history, society and language. This understanding of humanism has passed into the twenty-first century. In *Culture after Humanism* (2001), for example, Iain Chambers succinctly characterises the humanism which has become dominant as 'an inherited sense of the world in which the human subject is considered sovereign, language the transparent medium of its agency, and truth the representation of its rationalism'.[57] It is a moot point as to whether this version of humanism achieved hegemony as a result of its promulgators or critics, but whichever is the case, it has been difficult, despite the emergence of various other descriptions of humanism, to topple the image of humanism as a conceited, bourgeois ideology founded upon an inflated concept of 'man'.[58] I shall subsequently refer to the humanism described by such anti-humanists as Belsey as 'mainstream humanism'. The title gives it its due, as an ideology which has been and still is influential both in its own right and as a result of its high profile within anti-humanist discourse, but it also signals the existence of other humanisms. The problem with not providing any kind of distinctive title or qualifier is that it makes humanism appear as a singular, uncontested phenomenon, the effect of which is to render suspect all references to 'the human' on the basis that they must belong to the same discredited ideology.[59]

To give a concrete example: there are different ways of articulating a belief in human nature. In mainstream humanism, this belief is often articulated in terms of transcendence. In Jonathan Dollimore's *Radical Tragedy* (1984), another text written at the high point of anti-humanist criticism and theory and recently republished (2004), there is a section entitled 'Origins of the Transcendent Subject'. In it, Dollimore describes mainstream humanism's essentialist belief in human nature as follows:

> In effect the individual is understood in terms of a pre-social essence, nature or identity and on that basis s/he is invested with a quasi-spiritual autonomy.

> The individual becomes the origin and focus of meaning – an individuated essence which precedes and – in idealist philosophy – transcends history and society.[60]

To conceive of the belief in an essential humanity in terms of quasi-religious transcendence accords very well with the hubris of mainstream humanism, for transcendence raises us above 'history and society' and bolsters a sense of our autonomy. However, it is possible to articulate a belief in human nature, not in terms of hubristic transcendence but more humbly, as an acceptance of human limits. The limits to what we can do or be also assume a concept of 'nature' but, unlike the model of transcendence, the notion of limits leads to a far less inflated sense of humanity. However, this way of thinking about human nature – in terms of limits – is difficult because the model of transcendence has tended to monopolise essentialist descriptions of nature.

It is also worth pointing out that the idea of transcendence also paradoxically pushes in an anti-essentialist direction. In the passage from Dollimore, the sovereign individual is free from determination by 'society and history' because of his or her 'pre-social essence, nature or identity'. However, the principle of freedom can be extended to mean freedom from *all* determination, which recognises no such thing as a pre-defining human essence. Rather than being 'pre-made', we make ourselves in the manner of the existentialism of Jean-Paul Sartre.[61] The uncritical assumption that we are free to do as we will was described by the French anthropologist Claude Lévi-Strauss in the French newspaper *Le Monde* in 1979 as 'unbridled humanism':

> What I have struggled against, and what I feel is very harmful, is the sort of unbridled humanism that has grown out of the Judeo-Christian tradition on the one hand, and on the other hand, closer to home, out of the Renaissance and out of Cartesianism, which makes man a master, an absolute lord of creation.[62]

Despite the fact that within mainstream humanism (as described by its antagonists), there can be significant differences of emphasis, with Lévi-Strauss's 'unbridled humanism' somewhat at odds with Dollimore's notion of a 'pre-social essence', what binds it together is its inflated view of humanity. Master, lord of creation, transcendence, sovereignty, ' "man" as the origin and source of meaning, of action, and of history', as Belsey puts it: these are some of the watchwords and catchphrases of mainstream humanism as described by anti-humanists. But how do these descriptions match the (historical) reality? For example, does this version of humanism capture the reality of Renaissance humanism?

Renaissance Humanism

Renaissance texts and Renaissance humanists can be and have been enlisted on behalf of mainstream humanism. Ever since Jacob Burckhardt's *The Civilization of the Renaissance in Italy* (1860) and the claim made there that in thirteenth-century Italy 'the ban laid upon human personality was dissolved',[63] the Renaissance has been located if not as the unprecedented source of individualism, then as a key agent in its development. Although individualism itself is not a singular phenomenon, it is not difficult to find examples of individualism in the Renaissance which correlate with mainstream humanism.[64] The spectacular individualism represented in Renaissance drama by figures such as Tamburlaine, Faustus, Iago, Edmund, the Macbeths and Coriolanus, to name but a few, is an individualism of autonomous subjects aspiring to the heights of absolute sovereignty and transcendence. Critics such as Belsey in another of her books from the 1980s, *The Subject of Tragedy* (1985), have therefore found little resistance to their backdating of mainstream humanism to the Renaissance. Autonomous subjectivity may be embryonic but the signs of its emergence are unmistakable: the 'precariously unified protagonist of Renaissance drama', writes Belsey, 'points forward to a fully-fledged humanism rather than backwards to the Middle Ages'.[65] Ronald Knowles in a more recent article, '*Hamlet* and Counter-Humanism' (1999), agrees with the views of critics such as Belsey, arguing that subjectivity 'is not an anachronism retroactively conferred by the culture of bourgeois individualism, the essentialism of liberal humanism'.[66] However, in Knowles's account, the liberal humanism as represented by Hamlet conflicts with Renaissance humanism, for according to Knowles, Hamlet's mournfully alienated subjectivity is at odds with the optimistic image of 'homo erectus' projected by the latter. 'Renaissance celebrations of man', writes Knowles, 'took up the Patristic echo of [the] Biblical theme of man's uniqueness in creation, for he was the only one of God's creatures to be created erect in order to worship the heavens'.[67]

Despite Knowles's distinction, prompted by *Hamlet*, between liberal and Renaissance models, they can be mutually reinforcing, so much so that the umbrella term 'humanism' is used to cover both. The value of Knowles's own use of the commonplace of 'homo erectus' to characterise Renaissance humanism is that (with the exception of *Hamlet*) it does successfully identify a 'strong' type of humanism in the Renaissance which encompasses the individualistic hubris of a Coriolanus as well as, say, the 'erected wit' referred to by Philip Sidney in *A Defence of Poetry* (1595) as the counterpart to 'our infected will'.[68]

And it also makes sense of Renaissance humanists' faith in a classically inspired education to restore humanity's status as 'homo erectus'. This is the narrative given by Thomas Wilson in *The Arte of Rhetorique* (1553):

> Man (in whom is poured the breath of life) was made at the first being an ever-liuing creature, unto the likenesse of God, endued with reason, and appointed Lorde ouer all other thinges liuing. But after the fall of our first Father, sinne so crept in [that] our knowledge was much darkened, and by corruption of this our flesh mans reason and entendement were both overwhelmed.[69]

Reason is overwhelmed but does not wither completely, as the 'gift of speech and reason' is what distinguishes humans from animals and confirms our special place in creation.[70] An education in the art of rhetoric is for Wilson, as for other Renaissance humanists, the means of reclaiming our divinity.

An iconic text for this version of Renaissance humanism is Pico della Mirandola's *Oration on the Dignity of Man* (*c.*1486). This text has often been used to represent Renaissance humanism as mainstream humanism on the basis that, as Andrew Hadfield puts it in *The English Renaissance* (2001), Pico sets out 'an appealing vision of freedom of movement, action and intellectual enquiry'.[71] This is the often-quoted passage from Pico:

> Therefore He [God] took up man, a work of indeterminate form; and placing him at the midpoint of the world, He spoke to him as follows:
>
> 'We have given to thee, Adam, no fixed seat, no form of thy very own, no gift peculiarly thine, that thou mayest feel as thine own, possess as thine own the seat, the form, the gifts which thou thyself shalt desire. A limited nature in other creatures is confined within the laws written down by Us. In conformity with thy free judgement, in whose hands I have placed thee, thou art confined by no bounds; and thou wilt fix limits of nature for thyself. I have placed thee at the center of the world, that from there thou mayest more conveniently look around and see whatsoever is in the world. Neither heavenly nor earthly, neither mortal nor immortal have We made thee. Thou, like a judge appointed for being honorable, art the molder and maker of thyself; thou mayest sculpt thyself into whatever shape thou dost prefer. Thou canst grow downward into the lower natures which are brutes. Thou canst again grow upward from thy soul's reason into the higher natures which are divine.'[72]

This appears to correspond with many of the attributes associated with what I have been referring to as mainstream humanism: sovereignty, unbridled freedom, autonomy and a magnified image of humanity. It has nevertheless been interpreted in quite different ways, depending on the type of humanist lens through which it is viewed.[73] For Dollimore, for example, who conceives of humanism only as an essentialist doctrine, Pico's anti-essentialist emphasis on indeterminacy ('We have given to thee, Adam, no fixed seat, no form of thy very own, no gift peculiarly thine') undermines the humanism often attributed to the *Oration*. Anti-essentialism for Dollimore cannot be described in the humanist terms used by Hadfield as 'freedom of movement, action and intellectual enquiry', because anti-essentialism for Dollimore is exclusively represented by social thinkers such as Gramsci, Machiavelli and Marx who are taken as repudiating the existence of an essential human nature impervious to society and social forces.[74] It follows for Dollimore, therefore, that because Pico's *Oration* is, for him, 'anti-essentialist', it subverts humanism: in other words, rather than exemplifying the 'humanist' freedom to choose one's own nature, Pico's protean, nature-less self lends itself to the view that identity is socially constructed.[75]

Headlam Wells in *Shakespeare's Humanism* disagrees with Dollimore about Pico. Although he still thinks about humanism in essentialist terms, these terms are different. For Dollimore, mainstream humanism is essentialist because it appeals to such idealist and transcendent categories as the human spirit. For Headlam Wells, Renaissance humanism is essentialist because it had a clear idea of humanity's essential duality, one aspect of which is again 'homo erectus', aspiring to heaven:

> far from being anti-essentialists, the great Renaissance humanists had a clearly worked-out sense of humankind's essentially divided nature: as a species we are capable of realising our human *telos* and aspiring to heaven, or of descending to the level of brutes.[76]

For Headlam Wells, Pico is therefore still a humanist.

For all of their differences, neither of these interpretations countenances the notion that humanism can be an anti-essentialism. However, as I suggested earlier, there is a natural progression from the idea that human beings are undetermined by society and history to the idea, which on one reading Pico seems to embrace, that they are *completely* undetermined and therefore free to take on any form whatsoever. I reiterate this aspect of mainstream humanism because it shows how it can – perhaps paradoxically – begin to operate without a concept of the human: since the human is understood to be infinite rather than finite, we can make and remake ourselves in any number of guises. However, whether mainstream humanism is couched in terms of transcendent essences (Wilson, Dollimore) or infinite possibility (Pico, Lévi-Strauss), the picture is in each case still familiar: the freedom and sovereignty of 'homo erectus'. Either we are free (of society and history) because we have transcendent essences or we are free (of everything) because we have none.

Mainstream humanism *can* therefore be read back into the Renaissance and Renaissance humanism. However, several notable scholars regard the educational aspirations of Renaissance humanists as having very little to do with the 'secular religion' that humanism subsequently became.[77] There are different versions of what is taken by such critics to be the anachronism of associating the concerns of Renaissance humanists with mainstream humanism, but what they share is a tendency to scale down Renaissance humanism from being a 'big idea' with an (inflated) philosophy of 'man' at its centre to a downsized and, in some historians' eyes, rather disparate enterprise. Paul O. Kristeller and John Herman Randall Jr, for example, in the introduction to *The Renaissance Philosophy of Man* (1948), write that 'during the Italian Renaissance the term "Humanism" denoted primarily a specific intellectual program and only incidentally suggested the more general set of values which have in recent times come to be called "humanistic" '.[78] Isabel Rivers in *Classical and Christian Ideas in English Renaissance Poetry* (1979) advances a similar particularity of perspective when she differentiates Renaissance humanism from the 'broad current meaning' of humanism as 'a view of life which displaces God and puts man at the centre', arguing that the 'expression "Renaissance humanism" needs to be used much more precisely if it is to have any value'.[79]

More recently, Tony Davies, in *Humanism* (1997), limits the scope of Renaissance humanism still further, by doubting its coherence as the intellectual programme that Kristeller and Randall describe it as, and by suggesting that such iconic Renaissance humanists as Pico may not have been all that interested in a 'generic entity called "Man" '. Noting that the title to Pico's discourse was 'not given to it by Pico himself', Davies writes:

> The phrase 'dignity of man' does not occur in the text itself, and it is striking how little interest Pico shows, after the opening allegorical flourish of God's apostrophe to Adam, in defining the properties of a generic entity called 'Man'. In Latin, in any case, the distinction between 'a man' (any), 'the man' (particular) and 'man' (universal) is grammatically indifferent, since the language lacks both definite and indefinite articles: the Basle title, *De hominis dignitate*, could as easily be translated 'On a man's worthiness'. The usual version, with its portentous evocation of a transcendent 'Man', belongs, like so much else of Renaissance 'humanism', not to the fifteenth century but to the nineteenth.[80]

This is a useful corrective against flattening the term 'humanism' and backdating it uncritically to the Renaissance. However, the problem with these appeals to more historically precise descriptions is that in resisting Renaissance humanism as a 'big idea' and questioning, as

Davies does, the interest of the likes of Pico in 'a generic entity called "Man" ', they scale down Renaissance humanism too much. A caricature of such scaling down would be to treat Renaissance humanists as primarily philologists in a narrow sense, which of course they were not. But the point of the caricature is this: while mainstream humanism is granted a monopoly on portentousness and issues relating to 'Man', other accounts of humanism that are contrasted with this are in danger of being too microcosmic. What characterises many Renaissance humanists (and perhaps Renaissance thinking more generally) is the ability to shuttle between the particular and the general, microcosm and macrocosm, or, to recall the terms used earlier, between the roles of specialist and generalist.[81]

Erasmus, another iconic humanist figure, is an example. As a critical philologist, he was aware of the complexity of the human transmission of texts, arguing in his *Letter to Martin Dorp* (1515) for care and attention to detail in the attempt to restore both classical and religious texts to some kind of authenticity.[82] However, the ultimate aim of philology is not scholarship for scholarship's sake, for this would be in Erasmus's eyes to repeat the mistakes of the scholastic past. In his *Praise of Folly* (1509), the narrator Folly ridicules medieval scholastics for their supersubtle intellectualism which results in over-interpretation of the Bible. The satire on their 'subtle refinement of subtleties' depends upon the recognition that the theologians' professional over-concern with technicalities has taken them far away from the spirit of the Bible and its perceived relevance to human experience.[83] Erasmus wants a Bible which is accessible and which speaks to people's need, as he sees it, for meaning, purpose and sustenance. He has little use for a Bible as the exclusive property of professional critics. Erasmus wants theologians to come out of their ivory towers (or monastic equivalent) and proselytise, as a way of reversing the tendency for ideas to become so specialised that they cannot be transported beyond the realm of professional interpreters.

Moreover, when the Renaissance humanist in his role as generalist waxes expansive about the nature of existence or humanity, it is not solely to present magnified images of man and man's special place in the cosmos, for there are other ways of being 'portentous' than this. Addressing the question 'how to live' is one of these ways, and I would argue that it is this question, as much as the image of man as transcendent or infinite in capacity, which preoccupies Renaissance humanists. Pico, for example, does not embrace only infinite possibility and limitless freedom, for the freedom of movement is within certain limits: up, towards heaven, or down, towards 'brutes'. We may be able to 'sculpt' ourselves 'into whatever shape' we prefer, but such images of excess (endless self-fashioning, infinite moulding and remoulding) are balanced by the laying down of ethical boundaries. Martin Andic in 'What is Renaissance Humanism?' (1991) goes as far as to suggest that 'the humanists and philosophers of the Renaissance' discussed in his essay 'would mostly react with horror' to the idea of limitless human freedom.[84] We may have it in our 'nature' to be 'nature-less' and to live in a permanent state of 'free becoming', as Mikhail Bakhtin describes Pico's vision in *Rabelais and His World* (1965), but this is countered in the passage from Pico by an emphasis on ethical limits and the notion that we are intrinsically moral beings.[85] I shall examine further the tension between excess and limits as ways of defining the human in subsequent chapters.

In a sense, the 'how to live' question of *literary* humanism is so appropriate to Renaissance humanism as to be blindingly obvious. A Renaissance humanist, writes Rivers in a simple and succinct description, 'was a classical scholar with two complementary aims: to recover the moral values of classical life, and to imitate the language and style of the classics as a means to that end'.[86] The repositories of wisdom in the heyday of the Arnold-inspired literary humanism of the twentieth century were of course different – vernacular literature (mainly) rather than the classics – but the principle is similar: good books are good because they guide, nurture and nourish, and create a space (some more than others) for portentous existential questions. The line of descent from, say, Erasmus to Eagleton is hardly direct, but the existence of any kind of afterlife for Renaissance humanism can be overlooked in the understandable keenness of historians, acting in the interests of historical specificity, to isolate Renaissance humanism (or humanisms) from anachronistic readings.[87]

There is, however, a bridge between Renaissance humanism and modern literary humanism. The bridge's name is Shakespeare, that vernacular playwright who broadens and deepens the Renaissance humanist preoccupation with 'how to live', who intensifies the existential significance of otherwise abstract ideas and precepts by converting them into vividly realised forms of life, and who still manages despite his own complex rendering of life to preserve a sense of what 'really matters'. The second half of this book will focus on the art and the ethics of living, using Shakespeare for inspiration.

Scepticism

But Shakespeare, as several critics have shown, staged a series of sceptical positions, which question rather than affirm such foundationalist-sounding notions as wisdom, authenticity, human flourishing and what 'really matters'.[88] In a sense, Shakespeare's scepticism and Renaissance scepticism more generally are the natural consequences of Renaissance humanists' 'respect for complexity and diversity', as Toulmin puts it.[89] Indeed, for Toulmin, it is (a certain kind of) scepticism, based on the acceptance of 'plurality, ambiguity' and 'lack of certainty', which above all characterises sixteenth-century humanism.[90] I want, in the rest of the Introduction and subsequently in Part I, to follow the sceptical route, for the following reasons: first, as suggested above, because without properly considering sceptical standpoints, the case I want to make for literary humanism will be weaker; second, because the sage and sceptic in Shakespeare are constantly conversing with each other and the one therefore cannot be properly understood without the other; and third, because scepticism and its close companions disengagement and disenchantment are features of modernity, and I am keen to show how literary humanism arises out of the need to attenuate the effects of modernity.

Locating 'the general historical beginning' of modernity in 'disenchantment with . . . older meaning-giving myths and structures',[91] Lars Engle in '*Measure for Measure* and Modernity: The Problem of the Sceptic's Authority' (2000) suggests that the 'most obvious early modern discourse which might model anti-foundationalism for Shakespeare is scepticism, which enjoyed a vigorous revival in the sixteenth century'.[92] If Shakespeare is in this respect modern, then for Engle in *Measure for Measure* he is simultaneously pre- or anti-modern, 'treating scepticism itself rather sceptically'.[93] Adapting Engle's perceptions to the argument of this book, we might say that in Shakespeare the sage and the sceptic meet, foreshadowing future meetings and/or collisions between the literary humanist perception of literature as an enchanted, quasi-sacred space that shelters the human from the more corrosive effects of modernity and an irreverent scepticism which enlists literature on behalf of its suspicion of all received wisdom, reconceived as ideology. Both perspectives will be attended to in this book. As much as the literary humanist in me might want to treat Shakespeare as an oracle of human wisdom, it would be ethically irresponsible to ignore sceptical perspectives of the kind which demonstrate the ideologies in which literary humanism has been heavily implicated. Two telling examples are Ian Hunter's *Culture and Government* (1988) and Gauri Viswanathan's *Masks of Conquest* (1989). Hunter shows how the Romantic ideas of self-expression, wholeness and 'unalienated human fulfilment'[94] which were central to literary education from the late nineteenth century onwards became 'an instrument of moral supervision in a governmental pedagogy'.[95] Meanwhile, Viswanathan, concentrating on literary education as an instrument of empire, demonstrates how an 'approach to civilization as the humanization of man through various influences, including literature and the arts' was used to maintain British colonial rule in nineteenth-century India.[96] The sceptically oriented question which these books raise for this present study is whether literary humanism is redeemable, whether it ultimately impedes or contributes to human well-being. While an extreme scepticism might justifiably give a negative answer, on the basis that all appeals to authentic humanity and humanisation have been and always are implicated in ideology, a milder scepticism would question such appeals in the hope that a 'better' humanism might emerge.

The place between scepticism and belief is where I want to locate Shakespeare, for if his plays invite mockery of such complacent ethical advisers as Polonius, then they also distance themselves from the nihilism and individualism of an Iago. If they imply criticism of such racist appeals to the human as occur in *Othello*, then they draw back from the conclusion that distinctions between the inhuman and human are always and everywhere unethical or invalid. Literary humanism is therefore challenged but not demolished by scepticism. It needs to be challenged if it is to avoid the complacency and exclusivity of a 'more fully human than thou' attitude. But it needs to be saved from the kind of complete demolition which would deprive us of any means of distinguishing between the human and the dehumanising. Moreover, as subsequent chapters will argue, although mainstream humanism has often been regarded as a weapon *of* (bourgeois) ideology – and with good reason, as Hunter and Viswanathan show – it is possible to locate other expressions of humanism which have acted *against* ideology.

Scepticism and Modernity

I want further to embed scepticism within the context of modern life, for this will make its implications for literary humanism richer. Given, first, the inherent complexity of the phenomenon of modernity; second, the intellectual drive towards continual redescription; and third, postmodernism's suspicion of grand narratives, it is unlikely that there will ever be absolute consensus about either the origins or the nature of modernity.[97] But if we were to risk a selective glossary of key concepts and tendencies associated with modernity, and one which resonates with some of Shakespeare's own dramatisations of the old and the new, it might include the following.

1. Sceptical and/or ironic detachment from received ideas, habits and customs. In its postmodern form, sceptical detachment might be seen

as manifesting itself in the widely appealed to notion that meanings are always and everywhere 'constructed' through society and language rather than given, and in a 'hermeneutics of suspicion' which doubts the existence of any foundational principles, including human nature.
2. The disenchantment, detraditionalisation and desacralisation of world-views set in motion either by the exercise of a sceptical critical reason or by 'instrumental rationality' (or both).
3. The denaturing of the so-called natural, accompanied by the replacement of animist conceptions of nature by a secular, instrumental attitude towards nature as inert resource.[98]
4. The replacement of 'charismatic' or customary authority by the need for rationally justified authority.
5. The opening up of gaps between values and facts, mind and world, knower and known.
6. Specialisation and the division of the spheres of art, morality and science (implying a scepticism about the universality of any one of them).
7. The separation of 'roles', viewed as inauthentic and merely external, from 'selves'.
8. Alienation, anomie and the sense that modern life has lost direction, foundations, meaning and *telos*.

A certain nostalgia for the pre-modern is implied by some of these associations, for example by the association of modernity with a disorienting loss of foundations, but this nostalgia is balanced by more positive characterisations of modernity in terms of its healthy scepticism. This kind of double critique (of the present by the past, and the past by the present), could itself be construed as 'modern' because it involves holding both the past and present at a sceptical distance, but 'pre-modern' in that it also looks, as literary humanism does, for guiding principles.

A companion glossary, for pre-modernity, would feature counter-concepts to modernity and be a similar mixture of positive and negative characterisations. Such a glossary might therefore include: the idea of living 'inside' traditions, habits and customs, which are treated as though they are part of the natural order of things; a sense of the sacred; the notion that meaning is 'immanent', that is, already 'in' the world rather than attributed to it by subjects who are shaped by society, history and language; magic and animism as examples of immanence and the idea that 'soul' or 'spirit' inheres in the natural world; solidity as opposed to liquidity; the convergence of mind and world, value and fact; ideas of wholeness; the sense that roles are not merely roles but contain existential meaning and value; and the efficacy of ritual as a way of dealing with perennial human fears and longings.

The 'pre-modern', or a version of it, might be returning. In the wake of the September 11 attack on the World Trade Center in New York City, Roger Rosenblatt in *Time* magazine declared that 'one good thing could come from this horror: it could spell the end of the age of irony'. He continued: 'For some thirty years – roughly as long as the Twin Towers were upright – the good folks in charge of America's intellectual life have insisted that nothing has to be believed in or taken seriously. Nothing was real.'[99] If there is a grain of truth in this caricature, then it is important not only to contest the nature of the foundations which might be returning, but to uphold the positive features of the sceptical tradition. Shakespeare can help with both of these endeavours, for it is possible to find in the 'myriad-minded' playwright described by Coleridge many, if not all, of the above associations and meanings of modernity and pre-modernity.[100] His work both 'enchants' and 'disenchants', rescues foundations and questions them, closes and opens gaps between mind and world, and it does each of these things in a variety of ways. The broad literary humanist question of how to live in a 'groundless world', as Stanley Cavell describes it in *Disowning Knowledge* (1987), or a world simultaneously anchored and unanchored, sacralised and desacralised, 'magical' and robbed of magic by a scepticism that sometimes verges on cynicism, is as urgent in Shakespeare's work as it is utterly fascinating.[101] If in 'the bourgeois epoch' as described by Karl Marx and Friedrich Engels in *The Communist Manifesto* (1848) 'all that is solid melts into air', then the need for at least a small parcel of solid ground on which to stand seems both understandable and necessary.[102] Shakespeare's work is a search for that solid ground. It is an attempt to answer the question of what remains of the human, when 'the human' like all else is liable to evaporate.

Hugh Grady in *Shakespeare's Universal Wolf* (1996) makes the insightful point that the 'categories of the various modern humanisms arose to provide normative concepts to substitute for those of evacuated public and religious spheres'.[103] Disenchantment and desacralisation in other words left a vacuum which was filled by the foundationalist aspirations of 'modern humanisms'. However, what Grady's perspective does not take full account of is the disenchanted scepticism to which the human as a potential norm-giving source is also subjected by Renaissance writers and playwrights, including, or perhaps even epitomised by, Shakespeare.

Varieties of Scepticism

Scepticism in Shakespeare is varied. The first two versions of scepticism which I shall examine, via *Hamlet* in Chapter 1 and *Othello* in Chapter 2, represent what might be termed the 'acceptable' and 'unacceptable' faces of scepticism: one, the acceptable version, is embodied in the figure of Hamlet; the other, the unacceptable version, is represented by the nihilistic and instrumentalist Iago. These two versions of scepticism roughly correspond to the models of rationality described by Jürgen Habermas, with the latter, the Iago model, also coinciding with that aspect of mainstream humanism based on a 'narcissistically overinflated autonomy', as Habermas puts it.[104] It is to Habermas I now want to turn because he offers a framework for understanding Shakespeare's own contribution to, and fears about, the sceptical use of reason and its implications for ideas of human nature.

Rationality has come under attack in the twentieth and twenty-first centuries from various counter-Enlightenment quarters. To the tendency of Weber, and later Adorno and Horkheimer, to condemn Enlightenment reason for its instrumentality, Habermas in *The Philosophical Discourse of Modernity* (1985) responds by differentiating what he calls communicative rationality from its instrumentalising counterpart:

> both cognitive-instrumental mastery of an objectivated nature (and society) and narcissistically overinflated autonomy (in the sense of purposively rational self-assertion) are derivative moments that have been rendered independent from the communicative structures of the lifeworld, that is, from the intersubjectivity of relationships of mutual understanding and relationships of reciprocal recognition.[105]

The concept of 'lifeworld' is a central one in Habermas's work. Habermas uses the term 'lifeworld' (*Lebenswelt*) to designate the unspoken values, beliefs and assumptions which all human communities draw upon in order to understand and communicate with one another. The concept of the lifeworld also comes closest in Habermas's writing to the way mythical thought is seen by him as functioning, for both share the tendency of their world-views to become so naturalised that they are not visible as world-views. What happens to lifeworlds in modern societies, however, is that they become denatured. As a result, reason begins to play a hugely significant role in modernity, since once values and consensus are no longer givens, they have to be rationally argued for: in other words, reasons have to be given for the beliefs that a community holds where formerly no such rationalisation was necessary. 'A lifeworld', writes Habermas, 'can be regarded as rationalized to the extent that it permits interactions that are not guided by normatively *ascribed* agreement but – directly or indirectly – by communicatively *achieved* understanding'.[106] If the important difference between pre-modern and modern lifeworlds is 'reason', then their equally important shared characteristic is the 'inherent telos of human speech' of 'reaching understanding' with one another.[107] Rationalised lifeworlds may thus denature the apparently natural, but Habermas maintains a foundationalist concept of the natural through the idea that humans are naturally communicative and that communication inherently tends towards cooperative understanding.

However, what prevents members of a rationalised lifeworld from realising their potential as communicating, deliberating, reflexive citizens in search of a non-coercive consensus is the colonisation of the lifeworld by the negative forms of rationality embedded in capitalist and administrative systems. Capitalist rationality privileges 'egocentric calculations of success' over authentic communication.[108] Meanwhile, state administration and the capitalist economy itself constitute 'increasingly complex, formally organized domains of action' which hinder the lifeworld from exercising its different form of rationality.[109] In the absence of a shared mythical world-view, two conflicting models for achieving consensus present themselves: an organic as well as populist model rooted in the natural features of ordinary, everyday communication ('lifeworld') versus an inorganic, externally imposed, administered consensus.

Shakespeare's plays create a lifeworld of the modern, rationalised variety, which provokes debate on a wealth of subjects, from love to issues of authority to questions of 'how to live' and what it is to be human.[110] Proficiency in debate and argument was, after all, one of the outcomes of a Renaissance humanist education in rhetoric. Rhetoric might have been regarded as an effective means of conveying the wisdom of the ancients, but it had its own significant effect upon wisdom. An extreme version of this, satirised in *Love's Labour's Lost* (the focus of Chapter 7), is that rhetoric could become an end in itself rather than a means to the end of wisdom. Less extremely, rhetoric could unsettle wisdom by dialogising and contextualising it. Classical wisdom is registered ubiquitously in Renaissance texts and handbooks, Thomas Wright's use of Socrates to recommend frugal living in *The Passions of the Minde* (1601) being one of innumerable examples: 'Socrates was woont to say, that those men which liue continently and frugally, had more pleasure, and lesse paine than those, who with great care procured inticements to pleasure'.[111] However, not only was classical matter encyclopaedically diverse, but the rhetorically inspired awareness of audience and context created a 'flexible' wisdom, a wisdom attuned to the contingencies of particular situations. Because training in rhetoric also nurtured the ability to argue either side of a case, it belonged to the realm of probable rather than certain knowledge.[112] It therefore contributed towards the construction of a rationally oriented lifeworld in which rather than being given in advance, consensus has to be argued for. Of course, the origins of the exercise of critical reason are not to be located exclusively in the Renaissance. However, the plays of Shakespeare and his contemporaries can be thought of as constituting a popular forum for public debate and discussion which expanded the exercise of critical reason beyond privileged sectors of society, and which at the same time drew on already existing sceptical and desacralising elements of popular culture (such as were present, for example, in certain forms of carnival). Combining as he does elements of high culture (prince) and low culture (jester), Hamlet represents some of the positive components of a rationalised lifeworld, oriented, amongst other things, towards considering 'What a piece of work is a man' (II, ii, 305).

One source of scepticism, then, is Renaissance humanism itself. However, it is important not to exaggerate its anti-foundationalism. Toulmin (though himself no great supporter of foundationalism) differentiates between the method of 'systematic doubt' introduced in the seventeenth century by Descartes and the scepticism of the humanists, on the grounds that the latter 'no more wished to *deny* general philosophical theses than to *assert* them'.[113] It is also important not to exaggerate Renaissance humanists' embrace of the contingent and the particular. Theirs was a practical ethics, it is true, which proceeded 'case by case' rather than according to abstract principles, given in advance, but as I suggested earlier, the particular and the general were not mutually exclusive. Although Thomas Wilson in *The Arte of Rhetorique* (1553) takes pains to point out that 'thinges generally spoken without all circumstaunces, are more proper unto the Logician, who talketh of thinges uniuersally, without respect of person, time, or place', while 'particuler matters' fall within the ambit of the orator, he then proceeds to undo this opposition:

> And yet notwithstanding, Tullie doth say, that whosoeuer will talke of particuler matter must remember, that within the same also is comprehended a generall. As for example. If I shall aske the question, whether it bee lawfull for William Conquerour to inuade England, and win it by force of Armour, I must also consider this, whether it bee lawfull for any man to vsurpe power.[114]

Whether the particulars in question are the particulars of specialist philological knowledge, contingent historical circumstance or human embodiment, it would be a mistake to place Renaissance humanists on the side of a particularism sealed off from generalist interests and questions of the kind signalled in the above passage by Wilson. Where examples from the past (such as William the Conqueror's invasion of England) are too particularised, the orator's attempt to make examples 'exemplary' and speak beyond their own time and place is thwarted. For 'particuler matters' to become subjects for reasoned debate within a quasi-Habermasian public sphere, their 'absolute' particularity has to be transcended.

The counterpart to the 'healthy scepticism' of rational debate, sometimes (though not always) embodied by Hamlet, is the cynicism and instrumentalism of Iago. Iago does not test and question so much as demolish ideas about human nature, so that others become putty in his hands. He is that version of cold, calculating rationality based according to Habermas on 'both cognitive-instrumental mastery of an objectivated nature (and society) and narcissistically overinflated autonomy (in the sense of purposively rational self-assertion)'. 'Nature' can be taken to refer here to both the natural world and to human nature. 'Nature' of either kind is not something in which Iago participates. He is not part of or restricted by 'nature', but holds it at a distance, as an object that he works on and manipulates for rational self-interest. Human nature is for other people, not for Iago. Disengagement, to recall Charles Taylor, 'demands that we stop simply living in our bodies or within our traditions or habits, and by making them objects for us, subject them to radical scrutiny and remaking'.[115] Neither Hamlet nor Iago lives in his body or by 'instinct' (although Hamlet sometimes wishes he could). Both stand outside traditions and habits. And both therefore turn them into 'objects' in the sense of being removed from them. But where Hamlet treats traditions and habits as objects of *enquiry*, Iago treats them as objects for *manipulation*.

Iago's self-interested appropriation of reason also makes the rhetorical culture of the Renaissance look quite different from its use as a means of critical enquiry. Rhetoric begins to look less like healthy debate and to resemble instead Stephen Greenblatt's description of it in *Renaissance Self-Fashioning* (1980): '[Rhetoric] offered men the power to shape their worlds, calculate the probabilities, and master the contingent, and it implied that human character itself could be similarly fashioned, with an eye to audience and effect'.[116] Rhetoric is a tool for men on the make – self-fashioning men – rather than a spur to argument and debate.

Having considered two contrasting versions of disenchanted scepticism in the figures of Hamlet and Iago, the following two chapters will focus on irony (contemporary and Shakespearean) and historicism (contemporary, Renaissance and Shakespearean) as further examples of ways in which 'the human' can be set at different kinds of distance: it can be questioned (Hamlet), emptied (Iago), ironised or historicised. However, because of the ways that irony and history are also humanised, these two chapters (3 and 4) will anticipate Part II. Part II will consider the possibility that there is such a thing as 'existential wisdom', that Shakespeare has it, that an ethics of how to live can be built around concepts of human need and human nature, and that human beings therefore have a chance of one day becoming human.

Part I

Denaturing Human Nature

Chapter 1

Questioning the Human: *Hamlet*

At a sometimes critical, sometimes mournful distance from the instinct on which revenge is purportedly based, Hamlet is a conspicuous example of a character standing outside traditions, habits, rituals and supposedly natural human impulses. Rather than acting as sources of identification, human nature and human existence become the site, for Hamlet, of uncertainties and questions. He is exposed to a variety of beliefs and behaviours, each with its own assumptions about what it is to be human, but as a disengaged, disenchanted sceptic he remains at a critical distance from them.

But what does it mean, in the context of *Hamlet* (1600–1), to hold an engaged or 'enchanted' view of life?[1] We need to understand this and the part it plays in Hamlet's own imagination before we can fully understand what it means in this play to be disengaged and disenchanted. In Act IV the deranged Ophelia distributes herbs and flowers, each of them attributed with symbolic meaning:

> There's rosemary, that's for remembrance. Pray, love, remember. And there is pansies; that's for thoughts . . . There's fennel for you, and columbines. There's rue for you, and here's some for me. We may call it herb-grace o' Sundays. O, you must wear your rue with a difference. There's a daisy. I would give you some violets, but they withered all when my father died. They say a made a good end.[2]

Ophelia's folklore is an anthropomorphicisation of nature and at the same time an affirmation of the 'objective' existence of perennial human feelings. That nature 'feels' what human beings feel – 'I would give you some violets, but they withered all when my father died' – conflates the natural world with the human world in a way which corresponds to what Jürgen Habermas, drawing on the work of Claude Lévi-Strauss, refers to as mythical thought. From the 'reciprocal assimilation of nature to culture and conversely culture to nature', there results, writes Habermas,

> on the one hand, a nature that is outfitted with anthropomorphic features, drawn into the communicative network of social subjects, and in this sense humanized, and on the other hand, a culture that is to a certain extent naturalized and reified and absorbed into the objective nexus of operations of anonymous powers.[3]

In other words, nature is humanised and the human is naturalised. There is continuity between psychological and physical, or inner and outer worlds. Ophelia may have been deprived by others of self-expression for most of the play, but here at least her outward behaviour is an expression of her inward grief, and both are given universality via their association with the natural world.[4]

The term which brings these ideas together is ritual. Ophelia's leave-taking is an improvised ritual. Rituals seem timeless; they seem to express an 'eternal present', as Richard van Oort in 'Shakespeare and the Idea of the Modern' (2006) puts it.[5] The impression of permanence is created because rituals repeat themselves and appear to express perennial human emotions which are also expressed by and in nature. To put it at its simplest: human beings experience sorrow and loss, fears and anxieties, just as they also have hopes and dreams. From the perspective of ritual, emotions such as sorrow and loss are not only 'facts' of human nature but of nature, as expressed in Ophelia's ritual by the herb rue.[6] These aspects of ritual, connecting the human order to the natural and often, as well, to a sacred order, are also expressed in Perdita's equally ritualistic distribution of flowers in *The Winter's Tale*. This ritual expresses different emotions and urges (a sense of renewal and recovery rather than loss), but through ritual both Perdita and Ophelia bring nature back into the 'denatured' world of human artifice. Writing of the function of social ritual in Shakespearean comedy, C. L. Barber in *Shakespeare's Festive Comedy* (1959) argues that what is achieved in the festive comedies is a 'heightened awareness of the relation between man and "nature" '.[7] As Chapter 9 will discuss, the thorny question of what belongs to art and what belongs to nature is explicitly debated in *The Winter's Tale*, but such debate, coupled with the more obvious 'seasonal' patterning of the play, can be taken as evidence of a desire for art to be in some sort of contact with nature and so counteract the total alienation of human beings from both nature and human nature.

In stark contrast to Ophelia's immersion in ritualistic performance is the situation at the beginning of the play, where ritual, as far as Hamlet is concerned, has lost its eloquence, its meaning, its authenticity. Correspondences between inner and outer worlds are severed, most notably when Hamlet near the outset famously lays claim to an interiority – 'I have that within which passeth show' (I, ii, 85) – which is seen by him as deeper and more authentic than the outward displays of grief he sees around him at court:

> 'Tis not alone my inky cloak, good-mother,
> Nor customary suits of solemn black,
> Nor windy suspiration of forced breath,
> No, nor the fruitful river in the eye,
> Nor the dejected haviour of the visage,
> Together with all the forms, moods, shows of grief
> That can denote me truly. These indeed 'seem',
> For they are actions that a man might play;
> But I have that within that passeth show –
> These but the trappings and the suits of woe.
> (I, ii, 77–86)

How has it come about that for Hamlet rituals have lost touch with the inner human realities they purportedly express?

In its attack on Catholic ideas, such as the concept of purgatory, Protestantism, according to Stephen Greenblatt, deprived people of their need to 'negotiate with the dead'.[8] He suggests that Shakespeare was 'part of a very large group, probably the bulk of the population, who found themselves still grappling with longings and fears that the old resources of the Catholic Church had served to address'.[9] It is difficult exactly to determine Claudius's religious affiliation, but the truncated (in Hamlet's opinion) ritual of mourning over which he presides at the beginning of the play suggests that the human significance and value of ritual have been compromised. The downgrading of the Catholic doctrine of justification by works in favour of justification by faith may have contributed further to the 'silencing' of the external, public world, because outward signs were thereby rendered less expressive than the faith that supposedly came from within. Insofar as the collective life of a society is its religious life, and insofar as that religious life is composed of rituals which do manage to address human 'longings and fears', then it is possible to speak of the connectedness of inner to outer worlds. However, *Hamlet* via its central protagonist dramatises the alienation of feeling from public life and the sense that public rites and ritual have been 'damaged', to use Greenblatt's word,[10] or 'maimèd', which is Hamlet's description of Ophelia's burial ceremony (V, i, 214).

The play presents three kinds of response, via Hamlet, to this situation. One is to go along with the transfer of meaning and authenticity from outer to inner worlds and to think of the self, which Hamlet partly does, as a more authentic source of meaning than the world of fake or damaged ritual. 'I have that within which passeth show' is the expression of this transfer. 'In refusing to resign his private grief to the public world of debased value masked by rhetoric', argues Ronald Knowles, 'Hamlet refuses to communicate meaningfully, but is meaningful to himself'.[11] A second response is to try to mend the rift between inner and outer worlds, which is effectively what Hamlet, at the very beginning of his speech against false appearances, does when he responds to his mother's question 'Why seems it [grief] so particular with thee?' with 'Seems, madam? Nay it *is*' (I, ii, 76). From this perspective, Hamlet's 'nightly colour' (I, ii, 68), referred to by Gertrude, is *not* inauthentic for his outward appearance *does* reliably denote his inner condition. Although in the rest of his speech Hamlet suggests that all externals are inexpressive, at the beginning of it Hamlet holds onto the idea that shared, public signs can be expressive. He demonstrates this in his relationship with, and attitude to, both Horatio and the players. The third response is scepticism or 'disengagement', but not the kind of Iago-like disengagement which involves an unerringly exploitative attitude towards discourses by which others are enchanted. Hamlet's disengagement is instead based on testing traditions, ideas and rituals which lay claim to authenticity or customary status on the basis that they are adequately expressive of the inner human being. If 'I have that within which passeth show' encapsulates the drift of value and authentic human feeling from outer to inner worlds, whereas 'Nay, it *is*. I know not seems' affirms the possibility of their reconnection, then the 'motto' which sums up the sceptic's suspicion of *all* designs upon him is: 'I'll have grounds / More relative than this' (II, ii, 605–6). Referring to the uncertain 'grounds' for vengeful action represented by the ghost – 'The spirit that I have seen / May be the devil, and the devil hath power / T'assume a pleasing shape' (II, ii, 600–2) – this assertion of scepticism involves denaturing the natural and subjecting all appeals to seemingly natural courses of action and natural human feeling to intense scrutiny.

Hamlet is the fictional equivalent of Shakespeare himself in his inheritance of a variety of traditions. Each of these traditions advances an idea of what human nature is or should be. So, for example, in the tradition of classical revenge tragedy, represented by the ghost, retributive vengeance – an eye for an eye – is a primal instinct.[12] The desire for vengeance is what any self-respecting son should feel – on the pulse – for a father who has been murdered by his brother. The ghost itself appeals to 'nature' in its first encounter with Hamlet. Referring to his untimely death and the state of unconfessed sin in which he existed, the ghost of old Hamlet puts human instinct at the centre of the revenge plot: 'If thou hast nature in thee, bear it not. / Let not the royal bed of Denmark be /A couch for luxury and damnèd incest' (I, v, 81–3). The normative appeal to instinct is prefaced by an 'If' ('If thou hast nature . . .'). This is probably meant rhetorically by the ghost, but Hamlet will fasten onto this 'If' and hear it differently, as an 'ought' rather than an 'is', a statement about value rather than a statement of fact. These 'facts of nature' are a source of nostalgia for Hamlet; they contribute to a simplified view of how things used to be, when men were 'real' men. He will admire or, to borrow the theatrical language which pervades the play, he will 'act out' admiration for the player who himself acts out authentic-seeming passion in the classical revenge narrative of Pyrrhus and Priam. And he will shame himself for not being able to manage the same manly passion:

> O, what a rogue and peasant slave am I!
> Is it not monstrous that this player here,
> But in a fiction, in a dream of passion,
> Could force his soul so to his whole conceit
> That from her working all his visage wanned,
> Tears in his eyes, distraction in's aspect,
> A broken voice, and his whole function suiting
> With forms to his conceit? And all for nothing.
> For Hecuba!
> What's Hecuba to him, or he to Hecuba,
> That he should weep for her? What would he do
> Had he the motive and the cue for passion
> That I have?
>
> (II, ii, 552–64)

The speech Hamlet asks the player to perform is from a hazily remembered past: 'I heard thee speak me a speech once, but it was never acted, or, if it was, not above once; for the play, I remember, pleased not the million' (II, ii, 437–9). Like the players themselves, the speech and the antiquated heroic passion it enacts – 'The rugged Pyrrhus, he whose sable arms, / Black as his purpose, did the night resemble' (II, ii, 455–6) – are an antidote to a complicated present. But the complicated present is still very much in evidence owing to the fact that the language used in the speech sounds antiquated, not just to us, but to Hamlet, because it and the players are said to be not of the present, they are no longer 'the fashion' (II, ii, 342). Even when the players were in vogue, the speech, it seems, wasn't, for it 'pleased not the million'. The 'nature' represented in the speech is therefore not just once but twice removed from the present, although that does not stop Hamlet, or a part of Hamlet, wishing that he could enact this version of the past in the present and treat the mighty passion for vengeance as a fact of nature. The complicated present is also registered in the use of theatrical language. Shakespeare makes strikingly varied uses of the world-as-theatre metaphor, but here theatrical language is a signifier of both authenticity and inauthenticity: the player's imitation of heroic passion is an inauthentic simulation of an authentic passion. In applying theatrical language ('cue for passion') to his own situation, Hamlet partly theatricalises, in the sense of rendering inauthentic, his passion for revenge and treats it more like a 'role' rather than a 'self'.

Or therein lies the rub, because Hamlet never fully exteriorises roles in the way that Iago does. A role for Hamlet is a possible self, or possibly even an anti-self masquerading as a self, but it is not merely a role. In this respect, Hamlet is not fully 'disenchanted'. The roles which the world offers are not fully separated off from a 'self' that is defined in total opposition to them. At the same time, Hamlet remains at a critical distance from those 'roles' which are presented to him as 'selves'. In 'On the Value of Being a Cartoon, in Literature and Life' (2001), Sharon O'Dair contests what she sees as a Romantic prejudice against social roles, institutions and conventions. With the help of Robert Weimann, she argues that, for Shakespeare, 'society is not an obstacle (or, at least, not only an obstacle) to the development of selfhood, but the means to achieving it'.[13] Insofar as Hamlet conceives of roles as selves or possible selves, he is pre-Romantic. But when roles are instrumentalised and thereby drained of existential meaning, he takes steps in a Romantic direction, inwards, towards a self defined in opposition to role. The place between role and self is the place for a critical consciousness which regards the authenticity of roles, such as that of the revenger or public mourner, with scepticism, but simultaneously suspects that withdrawal into a separated self might also constitute a form of alienation.

The classical revenge tradition, with its emphasis on primal passion, is one of several traditions to which Hamlet is heir. Traditions, and the ideas of nature and human nature they embody, are not only multiple but hybridised. For example, the classical ghost from Senecan, and before that Greek revenge tragedy, does not emerge from the classical underworld, as Kyd's vengeful ghost does in *The Spanish Tragedy* (*c.*1589), but from purgatory, which as already mentioned is a pre-Reformation Catholic concept. And Christianity is itself hybridised, reflecting real life in post-Reformation England, because it is mediated not just through Catholicism via the concept of purgatory but through Protestantism: Hamlet's place of study, 'Wittenberg' (I, ii, 113), was Martin Luther's university and therefore associated with Protestantism.[14] It is also possible, as previously suggested, that Protestantism is present in Claudius's foreshortening of the ritual of mourning.

The variegated Christianity represented in the play gives Hamlet a number of further ideas of what it is to be human, some of which, most notably the New Testament injunction 'Vengeance *is* mine; I will repay, saith the Lord' (Romans 12: 19), are in direct opposition to the idea of human nature supplied by the classical revenge tradition.[15] Vengeance, from a Christian perspective, is a violent appropriation of divine justice, an act of hubris, which deforms the self. Christ was a man of peace and, as Ewan Fernie suggests, Hamlet at times echoes this pacifism in his shocked reactions to killing. These reactions, writes Fernie, 'evoke a religious conscience passionately averse to violence'.[16] The ghost implies that the vengeance pursued by a son on behalf of a father is a fulfilment of self and what is natural to the self, whereas the Christian tradition implies that vengeance and its accompanying hatred imperil the soul.

Christianity in both its Catholic and Protestant guises also bequeaths to Hamlet the idea that humanity is innately depraved, although Catholicism more than Protestantism allowed through its rituals of expiation for a degree of relief from this 'fact' of nature. Images of a fallen humanity, naturally prone to corruption and sin, pervade the play from the pre-Reformation ghost's concern that he was deprived of the chance to absolve himself of his 'imperfections' (I, v, 79), to Marcellus's diagnosis that 'Something is rotten in the state of Denmark' (I, iv, 67), to Hamlet's own sense of both his own and the world's depravity: 'I am very proud, revengeful, ambitious, with more offences at my beck than I have thoughts to put them in. What should such fellows as I do crawling between heaven and earth? We are arrant knaves, all' (III, i, 126–31). The upward glance to heaven suggests the possibility of a redeemed humanity and the reclamation of a spiritual self. By definition, tragedy dramatises the falling away from grace and the gap that opens up between human beings and the 'better selves' ostensibly represented by religion, but tragedy's protagonists and survivors also make last-hour attempts to crawl their way back to 'heaven', even as the 'earth' still clings to them. Tragedy in this respect reflects Pico della Mirandola's vision of humans, discussed in the Introduction, as half-god and half-beast.

More expansively as well as more optimistically, the notion of a God-created universe is an example of what Charles Taylor calls an 'ontic logos'. An 'ontic logos' promotes an immanent theory of meaning, whereby things are understood as having meaning and value in themselves rather than being dependent on a subject who attributes value to them. 'As long as the order of things', writes Taylor, 'embodies an ontic logos, then ideas and valuations are also seen as located in the world, and not just in subjects'.[17] Human beings do not therefore have to strive for meaning, because meaning already exists. When Hamlet after the 'sea-change' which he appears to have experienced says towards the end of the play that 'There's a divinity that shapes our ends, / Rough-hew them how we will' (V, ii, 10–11), he is implying that purpose and meaning are built into the scheme of things (by God). We may not always be able to see them because of the way we 'rough-hew' them, but they are nonetheless present and exist independently or semi-independently of our perceptions. Hamlet in the last act seems to express a Zen-like acceptance of his situation, as though the meaning of his life, and of human life in general, is no longer dependent on his agonised attempts to *find* meaning.

These are some of the traditions inherited by Hamlet (and by implication by Shakespeare), each with its own vision of human nature and human life. They do not correlate particularly with the mainstream humanism discussed in the Introduction. Some defenders of mainstream humanism would say they are the exact opposite, for what is religion if not a determination from elsewhere – from beyond the human – of humanity? But they are humanist in the broad literary sense described in the Introduction, for they engage questions of what it means to be human. And these traditions are humanist in a literary sense, as well, because Shakespeare makes them so, through his skill at embodiment. He turns them, that is, into 'selves' or possible selves. He turns them into ways of being and living, into ways of being human. Some of them – for example, the revenge tradition – are already this, but Shakespeare thickens their existential significance. This is also true of religious principles. As I suggested in the Introduction, Hamlet's intuition in the last act that there is a 'divinity that shapes our ends' is not just abstract doctrine but *embodied* as an emerging attribute of character which makes him less restless, less agonised. We can adapt an insight of Amanda Anderson's in *The Way We Argue Now* (2006) to Shakespeare's skill at embodiment. She suggests that recent theoretical developments 'join in a desire to correct for, or answer to, the overly abstract elements of earlier forms of theory' and 'reflect a persistent existential movement toward thicker characterological conceptions of theoretical postures and stances'.[18] Two models for such 'thicker characterological conceptions' are literature and, as the epitome of this model of literariness, Shakespeare, for Shakespeare has long been admired for the 'life and body', as F. R. Leavis puts it, in his verse.[19] Because he is able to embody different perspectives, the resulting 'forms of life' contend with one another for existential significance. Therefore, as I argued in the Introduction, where a fully secularised version of mainstream humanism might claim that human beings can only fully apprehend their humanness independently of a religious perspective, Shakespeare, by intensifying the existential significance of religion, gives us cause to wonder whether the secular self is a freedom or restriction. He gives us cause to question which way of living might be a more or less authentic expression of what it is to be human.

The focus so far in this chapter has been on traditions which emphasise different kinds of essentialism. However, Hamlet is also the sceptically inclined inheritor of more anti-essentialist humanist ideas, such as the freedom and limitless human potential which Pico's *Oration on the Dignity of Man* (*c*.1486) seems to celebrate. Although Pico's text, as discussed in the Introduction, has sustained different interpretations of its purported humanism, there are elements of it which suggest a confidence in human capacities and freedom. It is this confidence which Hamlet denigrates in his famous disquisition on 'What a piece of work is a man':

> I have of late – but wherefore I know not – lost all my mirth, forgone all custom of exercise; and indeed it goes so heavily with my disposition that this goodly frame, the earth, seems to me a sterile promontory. This most excellent canopy the air, look you, this brave o'erhanging, this majestical roof fretted with golden fire – why, it appears no other thing to me than a foul and pestilent congregation of vapours. What a piece of work is a man! How noble in reason, how infinite in faculty, in form and moving how express and admirable, in action how like an angel, in apprehension how like a god – the beauty of the world, the paragon of animals! And yet to me what is this quintessence of dust? Man delights not me. (II, ii, 297–310)

Is the world – is human life – inherently meaningful or is meaning a matter of perception? Three times Hamlet repeats the phrase 'to me': 'seems to me a sterile promontory', 'appears no other thing to me', 'And yet to me what is this'. The subjective turn makes the meaningfulness or meaninglessness of life 'merely' a matter of perspective. This open-endedness is not a positive experience for Hamlet. Andrew Hadfield suggests that Hamlet's speech may even be a parody of Pico's *Oration*. According to Hadfield:

> Hamlet's words express a painful disillusionment with the Renaissance ideals so highly praised by Pico. While Pico sees a series of infinite possibilities of existence, Hamlet can only see the pointlessness of existence without any means of guidance . . . What Pico regards as the excitement of new discovery, Hamlet can only see as infinite drudgery.[20]

The tragic perspective on limitless possibility is a sense of loss and this sense of loss begins to corrode any optimistic narrative about human beings being free to create their own natures.

William Bouwsma in 'The Renaissance Discovery of Human Creativity' (1993) argues that although the principle of artistic creativity gained significant ascendancy over the principle of imitation during the

Renaissance, it was impeded because it generated a considerable amount of anxiety:

> The great obstacle to the notion of human creativity was, I think, the anxiety to which it gave rise, and to which it largely succumbed in the seventeenth century. Imitation implies, after all, that the artist is constantly working under the guidance of nature, and therefore that art has a dependable ontological foundation. The artist, in this conception, discovers a reality that is recognizably there, waiting for him to find. The notion of *human* creativity not only detaches the artist from any real world but makes every artistic decision a terrible choice among infinite possibilities.[21]

'A terrible choice among infinite possibilities', none of which has 'dependable ontological foundation': this accords well with Hamlet's perception of his situation for most of the play.

Hamlet therefore questions both limits and limitlessness, 'nature' and the eradication of nature. He questions the limits which others seek to impose upon him through their appeals to what is natural; but he also questions the contrasting scenario of a 'denatured' limitlessness, in which the natural is no longer an organising principle of life. The sense of limitlessness is in fact the direct result of the *variety* of naturalised roles with which he is presented: the classical revenge hero acting on instinct, the fallen human being tainted by original sin, and so on. What this 'choice' amounts to is an anti-essentialism, as instead of automatically inhabiting one of these naturalised roles, he is presented with several conflicting versions of the natural. However, the resulting anti-essentialism is not an occasion for celebration; it is not embraced by Hamlet as an opportunity for choice, but agonisingly experienced as an erosion of ground, a loss of a sense that life is inherently meaningful (or has an 'ontic logos', to use Taylor's term). The question of how to live is precisely a *question* for Hamlet rather than a given, and it is a question which for most of the play leaves him feeling disoriented, immobilised by choice and caught between divided dispositions.

The open-endedness of life is also a problem for Hamlet because open-endedness in tragedy (as contrasted with comedy) is a negative open-endedness which seems only to destroy (again in contrast with comedy, where destruction is more clearly part of a cycle of destruction/renewal). In *Hamlet* freedom also often equates to aimlessness and an 'anything goes' form of relativism. Variations on the 'it seems to me' formula are serially repeated. Hamlet's conversation with Rosencrantz and Guildenstern includes a wonderful encapsulation of Hamlet's sense of relativist/anti-essentialist malaise:

> *Hamlet*: What have you, my good friends, deserved at the hands of Fortune that she sends you to prison hither?

> *Guildenstern*: Prison, my lord?
> *Hamlet*: Denmark's a prison.
> *Rosencrantz*: Then is the world one.
> *Hamlet*: A goodly one, in which there are many confines, wards, and dungeons, Denmark being one o'th' worst.
> *Rosencrantz*: We think not so, my lord.
> *Hamlet*: Why, then 'tis none to you, for there is nothing either good or bad but thinking makes it so. To me it is a prison.
>
> (II, ii, 242–53)

Thought – and thought's concretisation in language – can do anything in *Hamlet*. Thinking can turn an uncle into a father, or so Claudius hopes when he invites the grieving Hamlet early on in the play to 'think of us / As of a father' (I, ii, 107–8). It can make revenge seem like an act of heroism or an act of barbarism. It can make persistent mourning for a dead parent an act of loving remembrance or an unnatural perversion – 'a fault to heaven, / A fault against the dead, a fault to nature' (I, ii, 101–2), according to Claudius. It can make human beings seem 'the paragon of animals' or 'the quintessence of dust' (II, ii, 309–10). It can transform a cloud into a 'camel', then 'weasel', then 'whale' (III, ii, 365–70). And the disturbing thing for Hamlet is that these thought experiments and linguistic reconstructions of reality command almost automatic assent from the 'yes-men' of the court, such as Polonius. This is how anti-essentialism is experienced by Hamlet. This is how anti-essentialism unfolds in the world inhabited by Hamlet.

Claudius is another of Shakespeare's dissolvers of the supposedly natural and essential. He is another example, though more muted than Iago, of the unacceptable face of disengaged rationality, a figure who seems to pay only lip-service to traditions and rituals and to the ideas of the human that they embody. Presiding, at the beginning of the play, over the hybridised ritual of funeral wake and wedding celebration, Claudius in his first speech makes a clear appeal to 'nature'. Nature refers to the ostensibly natural human feeling of brotherly love, and, because Claudius uses the royal 'we', the natural love which subjects feel – should feel – for their sovereigns:

> Though yet of Hamlet our dear brother's death
> The memory be green, and that it us befitted
> To bear our hearts in grief and our whole kingdom
> To be contracted in one brow of woe,
> Yet so far hath discretion fought with nature
> That we with wisest sorrow think on him
> Together with remembrance of ourselves.
>
> (I, ii, 1–7)

Of course, brothers might not feel unmitigated love for each other and the ties between subjects and sovereigns might not be as strong as

Claudius would like. In fact, Claudius has himself proved as much by murdering his brother, who was also his king. He has dissolved those 'natural' ties which he solemnly represents here as inviolable.

As already suggested, his expressions of grief are also truncated. 'Dear brother's death', 'one brow of woe', 'memory be green' are brisk, businesslike expressions of feeling. 'Discretion' has fought with 'nature', and discretion has won the day. Business as usual is shortly to be resumed. In his sermon to Hamlet about Hamlet's protracted (or 'so it seems' to Claudius) mourning, Claudius then tries to quantify grief by limiting it 'to a certain term'. He also begins to unsettle the term 'nature':

> 'Tis sweet and commendable in your nature, Hamlet,
> To give these mourning duties to your father;
> But you must know your father lost a father;
> That father lost, lost his; and the survivor bound
> In filial obligation for some term
> To do obsequious sorrow. But to persever
> In obstinate condolement is a course
> Of impious stubbornness, 'tis unmanly grief,
> It shows a will most incorrect to heaven,
> A heart unfortified, a mind impatient,
> An understanding simple and unschooled.
> (I, ii, 87–97)

Claudius destabilises the word 'nature' in this speech. Its use in the first line is specified to Hamlet, whereas in other uses of the word the particular and the general are combined, as in, for example, Claudius's phrase 'so far hath discretion fought with nature' and also in old Hamlet's 'If thou hast nature in thee'. These uses refer simultaneously to the nature that is or should be in the person and the nature which is in human beings in general. However, the specification of the word nature to Hamlet – 'your nature' – excludes Hamlet from the universal. Hamlet becomes a quirk of nature rather than an example of a general condition. This is reinforced in the second use of the word nature in the speech which establishes an alternative concept of general human nature which makes Hamlet's 'particular' grief seem perversely idiosyncratic.

Hamlet has two fathers or father figures. One uses the word 'nature' and means it, and means the same thing by it throughout the play. The other, the one who suggests that he might replace the 'natural', biological father, plays faster and looser with the word 'nature' and uses it conveniently, instrumentally, to suit his own purposes and exclude Hamlet from power and influence. Neither father is a good role model for Hamlet. The essentialism of the one and the anti-essentialism of the other are both inadequate. Or, to be more precise, the particular fleshly forms which essentialism and anti-essentialism take through Claudius and old Hamlet are inadequate. This does not stop Hamlet following in both of his fathers' footsteps. He can 'do' essentialism, as when, for example, he consigns his mother to the level of the subhuman: a 'beast that wants discourse of reason / Would have mourned longer!' (I, ii, 150–1). And he can equivocate with the best of them. But he also remains at a critical distance from both fathers and both versions of human nature, essentialist and anti-essentialist, which they represent. The acceptable face of disengaged rationality is a scepticism which extends to questioning disengagement itself, especially when it involves being so far removed from human needs and feelings that the human can become virtually anything at all.

There is another father figure in *Hamlet*: Yorick the jester, who 'appears' – in the form of a skull – in the gravedigger scene at the end of the play. Peter Stallybrass has suggested that it is as if the 'ghost of the jester displaces the ghost of the soldier-king'.[22] As a court jester, Yorick would have been an outsider and a mocker of the great and the good, but his wit in Hamlet's memory is combined with warmth: 'He hath borne me on his back a thousand times . . . Here hung those lips that I have kissed I know not how oft' (V, i, 181–4). Hamlet may have adopted the role of sceptic, distrustful of inherited traditions and the versions of human nature on which they rest, but in the graveyard he discovers or rediscovers through the example of Yorick a form of scepticism which coexists with tenderness. He mocks Yorick or what remains of Yorick, but the mockery is deeply affectionate:

> Where be your gibes now, your gambols, your songs, your flashes of merriment that were wont to set the table on a roar? Not one now to mock your own grinning? Quite chop-fallen? Now get you to my lady's chamber and tell her, let her paint an inch thick, to this favour [referring to Yorick's skull] she must come. Make her laugh at that. (V, i, 184–90)

Hamlet is in fact mocking mockery's tendency towards satire, cynicism and emptiness. The existential tremble which the graveyard sets off in Hamlet – the realisation that life ends or may end in only skull, bone and worm-eaten flesh – provokes an awareness of the need for humans to cling to each other for comfort. What remains of the human in the graveyard is this need for human solidarity. That Hamlet only finds this need answered by his memory of Yorick is a comment on the alienating, dehumanising world in which he has existed for most of the play.

Chapter 2

Emptying the Human: *Othello*

In *Hamlet* scepticism takes the form of a critical, questioning reason. This scepticism comes from inside the play through Hamlet and the critical distance he maintains (most, but not all, of the time) between himself and the belief systems which appeal to nature and human nature as their support. In *Othello* (1603–4), scepticism is monopolised by Iago and pushed in the direction of an instrumental reason. Questions about what is natural and unnatural are implied by the play, but there are no critical outsiders of the Hamlet variety. The first section of this chapter will take up the play's *implied* questioning of nature and human nature, and then examine Iago's distortions of critical consciousness. For Iago, I shall argue, questioning human nature is reduced to emptying it. So alarming is this emptying that the need arises to resurrect human nature as an ethical norm that can be used to measure the extent of the inhumanity to which humans are of course not immune.

In *Othello* various inhumane actions and speeches are performed in the name of the human. The racially mixed marriage between Othello and Desdemona is regarded by Desdemona's father, Brabanzio, as contravening 'the rules of nature' which according to him should order the human world.[1] The language used early on in the play by Iago and Roderigo to describe Othello draws on racist stereotypes in its categorisation of Othello as bestial and subhuman: he is 'an old black ram' (I, i, 87), 'a Barbary horse' (I, i, 113–14), a 'lascivious Moor' (I, i, 128). Given the 'many crimes', writes Alain Finkielkraut in *In the Name of Humanity* (1996), that have been 'committed in the name of higher values – in particular, humanity', any humanism which makes prescriptive appeals to norms may be highly questionable.[2] A glaring example, relevant to *Othello*, is the colonialist construction of western civilisation as the beacon of enlightened humanity, and non-European races as primitive and savage.[3] Another glaring example, also evident in *Othello*, is the treatment of women by men as only superficially trustworthy in their affections and loyalties, since deep-down they, too, have animal-like sexual appetites: 'centaurs' from the waist down, as Lear puts it.[4] This view of women is expressed by Othello after he thinks he has been cuckolded: 'O curse of marriage, / That we can call these delicate creatures ours / And not their appetites!' (III, iii, 272–4). Comparable gender stereotypes are expressed elsewhere in the play, by Brabanzio, for example, when he warns Othello that Desdemona 'has deceived her father, and may thee' (I, iii, 293).

Questions about the use of the concept of humanity as an ethical norm are implied by the play because of its positive treatment of the black Othello and the female Desdemona. Because they are not what the stereotypes say they are, the stereotypes tell us more about the prejudices of those who employ them. This principle can be extended to the demonisation of Iago at the end of the play. The description which the dying Roderigo gives of Iago – 'O damned Iago! O inhuman dog!' (V, i, 64) – raises the issue of whether Roderigo is simply perpetuating an ideology which projects onto demonised 'others' traits that are in fact part of the demonising self. Iago is from one perspective only joining a list of characters who have been previously regarded as 'unnatural' or beyond the pale of humanity, such as Othello, described by Iago himself as 'ram' and 'Barbary horse'. Scepticism might rightly warn us to be careful about accepting Roderigo's description of Iago, on the basis that such descriptions have been used in the play – and for many cultural theorists always are used – to save a culture's ideological face. The 'Human', writes Jean Baudrillard in *Symbolic Exchange and Death* (1976), is the 'institution of its structural double, the "Inhuman". This is all it is: the progress of Humanity and Culture are simply the chain of discriminations with which to brand "Others" with inhumanity, and therefore with nullity'.[5]

Alongside scepticism of the kind expressed by Finkielkraut and Baudrillard concerning ethical appeals made on behalf of the supposedly 'higher value' of humanity, we can place scepticism about the epistemological stability of the term 'human'. In *At the Borders of the Human* (1999), Erica Fudge, Ruth Gilbert and Susan Wiseman suggest that early modern and Enlightenment texts 'struggled to constitute the human' and that the 'boundaries between the categories of the human and its others were not . . . experienced as secure'.[6] They argue that contrary to the tendency to see the human as a once stable category which becomes increasingly unstable in modernity and postmodernity, the 'category of "the human" has never been stable or consensual', least of all during the Renaissance.[7] This instability undoes what they see as the violence of taxonomy in which 'non-humans' are 'violently expunged from the terrain of the human'.[8]

In *Othello*, the crossings and recrossings of the boundary separating the human from the non-human could be regarded as exemplifying the instability of a taxonomy which when it is nevertheless forced into some kind of stability is from Fudge, Gilbert and Wiseman's perspective only ever violent and exclusive. Appeals to humanity are from this viewpoint only ever weapons of ideology. Critical consciousness can perform ideological critique by locating beneath the veneer of civilised humanity a barbarism which is initially offloaded onto others, but comes to haunt the institutions of civilised society itself. This model of reversal, whereby the 'other' turns out to be part of the 'self', is evident in the way Cassio rues the drunken brawl which Iago has lured him into: 'To be now a sensible man, by and by a fool, and presently a beast!' (II, iii, 298–9). To be human is paradoxically to err from the supposedly 'higher value' of humanity, but what the erring do (though this is not particularly a characteristic of Cassio's) is to pretend otherwise by creating scapegoats. To be human, then, is not only to err, but to create scapegoats – sacrificial victims – who are made to carry the burden of humanity's inhumanity. However, because the line separating 'sensible man' from 'beast' is continually traversed, those who seem to exist comfortably inside their culture's definitions of what it is to be human can be suddenly placed outside of them and vice versa. As Ania Loomba, on the subject of outsiders and insiders in Renaissance drama, puts it:

> On Shakespearean and other early modern stages, the outsider is not safely 'outside' at all – like the older figure of the wild man, he or she threatens to cross over the boundaries of racial or ethnic or religious difference. Othello is not simply an alien who crosses over by marrying Desdemona, he is also the exotic outsider who alone is capable of defending Venice against other outsiders such as the Turks. Shylock as well as Portia draw attention to the unstable divide between 'the merchant' and 'the Jew' in Venice, and Jessica's conversion to Christianity reminds the audience just how fragile the boundaries between communities really are.[9]

If the boundaries between communities are fragile, then so too are the oppositions, between the human and inhuman, by which colonial or proto-colonial discourses seek to ground themselves.

Recent post-colonial criticism of Shakespeare has amongst other things focused on the ways in which such grounding oppositions are dismantled as a result of what Jonathan Burton refers to as cross-cultural 'trafficking' in difference.[10] As Loomba and Martin Orkin point out in *Post-Colonial Shakespeares* (1998), where Burton's essay appears, the reason for the urge to deconstruct oppositions is that 'the hybridity of colonial and post-colonial subjects' is viewed by many post-colonial critics as a 'potentially radical state, one which enables such subjects to elude, or even to subvert the binaries, oppositions and rigid demarcations imposed by colonial discourses'.[11] From this standpoint, oppositions between the human and subhuman are part of the armoury of colonial discourse which post-colonial criticism seeks to undo. As this chapter progresses, it will reclaim the human from its use or abuse within colonial discourse, but it is important to register the force of post-colonial and postmodern scepticism regarding foundationalist categories, for only then can a self-consciously critical humanism emerge. Earlier generations of post-colonial writers themselves questioned Eurocentric humanisms, but this was often in order to advance a better kind of humanism. Frantz Fanon in *Black Skins, White Masks* (1952), for example, argued for a 'new' humanist ethic of reciprocity which, instead of defining the self and the human against a dehumanised other, restores 'to the other, through mediation and recognition, his human reality'.[12] The example of Fanon suggests that although humanisms and appeals to humanity are subject to abuse, this does not mean that we should abandon them.

I have begun this chapter with examples of scepticism in its manifestation as critical consciousness from outside of the play (using representatives of contemporary critical consciousness), because inside the play there is, as I suggested at the outset, little scepticism of this kind. A sceptic such as Hamlet is, when he's not himself endorsing stereotypes, might have questioned some of the appeals that are made in the name of the human in *Othello*. The position of critical outsider is often taken by Hamlet, as a release from the limiting 'prison', as he sees it, of Denmark (II, ii, 253). It is a position from which he questions at least some of the values and norms of those who live 'inside' them. The position of sceptical outsider is briefly advanced in *Othello* towards the end of the play by Emilia, who highlights the double standards of men:

> What is it that they [men] do
> When they change us for others? Is it sport?
> I think it is. And doth affection breed it?
> I think it doth. Is't frailty that thus errs?
> It is so, too. And have not we affections,
> Desires for sport, and frailty, as men have?
> Then let them use us well, else let them know
> The ills we do, their ills instruct us so.
> (IV, iii, 95–102)

Emilia's scepticism involves questioning the divisiveness which elsewhere in the play leads to the perception that some individuals or groups of individuals are either 'more' or 'less' human than others. Her non-parochial, non-exclusive appeal to a common humanity reverses the self/other model on which other appeals to the human in the play rest, and in carnivalesque style also levels high-minded repudiations of the flesh. Men and women – white and black – are implicated in Emilia's all-encompassing characterisation of humans as subject to uncontrollable bodily appetites. 'Frailty' is not exclusively the name of 'woman', but of all human beings. Humanity is not appealed to by Emilia in the name of traditionally 'higher' values (spirit, soul, ethics, reason), but of 'lower' ones (appetite, desire). Emilia, then, is not only a sceptic but an essentialist whose conception of humanity in terms of the 'only human' will be examined in more depth in subsequent chapters. My current concern in this chapter, however, is with the relative paucity in *Othello* as compared with *Hamlet* of critical comment of the kind which puts one set of essentialist assumptions about who and what is properly human in contention with other assumptions.

One of the verbal tools of the critical outsider is abstraction. Abstractions, in the form of *sententiae*, place the outsider temporarily at a distance from the action of the play in order to comment upon it. As I suggested in the Introduction, the rhetorical culture which influenced the drama was a culture of embodied example rather than abstract precept, but as I also argued, particularity and generality of perspective were not mutually exclusive. Abstractions are 'lived out', therefore, by dramatic characters, but the outsider is never so immersed in his or her embodied existence as to close entirely the gap between life and critical reflection upon it. This gap is often the product of the *contending generalities* generated by rhetorical culture. The relativism of Hamlet's 'There is nothing either good or bad, but thinking makes it so' (II, ii, 244–5), as contrasted with the metaphysical certainty of 'There's a divinity that shapes our ends' (V, ii, 10), is an example. Emilia's question in *Othello* – 'have not we [women] affections, / Desires for sport, and frailty, as men have?' – is a 'rhetorical' question (in a different sense), but one nevertheless spoken above the immediate stream of events and in contention with other assertions or generalities about who and what is human/subhuman. Abstract debate is particularly rife in *Hamlet*, partly as a result of the dramatic device of the delayed revenge plot which leaves time for rival generalities as well as organically giving rise to them. This is in contrast with the plot structure of *Othello* which is more intense and compressed. Its theme of jealousy also involves a limitation rather than an expansion of perspective. But there is another reason – namely Iago – for the limitation of critical perspective in the play which I shall come to presently.

As a bridge to Iago, I want first to establish that there are fewer examples in *Othello* than in *Hamlet* of characters thinking critically above the stream of immediate events, and that where abstraction does occur it is significantly impoverished by being placed in the service of a 'mild' instrumentalism. The exchange between the Duke and Brabanzio at the end of the trial scene in Act I highlights this impoverishment. Brabanzio's irritated response to the outcome of the trial is: 'I am glad at soul I have no other child, / For thy [Desdemona's] escape would teach me tyranny, / To hang clogs on 'em (I, iii, 195–7). The Duke's reply to the moral drawn by Brabanzio is to draw another moral (or a parody of one), this time in tritely rhyming verse:

> Let me speak like yourself, and lay a sentence
> Which, as a grece or step, may help these lovers
> Into your favour.
> When remedies are past, the griefs are ended
> By seeing the worst which late on hopes depended.
> To mourn a mischief that is past and gone
> Is the next way to draw new mischief on.
> What cannot be preserved when fortune takes,
> Patience her injury a mockery makes.
> The robbed that smiles steals something from the thief;
> He robs himself that spends a bootless grief.
> (I, iii, 198–208)

This may not, in fact, be intended as a parody of a moral, but as a serious attempt to bring matters to a speedy conclusion so that the Venetians can turn their minds to pressing affairs of state: the 'Turkish fleet . . . bearing up to Cyprus' (I, iii, 8). Several times the Duke makes reference to the urgency of the situation: 'Valiant Othello, we must straight employ you/Against the general enemy Ottoman' (I, iii, 48–9); 'Th' affair cries haste, / And speed must answer it' (I, iii, 276–7). He is almost monosyllabic at times: 'Fetch Desdemona hither' (I, iii, 120); 'Say it, Othello' (I, iii, 127); 'Why, what's the matter?' (I, iii, 58). This is not the kind of spectacular, cloak-and-dagger Machiavellianism which was often presented on the English stage (and which Iago himself represents), but in his effective and efficient statecraft the Duke is nevertheless following broadly Machiavellian principles. *Sententiae* for the practically oriented Machiavellian statesman must be available, ready to hand and easy to use. *Sententiae* from this perspective are pseudo-traditional: they have the aura of the timeless about them, but they are in reality flexible resources for the instrumentally minded.

The published collections of *sententiae* in the sixteenth and seventeenth centuries frequently advertised themselves on this basis. Simon Robson's *The Choise of Change* (1585), for example, which contains the 'triplicitie of diuinitie, philosophie, and poetrie', is described as 'short for memorie, profitable for knowledge, and necessarie for maners', while Robert Cawdray's *A Treasvrie or Store-Hovse of Similies* (1600) promotes itself as 'pleasaunt, delightfull, and profitable, for all estates of men in generall. Newly collected into Heades and Commonplaces'.[13] Referring to the model of reading and writing recommended in Erasmus's *De Copia*, Lorna Hutson in *Thomas Nashe in Context* (1989) has suggested that Erasmus's plan is to 'have all the resources of future discursive invention at one's fingertips, in "ready money" '.[14] In similar vein, Richard Halpern in *The Poetics of Primitive Accumulation* (1991) argues that the 'technical procedures for producing copia contributed to the destruction of content'.[15] This he links to the 'rise of scepticism in early modern Europe':

> Tudor students were made to write Aphthonian themes *in utramque partem* on assigned topics, often drawing on materials stored under antithetical headings in commonplace books – a practice that tended to promote eloquence at the cost of dissolving content. It has been suggested that the rise of scepticism in early modern Europe, with its attendant religious and intellectual crises, owed less to the revival of Greek Pyrrhonism than it did to the consequences of the humanist educational program.[16]

The kind of scepticism apposite to the rhetorical practices described by Halpern is an empty scepticism, less healthily questioning of values and beliefs than unhealthily destructive of them. Halpern's and Hutson's above characterisations of humanist rhetoric constitute only one theory of the proliferation of collections of *sententiae* and commonplaces during the sixteenth and seventeenth centuries, for the availability of varied discursive resources could also lead to the kind of critical debate between contending perspectives which takes place in Hamlet's head.[17] In *Othello*, however, Halpern's and Hutson's model holds good, as abstract generalisation is placed in the service of what I described earlier as the mild instrumentalism of the Duke. Given the Duke's position, this is perhaps not surprising, although other Shakespearean heads of state, such as Richard II, do not yet inhabit the rationalised, disenchanted world of statecraft.

Brabanzio's response to the Duke, which is 'in kind' – in other words, in the same tritely rhyming verse – definitely pushes towards parody:

> So let the Turk of Cyprus us beguile,
> We lose it not so long as we can smile.
> He bears the sentence well that nothing bears
> But the free comfort which from thence he hears,
> But he bears both the sentence and the sorrow
> That, to pay grief, must of poor patience borrow.
> These sentences, to sugar or to gall,

> Being strong on both sides, are equivocal.
> But words are words. I never yet did hear
> That the bruised heart was piercèd through the ear.
> I humbly beseech you proceed to th'affairs of state.
> (I, iii, 209–19)

This illuminates both the possibility of critical debate and its foreshortening in *Othello*. Brabanzio not only parodies the Duke's moral by parodying his moralising style of speech, he also shows that the same abstract generalisation can be used for any number of different moral purposes (in support, for example, of the acceptance of the invasion of Cyprus by 'the Turk'). But whereas a Hamlet might have latched onto this and started ruminating about the problems of relativism ('There is nothing either good or bad but thinking makes it so'), Brabanzio winds up this truncated debate with: 'I humbly beseech you proceed to th'affairs of state'. Reasons of state nip these sceptics in the bud.

The main reason, however, for the absence of critical outsiders or at least for the weakening of their role in the play is Iago. There is no shortage of outsiders in *Othello*, some of whom, like Cassio, are created or, in the case of Othello, recreated as outsiders by Iago himself. When Iago assures Othello that 'I know my country disposition well' (III, iii, 205), he is reconstructing Othello as the cultural outsider which he was at the beginning of the play. This time Othello is cast by Iago as the 'innocent abroad', reliant upon his mentor's inside knowledge of gender subcultures and subterfuges. Othello's role as outsider is therefore disempowered by Iago, and his own role as outsider, which here involves pretending to be an 'insider' the better to manipulate Othello, is proportionately strengthened. Iago manages all the malcontents and displaced individuals in the play (Roderigo, Cassio, Othello), ensuring that his own brand of disenchanted consciousness dominates. Transforming the role of outsider into a pure instrumentalism, Iago makes certain that being an outsider for everyone else in the play is a position of abject need, which he can exploit.

A place from which critical consciousness can emerge is in the gap between mind and world, perceiver and perceived. Hamlet occupies this gap most of the time. Iago opens one up in Othello, but only to insinuate that what he sees in the world (Desdemona's fidelity) may not correspond with what is actually in the world (Desdemona's infidelity). In the case of the Othello who is subject to Iago, scepticism therefore equates to chronic fear and instability. For Othello, the gap between mind and world is utterly unbearable and he implores Iago to close it:

> By the world,
> I think my wife be honest, and think she is not.

> I think that thou art just, and think thou art not.
> I'll have some proof. My name, that was as fresh
> As Dian's visage, is now begrimed and black
> As mine own face. If there be cords, or knives,
> Poison, or fire, or suffocating streams,
> I'll not endure it. Would I were satisfied!
> (III, iii, 388–95)

As the denigrating reference to his own skin colour shows, the mind/world split is compounded by his reawakened sense of being a cultural outsider, an 'other' in the eyes of white Venetian society. For Othello, under Iago's control, the place of the outsider can only be a place from which he wants to escape. He therefore implores Iago to restore, if not the 'enchanted' world of love, then the (false) certainty that Desdemona is faithless. 'I'll have some proof', he says, removing Desdemona and his marriage from the realm of 'unthinking' habit, acceptance and enchanted belief into the realm of instrumentalised and subjectivised rationality presided over by Iago. His love for Desdemona is no longer a customary way of being; it is no longer the domestic equivalent of a traditional 'lifeworld', to recall Habermas's terminology from the Introduction.[18] Othello needs reasons for his beliefs or unbeliefs, but so chronic is his insecurity that he swallows Iago's instrumentalised reasons and proofs.

Iago is the place where all certainties, all faiths, all ideals and all optimistic beliefs in human nature are suspected, not in the name of critical reason, but to serve his own ends. *Potentially* the source of a Habermasian critical consciousness, Iago's detachment degenerates into a cold, unfeeling nihilism. The way Iago describes his body – as a garden that can be replanted at will – exemplifies a hard-headed, calculating rationality which also demonstrates the extent of his repudiation of all spontaneous intimacy:

> 'Tis in ourselves that we are thus or thus. Our bodies are our gardens, to the which our wills are gardeners; so that if we will plant nettles or sow lettuce, set hyssop and weed up thyme, supply it with one gender of herbs or distract it with many, either to have it sterile with idleness or manured with industry, why, the power and corrigible authority of this lies in our wills. If the beam of our lives had not one scale of reason to peise another of sensuality, the blood and baseness of our natures would conduct us to most preposterous conclusions. But we have reason to cool our raging motions, our carnal stings, our unbitted lusts; whereof I take this that you call love to be a sect or scion. (I, iii, 319–32)

Like Hamlet's disquisition on the nature of 'man', this also seems to echo Pico's *Oration on the Dignity of Man*, but it is an amoral version of it. Where Pico's anti-essentialism is framed in terms of human beings choosing forms of existence which might dignify or debase them, Iago's anti-essentialism demolishes the moral substance which traditionally clings to the question of 'how to live'. The body brought under the control of an unfeeling and valueless reason is simply an effective, sterile receptacle for the mere accumulation of attitudes, codes and linguistic resources. Language is thus also instrumentalised. Language does not matter to Iago in the way that it matters to other characters. Where other characters automatically invest in language because language is assumed to carry existential meaning and value, Iago 'externalises' language: he turns language into a series of exterior roles rather than 'selves' or possible selves. The roles he adopts are not 'experiments'; they are not somewhere on a scale between 'selves' and 'anti-selves'. They have nothing to do with the self. Roles and the language which is used to perform them are turned into 'objects', not for rational scrutiny, but for cool and calculating self-interest.

When language becomes instrumentalised, it is also dehumanised because it is shorn of affective and existential meaning. Signs and symbols are appropriated by Iago without any psychic or emotional investment. He ventriloquises languages, for example, the language of the tavern (II, iii), of advice to rulers (III, iii), of masculine homosocial bonding (III, iii), of feudal service (II, iii), of friendship (II, iii) and so on, without these discourses leaving any permanent traces or inscriptions on a body and mind purged of passionate entanglements. When he announces in Act I that 'for necessity of present life / I must show out a flag and sign of love' (I, i, 157–8), he is in effect announcing the existence of a self from whom signs have become totally alienated, disengaged. It is for others to be moved, manipulated or seduced by language and the ideas of the human embodied in it. A nomadic traveller between tongues, Iago remains an aloof observer of his own and others' verbal performances.[19]

This is no way to live. This might be the literary humanist message of the play. A human being devoid of emotion is no human being. Such a perspective is not anachronistic: it is not just a Romantic or post-Romantic reaction to the perceived impersonality of Enlightenment reason. The importance of the emotions in the Renaissance, and their centrality to human life and well-being, will be discussed in more detail in Part II, but we can anticipate some of this discussion by citing one of the principal claims of Richard Strier in 'Against the Rule of Reason' (2004). 'Insofar as self-consciously "Renaissance" figures defined themselves as committed to rhetoric over "mere" philosophy or logic,' writes Strier, 'they were committed to stressing the importance of the emotional and affective in life.'[20] Strier goes on to suggest that for some

Renaissance writers, the Italian humanist Coluccio Salutati, for example, 'sociality and affectivity are seen as defining the human, and as inextricably linked'.[21] That Iago's cold impersonation of sociality and affectivity has provoked such impassioned reaction goes some way towards proving the truth of Salutati's insight. Hugh Grady in *Shakespeare's Universal Wolf* (1996) specifies one kind of emotional response to Iago when he writes that: 'if Iago represents reification for Shakespeare, then clearly he wants us to be horrified by reification – horrified and fascinated, of course'.[22] The powerful emotional reaction to the emotionless Iago is a register of the extent of Iago's demolition of the human. We may be happy to follow Hamlet in his questioning of human nature but to empty it completely, as Iago does, abruptly returns us to the need to say what we mean by it. For the Renaissance writer Salutati, as for the contemporary critics Strier and Grady (despite the latter's avowed anti-essentialist position), emotion is a key constituent of the human.[23]

In some ways, of course, Iago does not represent the total demolition of human ties because of the conspiratorial intimacy which, as the 'villain', he strikes up with the audience. All villains do not equally beckon intimacy, but the characters who belong to Shakespeare's confederacy of villains, such as Aaron, Edmund, Richard III and Iago, frequently do.[24] The intimacy draws us to the villain, even as the villain gloats about his self-sufficiency, rejection of intimacy and autonomy from the rest of humanity, including the usual claims made on our humanity. The paradox of the Shakespearean villain, then, is that his bonding with the audience suggests an other-orientedness which is at the same time routinely denied. It may be questionable to attach psychological significance to a dramatic device, but Shakespeare often exploits opportunities for psychological effects, as an antidote to the danger of performance and psyche parting company. The relationship between Shakespearean villain and audience has, in any case, often been treated in broadly psychological terms. In *Shakespeare* (1989), Kiernan Ryan writes of *Othello* that a significantly 'disquieting feature of the play is the way that it encourages us, through the villain's downstage intimacy with the audience, to identify more with the viewpoint and values of Iago than with Othello'.[25] This is one effect, and one that Ryan thinks we should resist, but a countervailing perspective would be to say that intimacy does not begin and end with complicity with the villain's explicitly expressed world-view, alluring and fascinating as that world-view is made to be. To be drawn in by Iago and to find him fascinating may generate another kind of bond, a bond that involves us with Iago to the extent of looking beyond his surface motivations to other possible explanations of why he is as he is.

For example, Iago keeps other characters at a distance by routinely finding them stupid. He considers them stupid because they are trusting to the extent of being gullible. Of Roderigo, he says: 'Thus do I ever make my fool my purse – / I mine own gained knowledge should profane / If I would time expend with such a snipe / But for my sport and profit' (I, iii, 375–8). Later in the same speech, he talks of 'the Moor' as being of a 'free and open nature' (I, iii, 391). Getting on intimate terms with Iago means that we might begin to wonder why he fastens onto the attribute of trusting others as the epitome of stupidity. His description of Othello ends with more references to the idiotic gullibility of someone who 'thinks men honest that but seem to be so, / And will as tenderly be led by th'nose / As asses are' (I, iii, 392–4), but the beginning of the description ('free and open nature') sounds like something Iago wants but cannot have. Trust quickly becomes idiotic, but not before it has been fleetingly registered as a good. Was Iago himself stupid to trust Othello and believe that Othello would make him his lieutenant ahead of Cassio? Is he now projecting trust – as idiotic – onto Othello and compensating for his own perceived stupidity by trusting no one and instrumentalising all relationships?

The issue of Iago's 'motiveless malignity', as Samuel Coleridge described it, is a problematic one.[26] Whatever Iago's motivation or lack of it, the critical interest in it is the outcome of Shakespeare's preoccupation with affective psychology, a field of enquiry which he seems to anticipate. Thus where instrumentalisation strips the world of feeling, Shakespeare compensates by gesturing towards the idea that instrumentalisation might have its displaced source in 'recognisably' human situations and emotions. Iago's 'official' self may be cold and calculating, but the subtext of his speeches suggests damaged feelings and a damaged human being, who as a result of a past situation is unable to trust anyone in the present but himself: 'In following him [Othello] I follow but myself' (I, i, 58). 'Damaged' implies the possibility of 'healthy', or if this is too worryingly normative, then at least 'less damaged'. Othello and Desdemona initially represent this healthier state and it is one which seems all the more admirable by managing to rise above the culture of fear and distrust which has its source in Iago. Iago sows the seeds of distrust in the first scenes of the play, to Brabanzio about Othello and Desdemona, and to Roderigo about himself, and it spreads from there to envelop virtually all the main characters. It is against the background of both forms of distrust that Desdemona and Othello establish or re-establish trust as a model for human relationships.

Desdemona and Othello demonstrate faith in a faithless world. To the suspicion which Brabanzio casts upon Desdemona's fidelity – 'She has deceived her father, and may thee' (I, iii, 293) – Othello replies: 'My life upon her faith' (I, iii, 294). By at least temporarily resisting the virus of distrust, Othello and Desdemona reintroduce enchantment and sacredness to the disenchanted, desacralised world which eventually brings them down. It is easy to sentimentalise their relationship, but the disenchanted scepticism of some modern critics – prone, like Arthur F. Marotti in ' "Love Is Not Love": Elizabethan Sonnet Sequences and the Social Order' (1982), to reading love as a symptom of a desire for socio-economic power – makes what is easy quite difficult.[27] There are other modern critics, such as Walter Cohen, however, who have recognised the emotive power of the relationship. 'Why', asks Cohen, 'has Othello's failure [to recognise Desdemona's fidelity] been so moving to audiences and readers since the seventeenth century?' The 'answer', he suggests,

> is that *Othello*, unlike its source, emphasizes that Othello and Desdemona are special people who have done a special thing. Their unusual nobility of soul . . . leads most of the other characters to applaud a marriage that bridges gaps in age, nation, ethnicity, and culture.[28]

Kieran Ryan concurs and does not flinch from redeploying a word – 'barbarity' – which is used against Othello in the play: 'The destruction of Othello and Desdemona lays bare the barbarity of a culture whose preconceptions about race and gender cannot allow a love like theirs to survive and flourish'.[29] Othello and Desdemona stand for the possibility of human flourishing in a culture desperately in need of redemption from its cynical disillusionment, its distrust and its racism and sexism. We need to register this before we begin to subject love itself – as Shakespeare himself does – to radical scrutiny.

This chapter began with sceptical attitudes towards the ethical and epistemological viability of the term 'human', then moved on to examine Iago's complete emptying of the term, and ended with its resurrection as a foundational concept. The other trajectory of this chapter, which will be revisited and developed in Chapter 8, is from a 'top-down' scheme of values, in which the human acts as an ideological norm and is used against marginalised individuals and groups, to a 'bottom-up' model, in which the human constitutes a source of resistance to the dehumanising aspects of dominant or would-be dominant ideologies, such as the instrumentalism represented by Iago. The latter, bottom-up perspective is a useful corrective to the tendency of anti-humanist critics to treat all humanist taxonomies as inherently violent and abusive. To recognise how a concept can be abused through ideological misuse might just as well lead to an effort to rescue it from abuse as to the conclusion that it is inherently abusive. Moreover, as Shakespeare shows time and again, the destabilisation of categories such as the human is *itself* often violent and abusive. It is, after all, Iago's speciality. *Othello* suggests a need, as *Hamlet* does, not only to be sceptical of self/other, human/inhuman taxonomies, but also to be sceptical of a scepticism which homogenises all foundationalist appeals to the human. There is a need in the case of *Othello*, therefore, to differentiate between uses of terms such as 'nature', 'unnatural', 'human' and 'inhuman', so that the 'perceived' inhumanity of an Othello in Act I and of an Iago in Act V *is not* just a matter of perception. To agree with Roderigo that Iago's actions really are 'inhuman' is to rescue ethical language from the oblivion to which Iago consigns it.

Shakespeare does not allow for pious or complacent indignation, however, as the human beings depicted in the play are not immune to Iago's manipulation of them. The human is not so stable, in other words, that it cannot be alienated from itself, and characters are not so unswerving that they cannot be emptied of whatever essences they thought they owned. Roderigo, Cassio and Othello all prove to be malleable. They all become blank slates for Iago to write what he will upon. On the success of his first inscription of Roderigo, Iago gloats: 'Thus do I ever make my fool my purse'. To Iago, Roderigo is no longer a 'person' but a pawn, no longer a subject but an object. He is treated as 'less than human' by Iago. The horrific irony is that people can become pawns and humans robbed of whatever traits are thought to distinguish the human from its 'others': the inhuman or subhuman.

'To know', writes Dominique Janicaud in *On the Human Condition* (2002), 'that there is a monster lying dormant in each of us must render us more vigilant still'.[30] It is just such a vigilant humanism, born of an awareness of how 'nature, erring from itself' (III, iii, 232) can turn into its opposite, which Shakespeare's *Othello* shows to be necessary.

Chapter 3

Ironising the Human: *The Merchant of Venice*

The last scene of *The Merchant of Venice* (1596–7), which is set in Belmont and opens with a love scene between Lorenzo and Jessica, is suffused with such 'enchanted' images as these, from Lorenzo:

> How sweet the moonlight sleeps upon this bank!
> Here will we sit, and let the sounds of music
> Creep in our ears. Soft stillness and the night
> Become the touches of sweet harmony.
> Sit Jessica . . . Look how the floor of heaven
> Is thick inlaid with patens of bright gold.
> There's not the smallest orb which thou behold'st
> But in his motion like an angel sings,
> Still choiring to the young-eyed cherubins.
> Such harmony is in immortal souls,
> But whilst this muddy vesture of decay
> Doth grossly close it in, we cannot hear it.[1]

All is well between the lovers, and between the lovers and the universe. The conventional happy ending of comedy is at work here as part of the play's celebration of the triumph of harmony over strife, love over hatred, humane values over economic ones. Although Lorenzo presents a version of human embodiment, associating the body with decay, which makes such visions of cosmic love and harmony but dimly perceptible, Belmont, it seems, goes some way towards closing the gap between the ideal and the real.

Unsurprisingly, the final scene and play as a whole have divided critics. Perhaps more than any other critical disagreement over a single Shakespeare play, the divergence of critical opinion highlights the tension within modernity between enchantment and disenchantment: between the desire, on the one hand, to regard literature as epitomised by Shakespeare as the quasi-sacred vessel of human values and the sceptical imperative, on the other, to establish a critical distance from such values because of their perceived complicity with ideology. In the case of *The Merchant of Venice* this tension is manifested in the extent to which critics have read the play with or without a sense of irony. Lawrence Danson in *The Harmonies of The Merchant of Venice* (1978) has identified the centrality of irony to the play's critical as well as theatrical history.[2] However, since the publication of Danson's book, the significance of irony as a Zeitgeist has become especially pronounced because of the pervasive association of postmodernism with irony.[3] I shall subsequently examine two representative examples of approaches to the play which foreground in different ways the issue of irony. First, I want to give a broad sense of what reading with or without irony involves and how these approaches bear upon the issue of scepticism, on the one hand, and the 'how to live' question of literary humanism, on the other.

Reading with irony involves a continual alertness to those paradoxes and contradictions in the play which scupper affirmations of harmony and humane living. According to Catherine Belsey in 'Love in Venice' (1991), Lorenzo's 'way of talking about the body' in the last scene 'might seem, if not ironic, at least incongruous in an unqualified celebration of the joy of love'.[4] Reading with irony therefore involves being alert to the ongoing gap between the ideal and the real, as well as to the ideological nature of all appeals – idealising or denigrating – to the 'real': 'reality' has to be put in ironic quotation marks, as Richard Rorty does in *Contingency, Irony, and Solidarity* (1989).[5] Meanwhile, reading without irony or with only a weak sense of irony permits a search for, and embrace of, life-affirming moments, scenes, characters or philosophies which purportedly show us how to live a fulfilled life.

If irony is a form of detachment, then its absence or partial absence opens the way to attachment. Because literature from a literary humanist perspective has something we want (or need), we are seduced by the images of human fulfilment that it presents. In romantic comedy, fulfilment is based on the overcoming of obstacles, such as the inflexibility of the law, rigid class structures or an oppressive father bent on a daughter's marriage for economic gain, which stand in the way of existing or potential intimacies. This ethos of intimacy is present in romantic comedy not only as theme, but as dynamic between text and reader (or play and audience): romantic comedy beckons us to form an intimate relationship with it because it is supposedly about 'us' and our emotional needs, one of which is precisely the need to belong.

The French feminist critic Hélène Cixous implies that literary criticism should itself embrace something like the ethos of romantic comedy when she claims that: 'Everything begins with love. If we work on a text we don't love, we are automatically at the wrong distance'. She contrasts this affective attitude with what she sees as the lovelessness of theoretical approaches which treat the text 'as if it were an object'.[6] In *Reading after Theory* (2002), Cunningham draws analogies with religion to make a similarly impassioned plea on behalf of the idea that literature matters or should matter to us (in the way that a person we love and who loves us matters) because of the sustenance it provides:

> The Word of God, the body of Christ, become you: to your emotional, ethical, spiritual benefit. And so it is with reading where this model of reading as a selving, self-making process has prevailed. On this plan the words of the text that you seriously and closely engage with become you, get into you, have personal effect.[7]

Some might consider Cixous and Cunningham to be too uncritically attached to the idea of literature. But the opposite danger, which I discussed in the Introduction (and will return to in the next chapter), is for potentially meaningful human endeavours, such as literature and history, to become merely externalised objects, unhooked from human concerns. Irony does not always lead to this, for irony can itself be humanised as an 'ethos' or disposition. This is what Rorty does in *Contingency, Irony, and Solidarity* by continually characterising irony as 'the ironist'. The ironist nevertheless keeps objects of potential attachment at a distance, regarding them precisely as 'objects', while the 'evangeliser' enters into deep personal communion with them in the way that Cixous and Cunningham do with literature, because literature, to repeat, is felt to have something that we want.

So what does the ending of *The Merchant of Venice* have that we want or *might* want? I emphasise 'might' because of the ironist in me and because not everyone will be equally receptive to the same supposedly life-affirming moments. It is not possible to be programmatic about such matters. There is nevertheless the chance that something somewhere in a literary text is likely to 'speak to us' in a way that, say, a bus timetable cannot. As I have already implied, this chapter will argue that the urge for attachment is that 'something' which the ending of *The Merchant of Venice* identifies not only as a human principle but as a cosmic one. The ironies which also exist in the play and onto which sceptical critics have fastened may frustrate this urge, but my argument in this chapter will be that the frustration leads only to the search for another object of identification to replace that which has been blocked.

It is not my intention, however, to divide critics over-neatly into literary humanist and anti-humanist on the basis of the relative presence or absence in their work of an ironising scepticism. Irony and scepticism may not only cultivate detachment from putatively existential needs and wants. Hamlet, for example, is a sceptic but still looks to differentiate between more or less authentic expressions of the human. He still clings to an ethics which shows him the difference between the world in which he exists and the better, more fully human world in which he might exist. There are different kinds of irony, in other words, some of which are more *redemptive* than others. An example of the use of redemptive irony is Erasmus's *Praise of Folly* (1509). The character Folly lavishes ironically intended praise on a number of follies, from human self-love to scholastic overspecialisation, but some of them are so persuasively described as to cause our ironic guard to slip and make us see ourselves in the folly. The humbling of the reader paves the way for the humility required by the form of folly – Christian folly – which is ironically denigrated (and therefore affirmed) at the end of the book.[8] Erasmus's redemptive use of irony thus moves us from detachment through to identification and finally affirmation. So-called postmodern irony may similarly cultivate distance as its initial ploy, but the cool breeze of irony is often not an end in itself, but a means to the end of affirming that human life could be better than it is. A distinction can nevertheless be drawn between those critics of *The Merchant of Venice* whose confident humanism allows them to move beyond irony to affirm expressions of authentic humanity wherever and whenever they think that it 'obviously' exists, and those more sceptically inclined critics whose approach is more wary of the obvious.

For a confidently literary humanist approach to the play, which puts definite limits on the extent of the play's ironies, we can turn to C. L. Barber's influential *Shakespeare's Festive Comedy* (1959). 'No other comedy, until the late romances', he writes, 'ends with so full an expression of harmony as that which we get in the opening of the final scene of *The Merchant of Venice*'. 'And no other final scene', he continues, 'is so completely without irony about the joys it celebrates'.[9] For Barber, irony in *The Merchant of Venice* is limited and, by the beginning of the final scene, over. The 'ironies', he writes, 'have been dealt with beforehand in baffling Shylock; in the moment of relief after expelling an antagonist, we do not need to look for the limitations of what we have been defending'.[10] For later critics, however, ironies abound both at the end of the play and throughout, so much so that Michael Ferber in 'The Ideology of *The Merchant of Venice*' (1990) wonders whether the tendency towards irony may have more to do with the nature of contemporary criticism than with the play itself:

> The last word on the play's unity and 'harmonies' seems already to have been said, and the reigning spirit of literary criticism today is skeptical, analytical, deconstructive, relentless in its search for ironies. The inconsistencies and

> paradoxes that have been turned up, however, often seem arbitrary, either because they are not folded back into a general assessment of the play or, more important, because they are not traced to the ideas and practices of Shakespeare's historical moment.[11]

The pursuit of irony is or was not only 'the reigning spirit of literary criticism', but part of the Zeitgeist of postmodernism, a Zeitgeist which Rorty's *Contingency, Irony, and Solidarity* is often taken to embody. Rorty characterises 'an ironist' as someone who has 'radical and continuing doubts about the final vocabulary she currently uses' and 'does not think that her vocabulary is closer to reality than others'.[12] With echoes of Hamlet's 'there is nothing either good or bad but thinking makes it so', Rorty argues that, for an ironist, 'anything can be made to look good or bad by being redescribed'.[13]

Ferber's reading of *The Merchant of Venice* does not participate in the 'endemic' that is or was postmodern irony (as represented here by Rorty), because he does try to establish some sort of 'final vocabulary' which will bring him closer to the play's historical reality. Ferber himself detects ironies in the play, but instead of finding them everywhere as 'recent post-structuralist readings' of the play tend to do, 'with little reference to the actual ideologies mobilized in it', he invokes 'standards of relevance', by which he means 'conventions of reading, historical probabilities, available ideologies, and even common sense' to put limits on the extent of the play's ironies.[14] The limits on irony which Ferber wants to impose also make unexpected room – but only right at the end of his essay – for another kind of 'final vocabulary', for he concludes his piece with a quasi-enchanted endorsement of 'social warmth'. Critics who ironise 'the Venetians' friendly, gregarious banter', writes Ferber, 'forget the extent to which their own sensibility is colored by modern suspicions of courtesy and social warmth and by the shriveling of the public sphere'.[15] 'Venice', he concludes, 'may be unable to solve its problems by itself, but gay camaraderie is not one of its problems. It may be one of its saving graces'.[16] The final vocabulary towards which Ferber moves here is not a historical truth but an ahistorical, human ideal.

Notwithstanding Ferber's 'non-sceptical' belief in the ability of the cultural historian to uncover historical realities, the affirming ending of Ferber's essay is unexpected because the essay devotes most of its energy to substituting one kind of scepticism for another: the scepticism of a (post-structuralist) philosophy of language, regarded by Ferber as ahistorical, for the scepticism of cultural historicism, based on identifying historically specific 'truths' and meanings rather than universal ones. Both forms of scepticism foster critically alert disengagement rather than 'humanist' identification of the kind that leads to an affirmation of a putatively authentic way of living, marked as a 'saving grace'. Talk of saving graces is more in the style of an older generation of literary critic, such as Barber, who as we have seen writes with confidence about the life-denying and life-affirming forces at work in *The Merchant of Venice*, of 'the reduction of life to mechanism', for example, represented by Shylock.[17] Barber also represents the 'post-ironic' festive ending of *The Merchant of Venice* in terms of cathartic relief and relaxation. Conflict-free Belmont is a place to 'frolic', a place of 'idle talk' and 'casual enjoyment of music',[18] a place, to recall a phrase of Barber's quoted earlier, where 'we do not need to look at the limitations of what we have been defending'. For Barber, critical disengagement has no place in the relaxed world of Belmont. In Barber's Belmont, there is no need for the guardedness, the analytical labour or the suspicion of irony, because the final scene is 'completely without irony about the joys it celebrates'.

The list Ferber gives at the beginning of his essay – 'the reigning spirit of literary criticism today is skeptical, analytical, deconstructive, relentless in its search for ironies' – makes literary criticism sound exhaustingly defensive. If the ironic critic is always on the lookout for the loophole, the undermining inconsistency, the paradox that reverses a stated position – if the ironic critic is in other words holding off his or her object and keeping it at a critical distance – then affirmation and attachment are the salves which reunite a disaffected subject with its estranged object. In Belmont, despite the fact that, as Barber notes, 'a certain contemplative distance is maintained by talking *about* perception, *about* harmony and its conditions', the alienation of self from self and self from world is overcome.[19]

Barber writes about the final scene with considerable enthusiasm. The source of his enthusiasm is what Ferber refers to in a shorthand way at the end of his essay as 'social warmth' but what Barber as a more fully fledged literary humanist expands on more lyrically, such that warmth is identified as a general human principle as well as a principle of the universe. Barber's enthusiasm is basically for all the 'reaching out' that is going on in the poetry of the last scene: of lovers towards each other; of self towards world; of world towards self; and of nature towards itself in such images as 'In such a night as this, / When the sweet wind did gently kiss the trees' (V, i, 1–2). Barber generalises all these harmonising embraces as follows: the 'openness to experience, the images of reaching out towards it, or of welcoming it, letting music "creep in our ears," go with the perception of a gracious universe'.[20] The assumption is that the urge to reach out and become attached to the world is a naturally human urge which is allowed to flourish and flow in the last scene uninterrupted by any of the blocking mechanisms of irony. In the near-paradise that is Belmont, there are no alienating distances. In psychoanalytic terms, we might say that Belmont is a pre-Oedipal world. In the influential sociological terms derived from Ferdinand Tönnies, it is an example of *Gemeinschaft* rather than *Gesellschaft*.[21] In religious parlance, it is prelapsarian.

It is no wonder, perhaps, that the rich and the privileged should be able to feel 'at home' in the world. But the urge to become attached to the world and to make of the world a 'home' which accommodates rather than alienates is one which can survive less promising circumstances. To give an updated example of the representation of a 'paradise' far less wealthy than Belmont, we can turn briefly to a section, simply called 'Paradise', in Eva Hoffman's autobiography, *Lost in Translation* (1989). Hoffman describes the 'wonder' of 'what you can make a paradise out of':

> I grew up in a lumpen apartment in Cracow, squeezed into three rudimentary rooms with four other people, surrounded by squabbles, dark political rumblings, memories of wartime suffering, and daily struggle for existence. And yet, when it came time to leave, I, too, felt I was being pushed out of the happy, safe enclosures of Eden.[22]

The outside world, for the as yet unalienated Hoffman, is not really an 'outside' at all. Lying, aged four, in her bed in Cracow in 1949 in a half-conscious state, she describes her room, with echoes of John Donne, as 'an everywhere' which is 'enough to fill me with a feeling of sufficiency because . . . well, just because I'm conscious, because the world exists and it flows so gently into my head'.[23] The moral is not 'poor but happy', but the wonder of our predisposition to form attachments to whatever bit of the world we happen to be thrown into. Lauren Berlant in 'Critical Inquiry, Affirmative Culture' (2004) writes that to 'talk about the senses is to involve oneself in the optimism of attachment, the sociability of persons across things, spaces, and practices', which she argues 'represents a turn to the human without resurrecting, necessarily, a metaphysical subject'.[24] However, the human predisposition, evoked by Hoffman, to make a home of the world suggests that attachment might be more than a matter of optimism.

In contrast with Hoffman's sparse proletarian paradise, the soft lighting and generally congenial atmosphere of Belmont make attachment easy. Nevertheless, there are problems both in and with Belmont, problems which create various discordant ironies. Antonio, for example, remains detached when the likelihood is that he would prefer to be attached, in love, friendship and sex, to Bassanio. The exclusion of Antonio, according to Alan Sinfield, conforms to a pattern in Shakespeare whereby 'the erotic potential of same-sex love is allowed a certain scope, but has to be set aside'.[25] Antonio is instead left with the news, given to him by Portia, of the safe arrival of his ships: 'Unseal this letter soon. / There you shall find three of your argosies / Are richly come to harbour suddenly' (V, i, 275–7). Despite the fact that trade, or certain kinds of trade, have themselves been 'humanised' in the play, in the sense that they have been treated as though compatible with human attributes and aspirations, the pouring of human passions into ships is a poor substitute for human bonding. This is especially so, given that excessive person-to-thing attachments have themselves been heavily ironised in the play. Shylock's reported preference for 'ducats' over his 'daughter' (II, viii, 15) is so obviously a sign of Shylock's dehumanisation that the humanised Antonio cannot be overjoyed by being reunited only with his wealth. Antonio's 'marriage' to his ships is not the kind of 'authentic' coupling, of person-to-person rather than person-to-thing, which is the basis of a traditional comic ending.

The irony, if we see it that way, of Antonio's exclusion from the authentic person-to-person bonding of the last scene blocks the complete (or almost complete identification) with the human values of Belmont which a critic like Barber seeks. The perception of irony at this point can travel in one of two directions. It can be entirely negative and metaphorically 'trash' Belmont as an aristocratic, heterosexual 'club', whose humanism is exclusive. Such irony involves a complete and utter detachment, and only leaves the satisfaction of having demolished a cow held by the characters within the play and some critics outside it to be sacred. The other way in which irony can travel is in a more redemptive direction, meaning that our attachment to the values of Belmont is frustrated but that the frustration provokes a search for a better, more inclusive humanism. Redemptive irony thus saves rather than discards. It recycles rather than trashes. In the case of Belmont, it identifies loopholes and contradictions while retaining a sense that there is something there worth keeping. Redemptive irony chimes with what Ferber in his (qualified) endorsement of the 'social warmth' of the Venetians refers to as one of their 'saving graces'.

The treatment of Shylock is another major source of irony which complicates the Venetians' confident sense of their superior humanity and way of life. Should we therefore scorn or salvage the 'humanity' they represent? If the aim is to salvage, then it must take account of the various ironies as well as intricacies woven by the play around Shylock and the Venetians.

Shylock is vilified by the Venetians for purportedly putting economic above human and ethical values – ducats above daughters. When the deal between Bassanio and Shylock is being negotiated, Shylock ponders whether Antonio, who is offering himself as surety for the loan, is a 'good' man:

> *Shylock*: Antonio is a good man.
> *Bassanio*: Have you heard any imputation to the contrary?
> *Shylock*: Ho, no, no, no, no! My meaning in saying he is a good man is to have you understand me that he is sufficient. Yet his means are in supposition. He hath an argosy bound to Tripolis, another to the Indies. I understand moreover upon the Rialto he hath a third at Mexico, a fourth for England, and other ventures he hath squandered abroad.
> (I, iii, 12–21)

The ethical content of 'good' is irrelevant from the point of view of business. Shylock, here, is a further example of the instrumental rationality whose links to a burgeoning capitalism are apparent. Shylock is Shakespeare's prescient sign of the pervasiveness of market values, prescient because capitalism is of course now a global phenomenon whose effects on all aspects of human life are seemingly irresistible. In *The Merchant of Venice*, however, resistance comes paradoxically from within capitalism itself. Antonio is himself 'the merchant of Venice', but a merchant who in apparent contrast to Shylock's reductive economism asserts the primacy of human values, meaning that he puts affective ties (person-to-person attachments) above money, metal, gold and ducats. Where Shylock's imputed 'motto' is 'My daughter! O, my ducats' (II, viii, 15), Antonio's reverse motto is: 'when did friendship take / A breed of barren metal of his friend?' (I, iii, 131–2).

Although we may be tempted to locate an irony in the vilification of one type of capitalist by another, from the perspective of Antonio's benevolent practice of capitalism, there is *no* irony in the fact that a merchant should vilify a usurer for his lack of humanity, because the merchant represents or is seen as representing a form of capitalism which can accommodate – and even generate – human values. This is Barber's perspective when he suggests that '*The Merchant of Venice* . . . exhibits the beneficence of civilized wealth, the something-for-nothing which wealth gives to those who use it graciously to live together in a humanly knit group'.[26] In other words, because money makes possible an 'aristocratic' disregard for money, it poses no threat to 'social warmth'. For a more up-to-date perspective on the hope that capitalism might have a human face to offset its more disfiguring aspects – a hope that was partially supported in reality by the affective networks of credit and debt which developed in the sixteenth century – we can turn to Curtis Perry's 'Commerce, Community, and Nostalgia in *The Comedy of Errors*' (2003). Drawing on the work of Theodore Leinwand and Georg Simmel, Perry argues that:

> Shakespeare's England was neither the modern marketplace of individual commercial agents that Simmel describes nor the primitive culture he sets modernity against: in attempting to recover the 'socio-economically aroused affect' dramatized in the period's fictions, we need somehow to reconcile the disaffiliating force of early capitalism with the intense sociability fostered by the culture of credit.[27]

Capitalism and kinship, money and affect, could be reconciled. Such, at any rate, was the hope that had some anchoring in reality via the culture of credit. The mutuality of love and money is expressed on several occasions in the play: it is present in Bassanio's first description of Portia (I, i, 161–76) and in his testimony to his friendship with Antonio: 'To you, Antonio, / I owe the most in money and in love' (I, i, 130–1). Financial and emotional indebtedness go together.

The merchant *can* therefore vilify the usurer for reducing affective to monetary values without the irony of contradiction. Matters are nonetheless more complicated than this, as there are still multiple ironies at work in the Venetians' attitude to wealth and treatment of Shylock. However, I shall argue that these ironies do not so much 'block' affective attachment to the human values of the play, as re-route it.

One irony is that the reality of capitalism may be different from the partial reality which has it that commerce is compatible with human values. The 'assumption', writes Eric Spencer in 'Taking Excess, Exceeding Account' (2003), 'that brotherly solidarity results from free lending rings false, if we can judge by the failure of Venice's merchant community to come to Antonio's aid'.[28] The illusion that capitalism nurtures rather than negates human values is the stuff of ideology in the Marxist sense that it misrepresents reality in the interests of those who benefit most from capitalism. However, the illusion that can be unmasked by an ironic scepticism towards the 'so-called' truth does not compromise the desirability of those human values, though it *does* mean that we look askance at the capacity of the Venetians to embody them totally because they are part of the burgeoning capitalist culture.

Although the Venetians seek to represent the human face of capitalism and project its inhuman face onto the Jewish usurer Shylock, the irony is that they are themselves complicit in capitalism's inhumanity.[29] Shylock himself often takes the role of sceptic or ironist in the play, in that he stands mockingly outside belief systems and exposes the double standards of those around him. As Barber puts it, Shylock can be 'a drastic ironist, because he carries to extremes what is present, whether acknowledged or not, in their [the Venetians'] silken world'.[30] That the source of the Venetians' wealth might be their exploitation of people as commodities is indicated by Shylock when he refuses to act mercifully towards Antonio on the basis that the Venetians themselves are less than merciful towards their 'slaves', as Shylock refers to them. Why should he, in the name of human 'mercy' (IV, i, 87), give up the pound of flesh he has bought, when Venetian society is itself based on the buying and selling of human beings?

> You have among you many a purchased slave
> Which, like your asses and your dogs and mules,
> You use in abject and in slavish parts
> Because you bought them. Shall I say to you
> 'Let them be free, marry them to your heirs.
> Why sweat they under burdens? Let their beds
> Be made as soft as yours, and let their palates
> Be seasoned with such viands.' You will answer
> 'The slaves are ours.' So do I answer you.
> The pound of flesh which I demand of him
> Is dearly bought. 'Tis mine, and I will have it.
> (IV, i, 89–99)

The Venetians' reduction of people to 'asses', 'dogs' and 'mules' weakens their claim to represent human values. While the Venetians are good at identifying certain types of dehumanisation, such as the reduction of daughters to ducats, they are less good at identifying their own inhuman ways, such as their running of a slave economy.

The Venetians' blindness to their own dehumanisation of others extends, of course, to Shylock himself, who with his usual candour points out the nauseating treatment he has received at the hands of Antonio:

> You come to me, and you say
> 'Shylock, we would have moneys' – you say so,
> You, that did void your rheum upon my beard,
> And foot me as you spurn a stranger cur
> Over your threshold. Moneys is your suit.
> What should I say to you? Should I not say
> 'Hath a dog money? Is it possible
> A cur can lend three thousand ducats?' Or
> Shall I bend low, and in a bondman's key,
> With bated breath and whisp'ring humbleness
> Say this: 'Fair sir, you spat on me on Wednesday last;
> You spurned me such a day; another time
> You called me dog; and for these courtesies
> I'll lend you thus much moneys'?
> (I, iii, 114–27)

The basic but basically sound psychology appealed to by Shylock is that if you treat a person like a dog, then he or she may well act like a dog.

The scapegoat vilified for his inhumanity talks back here to the scapegoater and his inhumanity. Speeches like this one support the view that the play is neither anti-Semitic nor 'anti-anti-Semitic', but rather, as René Girard argues in *A Theater of Envy* (1991), both at once. Shakespeare, writes Girard:

> is so knowledgeable in regard to the paradoxes of mimetic reactions and group behavior that he can stage a scapegoating of Shylock entirely convincing to those who want to be convinced, and simultaneously undermine that process with ironic touches that will reach only those who can be reached.[31]

This is a good example of a redemptive form of irony whereby the Venetians' 'humanity', access to which has been blocked by Shylock's scepticism, is 'saved' by relocating human values outside the play, in Shakespeare himself. The character inside the play, however, who makes this identification possible is Shylock, the scapegoat and ironist who draws attention to the process of creating scapegoats.

For Girard, the play's subtly double message is a kind of secret code for the 'refined' to decipher. The 'most vulgar as well as the most refined audiences', he writes, 'will be satisfied by the anti-Semitism and anti-anti-Semitism respectively'.[32] For other critics, however, the ironies of the play, which work to undo the differences between scapegoat and scapegoated and insist instead upon their equivalence, are part of Shakespeare's routine dismantling of the boundaries between 'self' and 'other'. For Edward Berry, in 'Laughing at "Others"' (2002), for example, the trial scene in *The Merchant of Venice*, where 'Shylock's vengefulness comes to seem almost indistinguishable from a Christian charity that outwits and breaks him', is one of numerous examples from a range of comedies of selves sliding into their opposites.[33] Whereas for Girard this kind of slippage is noteworthy and controversial, for Berry it is just the kind of thing that routinely happens in Shakespeare. Berry's conclusion is that such slippages are evidence of a 'skepticism about the categorizing of social experience that divides "selves" from "others" in ways that are neither stable nor secure'.[34]

My own, somewhat different, conclusion is that the ironising principle of equivalence not only undermines the supposedly greater 'humanity' of one character or group, but calls for an acknowledgement of a common humanity. In negating difference, such irony affirms sameness. While the sameness in question can bring 'high' characters down to the level of the 'low', as is the case in Christopher Marlowe's *The Jew of Malta* (*c.*1589–90), where the Christians scarcely look better than the Jew Barabas, the affirmation of equivalence in *The Merchant of Venice* arguably draws a more hopeful picture of humanity. The irony that produces equivalence amongst characters is consequently redemptive rather than destructive of ethical appeals to humanity and how to live. The example of Shylock, upon whom I now want to focus in more depth, can direct us to this path of thinking about irony in the play.

Not only are the Venetians as inhuman as Shylock, but Shylock, like Iago, is not as irredeemably inhuman as first appears. Shylock often ventriloquises possible responses to his interlocutors: 'Shall I say to you'; 'Should I not say'; 'shall I bend low . . . and say'. These imagined Shylocks are themselves 'ironised' Shylocks. They are characters whom the ventriloquising Shylock knows to be the creation of others, such as Shylock the 'dog'. Shylock, so the ventriloquist implies, might be or might have been different. The difference of Shylock from the imagined or ventriloquised stereotype of him as the inhumanly money-driven 'Jew' has been noted by Katharine Eisaman Maus. Shylock, she writes, 'pretends that he thinks of people in purely material, economic terms', but, she suggests, 'he becomes a moving character precisely at those moments when he admits another kind of value'. The examples she gives are his 'grief over his daughter's defection' (which contradicts the rumoured economic source of his grief), his 'refusal' in the courtroom to be 'swayed by monetary appeals' (which contradicts the 'calculating prudence' he is famed for) and his sentimental response to the loss reported by Tubal of his turquoise ring:[35] 'Thou torturest me, Tubal. It was my turquoise. I had it of Leah when I was a bachelor' (III, i, 112–13).

The motivation behind the bond which Shylock seals with Antonio is also not strictly or narrowly economic. As Shylock himself says of the forfeit of the pound of flesh: 'what should I gain / By the exaction of the forfeiture? / A pound of man's flesh taken from a man / Is not so estimable, profitable neither, / As flesh of muttons, beeves or goats' (I, iii, 162–6). Bassanio's explanation for the forfeit suggested by Shylock implies that it is just the kind of mischief – or worse – of a villain: 'I like not fair terms and a villain's mind' (I, iii, 179). The perceived motivation of the villain is circuitous: evil for evil's sake, rather than economic. However, Shylock as we have seen through his ventriloquising of the role of scapegoat is more than a typical stage villain. He is given access to more viewpoints, more discourses, than this. These include the irony of the oppressed and an emotional/psychological depth. The prelude to the sealing of the bond is not coldly businesslike, but emotionally charged, with Shylock, as already discussed, inflamed by Antonio's appalling treatment of him. In his subsequent speeches, Shylock repeatedly makes out that he wants to be Antonio's friend and that his offer is an act of love and 'kindness': 'I would be friends with you, and have your love' (I, iii, 136); 'This kindness will I show' (I, iii, 142); 'To buy his favour I extend this friendship' (I, iii, 167); 'for my love, I pray you wrong me not' (I, iii, 169). Shylock is again almost certainly being ironic, by appealing to values – of love and friendship – that he knows are dear to the Venetians but have not ever been extended to him. Shylock is from this perspective speaking not out of calculated economic self-interest, but injury and resentment. Resentment is a substitute for friendship. It holds its object in an affectively loaded connection to itself and will not let go of it. This is what the 'bond' signifies. The bond is not a cold economic transaction but a sign of the depth of Shylock's grievance.

Bassanio and Antonio came to Shylock to talk money and terms, but Shylock insists on talking about friendship, love and the lack of them: 'You come to me, and you say, / "Shylock we would have moneys" – you say so, / You that did void your rheum upon my beard'. Antonio and Bassanio treat Shylock instrumentally, as an (economic) means to an end, but Shylock refuses to be so treated. He reminds them that he is a human being, who has been used badly. Economic relations are thus being saturated by affectively charged relations.[36] Economics in the play is not the prime mover which shapes, reshapes or misshapes human beings, but the outcome of human relationships which have turned sour. Calculated economic self-interest is from this perspective the institutionalisation of resentment. It is a sign of the failure of relationship. What *might*, according to Shylock, have made the world go round is neither money nor the resentment that underlies it, but love. This is the bond which might have been.

The irony here, then, is that 'economic man' turns out not to be so economic. In *Shakespeare's Universal Wolf* (1996), Hugh Grady examines what he refers to as an 'incipient differentiation' in Shakespeare's work between 'objectivist and subjectivist' spheres. By 'objectivist' he mainly means reification, defined as 'the property of social systems to act through their own objective logic, as if they possessed an autonomous intentionality'. The subjective sphere is according to Grady 'closely implicated' in 'the newly emerging objectivity', but it also 'becomes the container of all that the new objectivity has suppressed'.[37] In *The Merchant of Venice* the 'subjective sphere' which is only half-suppressed by the 'newly emerging objectivity' is represented by feeling, friendship and the natural human urge to form attachments. Shylock may represent an incipient form of economism, but its incipience means that feeling still clings to economic transactions. These are not the 'good' feelings (of love and friendship) that attach to the culture of debt and credit represented by Antonio and Bassanio, but their inversions or perversions. They are nevertheless feelings which resist the process whereby 'feeling' is expelled from a dehumanised public into a humanised private sphere. Shylock refuses to be a pure symbol of the exchange mechanism. Mocked for reducing 'life to mechanism', as Barber puts it, the irony is that he himself opposes such a reduction. Nowhere is this more apparent than in Shylock's famous 'Jew' speech:

> Hath not a Jew eyes? Hath not a Jew hands, organs, dimensions, senses, affections, passions; fed with the same food, hurt with the same weapons, subject to the same diseases, healed by the same means, warmed and cooled by the same winter and summer as a Christian is? If you prick us do we not bleed? If you tickle us do we not laugh? If you poison us do we not die? And if you wrong us shall we not take revenge? (III, i, 54–62)

Some critics have read this as further evidence of the reductiveness with which Shylock is associated in the play, for the human sameness it appeals to is the sameness of the flesh, as opposed to the spirit. From the perspective of the Christian characters in the play, it only proves Shylock's reductively materialist outlook. After this speech, writes Richard Halpern in *Shakespeare among the Moderns* (1997), the insinuations of Salerio of racial difference 'are never repeated', but the 'logic of difference, exiled from the flesh, proceeds to root itself in even more fertile ground: the realm of spirit'.[38] Just when Shylock might have thought that he had won the 'irony wars' and contra the 'logic of difference' proved the common humanity of Jews and Christians, the human/humane moves elsewhere, into the realm of 'spirit', away from the Jew and back towards the Christians. But it does not stay securely there either, because the Christians via Portia in the trial scene prove themselves adept at suspending the 'spirit' of the law when they need to and insisting instead on its 'letter'.

The conclusion I want to draw is that the multiple ironies in the play mean that the human as a source of identification in the play keeps shifting about: from Belmont to Venice, from Christian to Jew back to Christian, from capitalism via the affectively charged culture of debt and credit to the play's anti-capitalist critique. It may therefore be difficult to identify a definitive location for human values, but equally – and this is the basis for the redemptive kind of irony which I would argue that the play ultimately inspires – they are difficult to avoid. This is because the play keeps inviting identification with the human and the humanised as an antidote to the various kinds of dehumanisation present in the play, including the 'inhumanity' of a complacent humanism. Redemptive irony recognises the shortcomings of each and every appeal made 'in the name of humanity', but does not remain coldly detached from such appeals. Because the play urges the 'warmth' of human attachment rather than the 'coolness' of detachment, we keep looking for objects of identification as replacements for those which have been withdrawn or partly withdrawn. Shylock's irony is itself caustic and cutting, but it is at the same time redemptive in its insistence on his inhumane treatment: 'You come to me, and you say, / "Shylock we would have moneys" – you say so, / You that did void your rheum upon my beard'.

To end the chapter here, with the wounded Shylock's powerful accusation of inhumanity, is bound to be to some extent arbitrary. Once irony as a principle of the play or a critical principle has been set in motion, it is difficult to arrest, especially in a climate where, as Ferber suggests, the 'reigning spirit of literary criticism . . . is skeptical, analytical, deconstructive, relentless in its search for ironies'. It is easy to feel stupid and naive as a result of failing to notice an irony where one might have been intended or where one has been subsequently found by a critic. 'No modern Shakespearean', writes Danson, 'would want to be thought deficient in his sense of irony'.[39] Moreover, if irony according to Girard is 'not demonstrable', then its detection will make critics feel a cut above those who rest content at what Girard refers to as the 'cathartic level':

> Irony is not demonstrable . . . and it should not be, otherwise it would disturb the catharsis of those who enjoy the play at the cathartic level only. Irony is anticathartic. Irony is experienced in a flash of complicity with the writer at his most subtle, against the larger part of the audience that remains blind to these subtleties.[40]

Are ironists immune from the need for catharsis? If literary humanism has as one of its core principles the practical-ethical imperative – of how to live – then the complicating movements of irony need to be attended to without withdrawing the possibility of coming to rest somewhere. Peace, harmony, love and egalitarianism: *The Merchant of Venice* blocks immediate access to these values but flounders towards them nevertheless.

Chapter 4

Historicising the Human, Humanising the Historical: *I Henry IV*

In their introduction to *Historicism, Psychoanalysis and Early Modern Culture* (2000), Carla Mazzio and Douglas Trevor write that '"historicism" has become the default mode of critical practice'.[1] Historicism has taken a variety of different forms in the last thirty to forty years (cultural materialism, new historicism, materialist feminism, the new economic criticism, presentism), but one characteristic that many of them share is a scepticism about universals.[2] One effect of this has been to dehumanise history, to empty history of its human interest, scope and scale. There have of course been contrary effects, which I shall argue are mainly the product of the literary humanism still practised by cultural historicists, despite their avowal of anti-humanist positions: the 'very idea of a "defining human essence" is precisely what new historicists find vacuous and untenable', writes Stephen Greenblatt, yet one effect of Greenblatt's and other new historicists' recourse to anecdote has been precisely to humanise history.[3] The purpose of the first half of this chapter is therefore to locate the humanising, dehumanising and rehumanising tendencies within the cultural historicisms that have dominated literary studies in recent years. The second half of the chapter will discuss Shakespeare's own treatment of history in *I Henry IV* (1596–7), focusing on Falstaff's humanising and Hal's dehumanising influence upon it.

In *I Henry IV* – to anticipate briefly the second half of the chapter – political and historical issues are inseparable from existential issues. Hal might be on the way to becoming an effective king, but, we are invited to ask, at what 'human' cost? Present-day forms of cultural historicism tend to separate off the human from the historical and political, because appeals to the human smack of a discredited universalism and essentialism. 'Criticism for the past two generations', to recall Margreta de Grazia's comment from the Introduction, 'has tended to situate

Shakespeare in history rather than assume his universality'.[4] The waning of interest in Shakespeare's assumed universality means that existential questions (even though they might take the humble form of questions rather than assertions) are marginalised in favour of culturally specific issues and questions. 'Meaning' is no longer about the meaning of life. 'Meaning' is instead something that is produced by and within specific languages and cultures. One of the five (tentatively proposed) principles of the new historicism identified by H. Aram Veeser is the view that 'no discourse, imaginative or archival, gives access to unchanging truths or expresses unalterable human nature'.[5] From within the framework of a historicism which is doubtful of the permanence of human nature, it is not possible to say that Hal pursues his historical mission at a human cost, because the 'human' does not exist.

As de Grazia's and Veeser's comments imply, this kind of extreme scepticism has become the norm within literary criticism. Of course – and as I have already indicated – there are exceptions to the norm as well as currents within the mainstream which run in other directions. Nevertheless, the consolidation within literary studies of various kinds of cultural historicism has led to what sometimes appears to be a stark and irreconcilable opposition between the human and the historical. The bracketing off of existential from historical issues arguably impoverishes history, because it removes history from 'our', that is, human beings', sphere of concern. An analogy with politics might help to strengthen this point. Official politics, in our own time, seems remote from human concerns. It is what professional politicians do. It is not something which expresses, as it did for Aristotle, for example, a sense of who we are as human beings. 'It is our affections for others', he writes in *The Politics*, 'that causes us to choose to live together', and it is the city state or *polis* which for Aristotle 'belongs to the class of objects which exist by nature' as a means, initially, 'of securing life itself' and subsequently of securing 'the good life'.[6] For Aristotle, we are citizens first and individuals second, for the *polis* is held to be 'prior to the individual'.[7] Serving society is thus not a duty in the sense of an external imposition foisted upon reluctant individuals, for citizenship on this model is the true expression and fulfilment of what it means to be human.

A form of historicism from which all appeals to the so-called human have been expunged is a historicism which is in danger of going the way of such other 'alienated' objects or spheres of potentially meaningful human endeavours as politics. For history to matter it has to resonate with us at some level; it has to produce a sense of the past in which we feel we are meaningfully engaged, such as autobiography or family history. Of course, if history is only about identification, then it is in danger of becoming narcissistic. But the opposite danger of a historicism coldly dismissive of the idea of history as a 'human interest' story is that history becomes too remote. Present-day historicisms do not always avoid this danger: there is at times a forbidding rigour in the language and tone of contemporary cultural historicisms which imply that we should remain critically aloof from false, ideologically naive identifications with the past on the basis of its perceived continuities with the present. An example from the last chapter is Michael Ferber's rigorous historicist appeal to such 'standards of relevance' as 'conventions of reading, historical probabilities' and 'available ideologies'.[8] To speak of existential issues or history in terms of its human interest would seem out of place here.

The paradox of an impersonally contextualising historicism making use of literature, conventionally regarded as the opposite of cold and impersonal owing to its affective power, has not been lost on some critics, such as Edward Pechter. Pechter in 'The New Historicism and Its Discontents' (1987) criticises new historicism in particular for 'draining [Renaissance] plays of much of their potential to involve an audience', for de-emphasising 'passages whose affective power seems unusually great' and for 'reducing the power of the text' so as to increase 'the observer's power'.[9] Pechter's dismay at the new historicist's treatment of the text – as an object – recalls Hélène Cixous's similar dismay at the loveless instrumentalisation of texts by certain types of theory.[10]

Pechter's comments are now around twenty years old and in reaction to the iconoclasm of some new historicists, an iconoclasm which made any reference whatsoever to the human suspect. The cold detachment for which Pechter castigates the likes of Jonathan Goldberg, Leonard Tennenhouse, Jonathan Dollimore, Catherine Belsey and Frank Lentricchia does not by any means represent the whole of the field of contemporary cultural historicism. There is a new wave of historicism, representatives of which I will discuss later, who are much less 'cold', and there are numerous other historicist critics who register the affective power of Shakespeare's work in general and of his treatment of history in particular even as they doubt his universality. However, such recognition can often take the form of passing reference. David Scott Kastan in 'Shakespeare and English History' (2001) actually devotes an entire opening paragraph to the way Shakespeare's artistry 'animates the past':

> Shakespeare's artistry uncannily animates the past. As one near contemporary insists, in a commendatory poem in the second edition of Shakespeare's collected plays (1632), the plays energetically present 'what story [i.e.,

history] coldly tells', and they even more literally enliven history in their ability 'to raise our ancient sovereigns from their hearse'. The stage makes the past present and allows its audiences vicarious emotional participation. When historical characters are represented in the theatre, 'the present age / Joys in their joy and trembles at their rage'. For the commendatory poet, this is value enough; we are 'by elaborate play / Tortured and tickled'.[11]

Shakespeare's ability, with help of course from the stage, to breathe life into history may well be 'uncanny', to use Kastan's language, but the reluctance to acknowledge some of the basic and perhaps banal continuities of human experience will make it seem all the more uncanny. How can 'animation' of the past occur without some minimal sense of what a human being is? Kastan's use of the term 'animates' ('Shakespeare's artistry uncannily animates the past') depends upon us being able to recognise the source of history's means of animation: human beings. Although Kastan acknowledges, albeit via a third party, the animated history which Shakespeare was able to imagine, Kastan's overall commitment to a 'denatured' concept of historical difference means that such acknowledgement is only ever anecdotal rather than 'worked up'.

For more developed appeals to the importance of animated history, we can draw on the work of a combination of thinkers, starting with Raphael Samuel in *Theatres of Memory* (1994). Samuel contrasts what he calls 'living history' with 'Dryasdust forms of [historical] scholarship' exemplified by attempts in the 1950s to turn history into an exact science:

> It [i.e. living history] was much more attentive to the small details of everyday life than those different versions of 'total history' which were all the rage in the 1950s – the abstracted empiricism of the social scientists, with their geometrically plotted histograms and their social structure; the cliometrics of the economic historians, reducing mighty social changes to the squiggles of a graph; or the *longue durée* of those *Annales* historians who boldly declared that without quantification no serious history was possible.[12]

Samuel's 'living history' bears resemblance to what Fredric Jameson calls 'existential historicism', in which the past is imagined as the site of 'an existential experience, a galvanic and electrifying event'. Jameson's partial endorsement of this existential historicism is based upon its compatibility with his own Marxist-humanist concept of the past as that which 'speaks to us about our own virtual and unrealized "human potentialities"'.[13] A past which 'speaks' to us in this powerfully affecting way is contrasted by Jameson with the 'sheer mechanical and meaningless succession of facts of empiricist historiography'.[14] What Jameson's existential historicism might be thought of as doing is to *libidinise* history. Rather than making history the object of dispassionate enquiry or the dehumanised site of cultural difference, the concept of historical and cultural difference is itself humanised because the past has something to do with 'us' and the latent selves and ways of being that lie buried within us.

To Samuel's concept of 'living history' and Jameson's existential historicism, we can usefully recall the insight (quoted in the Introduction) of Paul Hamilton in *Historicism* (1996). In his exploration of eighteenth-century precursors to our own conceptions of history, Hamilton comments that for the philosophers Giambattista Vico and J. G. Herder, history 'had to be understood as something we are actively engaged in, like purposeful living, not external to, like the phenomena rationalized by scientific investigation'.[15] Samuel's examples of 'dryasdust' history are in the tradition of history conceived of on the model of science. Contrastingly, Samuel's living history and Vico's and Herder's purposeful human history constitute an alternative tradition of history conceived of more in aesthetic terms, in terms, that is, of how history plays out in the emotional, sensate lives of those 'entities' we still insist on calling human beings.

History mediated aesthetically, through literary texts, is more likely to move us and make history matter to us than when it is mediated through dry factual chronicle or 'squiggles of a graph'. I am not suggesting that contemporary cultural historicists depersonalise history to anything like this extent. But for all those whose discrediting of human nature does push them towards an impersonal distance, there are others, as already emphasised, who return to history an existential dimension. I shall call these forms of historicism *literary humanist* historicisms, on the basis that history mediated via literary texts or via literary critics (often in spite of their sceptical selves) is liable to be humanised and brought alive because of its engagement with the question of 'how to live'. For some cultural historians, the word 'culture' itself carries existential implications. Of his transition from intellectual to cultural historian, William Bouwsma in *A Usable Past* (1990) writes:

> I began instead . . . to call myself a *cultural* historian, understanding 'culture', somewhat as anthropologists do, less as a set of beliefs and values than as the collective strategies by which societies organise and make sense of their experience. Culture in this sense is a mechanism for the management of existential anxiety; it serves deeper needs than the 'ideas' to which I had first been attracted.[16]

Where, for Bouwsma, 'culture' unambiguously addresses existential needs and dilemmas, in the work of other cultural historians the term hovers more equivocally between being expressive and inexpressive of human concerns.

As an example of the cross-currents which exist sometimes within the same critic's approach, we can turn again to Kastan. In *Shakespeare after Theory* (1999), Kastan makes a comment which is characteristic of many contemporary cultural historicisms' repudiation of the human. He writes that although Shakespeare,

> does live on in subsequent cultures in ways none of his contemporaries do, it is not, I think, because he is in any significant sense timeless, speaking some otherwise unknown, universal idiom. Rather, it seems to me it is because he is so intensely of his own time and place.[17]

However, having discounted the possibility of timeless relevance, Kastan goes on to speak of history as a form of self-discovery. The language of self-discovery gives history an existential charge and implies a quasi-Hegelian conception of history as the expression of human spirit:

> [Shakespeare's] engagement with his world is the most compelling record we have of that world's struggle for meaning and value. If he is miraculously able to 'looke / Fresh to all Ages', as Leonard Digges claimed in the first folio, it is because he enables each age to see for itself what it has been, and, in measuring its distance from that world, to discover what it has become. In his historical specificity, then, we discover ourselves as historical beings.[18]

As argued above, the trouble with the total separation of the human from the historical is that history might cease to matter to us. Kastan does not want this. He wants history to 'matter'. The language of self-discovery he uses – 'we discover ourselves as historical beings' – gives history the existential twist that is needed to make it 'compelling', as Kastan puts it. History and historical difference become compelling when instead of being external to us, in the way that 'roles' become totally external to Iago, they are brought within the ambit of the human. But this can only be done by acknowledging the continuities of human being over time. Without these continuities, we would not be able to appeal to such an idea as animated history.

The example of Kastan demonstrates the point that there is a 'residual' literary humanism at work in forms of historicism avowedly sceptical of the existence of human nature. This residue is present because *literary* historicists, historicists whose primary training is in literary criticism, arguably still draw, implicitly if not explicitly, on aesthetic categories in their historical narratives. Ewan Fernie's previously referred to *Shame in Shakespeare* (2002) is another example of this. The broadly historical and historicising impulse of the book is indicated (as I suggested in the Introduction) in the titles of the first three chapters of the book – 'Shame before Shakespeare', 'Shame in the Renaissance' and 'Shame in Shakespeare' – but the history of shame mediated as it mainly is through literary texts makes the history come alive because literature is according to Fernie 'a living process'.[19] This perspective is not far removed from Philip Sidney's appeal in *A Defence of Poetry* (1595) to poetry as having the power to move people to virtuous action because of its sensuous embodiment of otherwise abstract (moral) ideas.[20] To discuss a concept such as shame in the abstract is not the same as experiencing it, and what literature does is to offer us virtual or, to use Sidney's terminology, 'feigned' experiences which transform moral philosophy into practical moral philosophy or moral philosophy with a human face.[21] This is part of what makes literature and poetry a 'living process', or, as Sidney puts it, a 'speaking picture'.[22] And it is what makes history come alive. Literature's ability to animate history belongs to that aspect of literary humanism that I described in the Introduction as the power of embodiment.

Fernie's book traces continuities between past and present at the same time as it practises as well as preaches historical difference. However, it is worth dwelling briefly on the concept of historical difference that a literary humanist historicism advances. Literature's inscription of difference is to transform it into sensuous experience and in so doing to 'existentialise' it. As Christophe Bode and Wolfgang Klooss put it, in *Historicising/Contemporizing Shakespeare* (2000):

> The aesthetic category of *experience*, or, more precisely, *the fact of experience*, is resistant to the claims of other discourses, although it is . . . informed and permeated by them. To historically contextualize Shakespeare seems as legitimate as it is legitimate to deliberately engage in 'contemporizing' acts of reception – a practice that *relates* the unfamiliar to us without taming its otherness.[23]

Appeals to historical difference which fail to relate the past to us will leave us unaffected by it, whereas historical difference which is aestheticised – turned in other words into sensuous experience – is again more likely to matter to us.

It is no coincidence either that a literary historicist, such as Fernie, should choose shame as his topic. Although literary historicists do not have a monopoly on the emotions, their interest in them accords well with literature's affective power. In Fernie's case this interest is more than 'academic', because, as I pointed out in the Introduction, shame viewed through the lens of Shakespeare has according to Fernie 'the potential radically to transform our lives for the better'.[24] Fernie expresses explicit interest here in the question of how to live and uses the emotion of shame to address this question. His approach is thus the opposite of the detachment from the emotions which Pechter identifies as one of the characteristics of new historicism, but there are other examples of critics, including Greenblatt himself, a figure central to new historicism, who tend towards topics of such seemingly immediate and perennial human interest as the emotions.[25] The topics often chosen by literary historicists, such as shame, by Fernie, or anxiety, by Greenblatt, or the emotions in general, by Gail Kern Paster (whose work I draw on in this and subsequent chapters), again reflect an attenuated or residual humanism, for such topics may be thought of as existing on the cusp of the familiar and the unfamiliar, the natural and the cultural. They suggest a foundation, in other words, in the guise of a recognisably 'human' phenomenon or experience, but that phenomenon will then more often than not be estranged, treated as culturally 'other'. However, despite the frequent repudiation of universalism – 'the very idea of a "defining human essence" is precisely what new historicists find vacuous and untenable', to recall Greenblatt's claim from the opening of this chapter – the recognisability of the phenomenon in question is still apparent. Anxiety is still recognisable as anxiety, shame as shame. We have an ordinary phrase – 'the same but different' – that does useful work for us in everyday situations in identifying patterns or personalities or experiences which almost but do not quite repeat themselves, but the idea of difference existing within sameness, or sameness within difference, has been more difficult for historicists to acknowledge in their self-consciously theoretical statements, even if it is implied by their practice.

However, recent work that attempts to put the 'literary' back into specifically Renaissance literary studies shows somewhat less embarrassment about combining historical with ahistorical perspectives. The so-called new formalisms examined in a collection of essays entitled *Renaissance Literature and Its Formal Engagements* (2002) are one example.[26] In 'The Politics of Aesthetics: Recuperating Formalism and the Country House Poem', Heather Dubrow's remedy to the demonised ahistoricality of form is to embrace that very ahistoricality – 'our pleasure in rhyme', she writes, 'is indeed sensuous, immediate and nonconceptual' – but at the same time to relate the formal characteristics of the Renaissance country house poem to its historically specific political agenda.[27] Elizabeth Harris Sagaser's contribution to the same volume makes even more expansively ahistorical claims on behalf of the 'personally communicative and expressive' power of poetry.[28] Indeed, for Sagaser, history is secondary to poetry's attempt to overcome it: 'immersing oneself in poetry in form', she writes, 'is an attempt to *name* time – to seize and control a part of the experience of time by rendering it linguistically palpable, identifiable, human-scaled, and ordered'.[29] Here, the enchantments of literature, as a discourse which puts us in touch with ourselves and our most fundamental urges, outweigh the historicist scepticism that always places such claims at a critical distance.

The kind of historicism which I have been referring to as literary or literary humanist historicism has affinities with Renaissance concepts of history. In both cases, there is an attempt to animate history and bring it alive. And in both cases, history has an important bearing on the question of how to live. In *A Defence of Poetry*, Sidney prefers poetry to both history and philosophy on the basis that poetry mediates between the dry abstractions of moral philosophy and the empiricism of the historian who, according to Sidney, 'is so tied, not to what should be but to what is, to the particular truth of things and not to the general reason of things, that his example draweth no necessary consequence'.[30] However, this is not the last word in the Renaissance – or even Sidney's last word – on history. As Hanan Yoran points out in 'Thomas More's *Richard III:* Probing the Limits of Humanism' (2001), history in the Renaissance was 'one of the *studia humanitatis*'.[31] As such, it contributed to Renaissance humanists' preoccupation with practical ethics. Following such classical authorities as Cicero, humanist historians differentiated between chronicle and history on the basis that, according to Yoran, the former supplied the bare historical facts, while the latter provided 'credible psychological descriptions' and explained 'the causal relation between events', and 'since history, like all humanist disciplines, had an educational purpose, the historian had to evaluate events, praise the worthy, condemn wrongdoers, and draw the appropriate moral lessons'.[32]

Timothy Hampton in *Writing from History* (1990) corroborates but also updates this perspective when he suggests that for 'humanist historiography – as, indeed, for all secular historiography up to Hegel – the past is seen as a reservoir of models for present action'.[33] We might update this idea still further by suggesting that when Michael Ferber refers to the 'social warmth' in *The Merchant of Venice* as one of the Venetians' 'saving graces', or when Ewan Fernie says that Shakespeare's understanding of shame has 'the potential radically to transform our lives for the better', or Terry Eagleton in only partial imitation of the sentiments of *King Lear* writes that to 'perceive accurately, we must feel', the past in the form of old texts is being raided for the ethical impact it might have on the present.[34] The past is being used to comment on the question of how to live, and it is no accident that literary texts should enable this. Such comments might only exist in the interstices of other, more distancing historicist priorities, but they once again indicate the presence of a residual literary humanism.

I suggested earlier that in *I Henry IV*, political and historical issues are inseparable from existential issues, and that consequently we are invited to measure the human cost of Prince Henry's apprenticeship in the technique of effective kingship. Hal, as he is affectionately known by Falstaff, embarks upon a historical mission, and that mission involves banishing 'humanity'. The play-acting scenes of Act II are, amongst other things, about Hal's anticipation of a historical role in which he will sever all connections with the fulsome humanity represented, needless to say, by Falstaff. Playing the part of King Henry, Falstaff says that to 'banish plump Jack' would be to 'banish all the world', to which Hal, anticipating his future self, answers: 'I do; I will'.[35] This is chilling, because history without Falstaff is history without a human face, history exclusively devoted to what A. P. Rossiter in *Angel with Horns* (1961) calls 'the State-order system'. Within such 'History', writes Rossiter, 'Shakespeare felt that men were constrained to be much less than their full selves'.[36]

But what is the nature of this full self, this human face? Falstaff, I want to argue, is all sensuous embodiment; he *is* the aesthetic, or that aspect of the aesthetic to do with embodiment. He represents the senses, the frailty of the flesh, the 'human' or 'only human' at its most quotidian.[37] To appropriate an apt phrase that Terry Eagleton uses to describe the aesthetic in *The Ideology of the Aesthetic* (1990), Falstaff is the record 'of how the world strikes the body on its sensory surfaces'.[38] Given his obvious corporeality, it is tempting to think of the idea of 'surfaces' in terms of merely physical rather than emotional sensation. Hal, as we shall see, tries to reduce Falstaff to a physical entity only, but the physical and the emotional are in fact inseparable in Falstaff. Pain and pleasure are registered on both levels simultaneously.

As the reference to Hal's view of Falstaff indicates, humanity is viewed through different lenses in the play. The lens mainly used by Hal helps him to keep his eventual banishment of Falstaff firmly in mind. So Hal keeps noticing the more extravagant and obvious manifestations of Falstaff's 'only human' humanity: his drinking, eating, debauchery, excess and immorality. These characteristics justify the reforming Hal's rejection of Falstaff. Falstaff is fallen man, 'that reverend Vice, that grey Iniquity, that father Ruffian', as Hal playing the part of his father puts it (II, v, 458–9). These attributes are just three in an extensive list of epithets and insults used by Hal to describe Falstaff. While the proliferation of names implies that Falstaff is excessive in more than one way – that he defies single description, for example – Hal stays focused on Falstaff's physical excess:

> There is a devil haunts thee in the likeness of an old fat man; a tun of man is thy companion. Why does thou converse with that trunk of humours, that bolting-hutch of beastliness, that swollen parcel of dropsies, that huge

> bombard of sack, that stuffed cloak-bag of guts, that roasted Manningtree ox with the pudding in his belly, that reverend Vice, that grey Iniquity, that father Ruffian, that Vanity in Years? (II, v, 452–9)

The 'more' that there is to say about Falstaff contributes to the same point, that he is the embodiment of Appetite, described in vividly physical terms. Hal's view of Falstaff corresponds with that of critics whose interest in Falstaff as a carnivalesque character seems naturally to lead to a focus upon his physical excess. François Laroque, for example, in 'Shakespeare's "Battle of Carnival and Lent": The Falstaff Scenes Reconsidered' (1998), refers to Falstaff as 'an apostle of extravagance', who represents 'the voracity of the carnivalesque body, emblematized by a gaping mouth and a swollen belly'.[39] Concentrating on these physical aspects of carnival leads Laroque to find an interesting parallel between carnival and war:

> we are made to understand the fundamental complementarity of tavern life and battleground, of Carnival exuberance and Lenten restriction or negativity: they are the two sides of the same coin. On the one hand, there is the slaughtering of cattle at Martinmas and the pigs butchered in Carnival time with vast amounts of wine or sherris sack being drunk to fill Falstaff's hungry belly and bottomless throat; on the other, we find the butchery of civil war that fattens the worms and offers fresh drink to a vampiric earth.[40]

The representation of Falstaff as 'hungry belly', 'bottomless throat' and 'gaping mouth' transforms him into an almost inhuman principle, like the 'vampiric earth'. If the emotional content of the physical is ignored, then it is relatively easy to confound, as Hal does, 'fallen humanity' with 'the inhuman'. Although, as previous chapters have shown, the human is not safely guarded from its other(s), to represent Falstaff only as a kind of physical mechanism – an eating machine – robs him of the emotions to which the physical is also connected.

One aspect of Falstaff unnoticed or ignored by the representation of Falstaff in exclusively physical terms is his childlike need. As war looms, the reluctant soldier Falstaff says to Hal: 'I would 'twere bed-time, Hal, and all well' (V, i, 125). Recalling Eagleton's phrase about the way the aesthetic has to do with 'how the world strikes the body on its sensory surfaces', we might think of children as being more 'struck' by the world than adults, who build up protective layers and learn to control their emotions. This is not just a modern but a seventeenth-century perspective. In *The Passions of the Minde* (1601), Thomas Wright argues that both the 'internall and immateriall' and 'external and materiall' expressions of passions are at their rawest and clearest in children and animals:

> Three sortes of actions proceede from mens soules, some are internall and immateriall, as the actes of our wits and willes: others be mere external and

> materiall, as the actes of our senses, seeing, hearing, mouing, &c others stand beetwixt these twoo extreames, and border vpon them both; the which wee may best discouer in children, because they lacke the vse of reason, and are guided by an internall imagination, following nothing else but that pleaseth their sences, euen after the same maner as bruite beastes doe: for, as wee see beastes hate, loue, feare and hope, so doe children. Those actions then which are common with vs, and beasts, we cal Passions, and Affections, or perturbations of the mind.[41]

Such primary emotions as those listed by Wright – of 'hate, loue, feare and hope' – are easily discernible in Falstaff. He registers fear on the battlefield as the body's natural response to danger. The human body is vulnerable when it comes into the world. It continues to be vulnerable, although the extent of its vulnerability depends to a large extent on social conditions and circumstances. The circumstances in which Falstaff finds himself threaten to expose that vulnerability. These are banal 'facts' about human bodies, but they have implications for the way we should live. Perhaps we should protect these bodies, rather than expose them to unnecessary danger? Falstaff also wants reassurance that all will be 'well'. The need to feel secure, as I shall argue more fully in the next chapter, may also be seen as a banal 'human' need. Hal's curt response, however, ignores these ordinary facts and needs: 'Why, thou owest God a death' (V, i, 126).

Characteristically, Hal harps on the 'payback' theme of Falstaff owing God a death because, for Hal, Falstaff has prolonged his indulgence in carnivalesque excess.[42] He does not engage with Falstaff on the level of pleasure/pain but on the level of debt/credit. This, of course, is the level at which Hal himself is currently operating, for the battle is his opportunity to pay back father, king and country for his (apparently) misspent youth. His former 'intemperature' (III, ii, 156), as he refers to his unregulated body in the repentance scene with his father, will be exchanged for a properly schooled and militarily disciplined body, subject to a regime of strict accounting. 'Percy', he tells his father, 'is but my factor . . . To engross up glorious deeds on my behalf; / And I will call him to so strict account / That he will render every glory up' (III, ii, 147–50). Hal's world is one of disciplined economic calculation, whose opposite is not only the unregulated bodily excess of Falstaff, but a sentimentality which uses the body as its touchstone. Where Falstaff sees the body in terms of physical needs which are at the same time emotional needs, Hal sees only a pile of organs. To Hal, Falstaff is all 'guts and midriff' (III, iii, 156). These organs are 'moralised' by Hal, but they are not 'sentimentalised'. They are a sign of gluttony and debauchery only: 'there's no room for faith, truth, nor honesty in this bosom of thine; it is all filled with guts and midriff' (III, iii, 154–6). Hal deliberately reduces Falstaff to mere body and appetite in order to ease his own banishment of one he knows to be a fuller human subject. An index of this fullness is that Falstaff keeps wanting to talk about the body in another, more emotional way. His answer, or part of it, to Hal's moral tirade is to say that because he has more 'flesh' he has more 'frailty' (III, iii, 168). This is a moral/Biblical proverb, but in the context of Falstaff's admission on the battlefield of vulnerability, frailty encompasses the sense of being more easily 'struck' by the world.[43] There is more of him, so there are more physical and emotional sensory surfaces to be struck.

Falstaff has many faults and foibles, but he is not without an ethical orientation. Others, both inside and outside the play, may not see this ethical orientation because their ethical systems are in denial of the body, whereas Falstaff's is based on the body. He tries, in other words, to derive values from biological facts. This is the basis of his diatribe against honour:

> Can honour set-to a leg? No. Or an arm? No. Or take away the grief of a wound? No. Honour hath no skill in surgery, then? No. What is honour? A word. What is in that word 'honour'? What is that 'honour'? Air. A trim reckoning! Who hath it? He that died o' Wednesday. Doth he feel it? No. Doth he hear it? No. 'Tis insensible then? Yea, to the dead. But will it not live with the living? No. Why? Detraction will not suffer it. Therefore I'll none of it. Honour is a mere scutcheon. And so ends my catechism. (V, i, 131–40)

It is significant that the word 'grief' in Shakespeare can mean the physical sensation of pain and the emotion of intense sorrow. Although it could be argued that physical pain is the more appropriate meaning here, Shakespeare's language, woven as it often is out of classical and Renaissance theories of the humours, slides physical and affective realms into one another. Wright encapsulates something of the spirit of such theories when he claims that 'passions ingender humors, and humours bred passions'.[44] In Falstaff's speech on honour, the tendency to see the human body in affective terms yields the 'moral' that moral codes ought to be 'sensible' rather than 'insensible', meaning that they ought to be more mindful of the body and its needs. Rather than a 'top-down', hierarchical model of morality based on the principle of 'higher equals holier', Falstaff's is a 'bottom-up', corporeal model.

Falstaff, as we have already seen in the work of Laroque, is often associated with carnival and carnival is frequently conceived as a kind of moral holiday which granted its participants temporary respite from the austerity of moral codes and allowed them to indulge themselves.[45] This characterisation fits most of what Falstaff does and says. But

Falstaff does not only debunk the official morality, or what was once an official morality, of honour and chivalry, but gestures towards a different, body-based morality.[46] While it is true that his preference for concrete words and material things speaks to a kind of hedonism of the senses, the warm, emotional glow which attaches to food, for example, is part of an ethic which sees more value in feasting than fighting:

> Well, to the latter end of a fray
> And the beginning of a feast
> Fits a dull fighter and a keen guest.
> (IV, ii, 79–81)

If Falstaff's values are the values of hearth and fireside, then his opposite number, Hotspur, cannot wait to get away from the hearth to the battlefield. While, according to Paster in *Humoring the Body* (2004), Hotspur's 'spiritedness, courage, and impulsivity' can be explained, in terms of the theory of bodily humours, as the outcome of 'hot-bloodedness',[47] Hotspur's dying words support Falstaff's view of honour as a code which is 'insensible':

> O Harry, thou hast robbed me of my youth.
> I better brook the loss of brittle life
> Than those proud titles thou hast won of me.
> They wound my thoughts worse than my sword my flesh.
> (V, iv, 76–9)

The loss of 'titles' is more wounding to Hotspur than the wounding of the 'flesh'. Hal has done what he promised his father he would do, which is to trade in his disreputable self for an honourable one by robbing Hotspur of his 'titles' which are, for Hotspur, his identity. If he had been able to articulate a humours theory of character, he might have been able to see that the passionate pursuit of honour was one, but not the only, outcome of a hot-bloodedness which was less alienable than his titles turned out to be. He might have been a passionate pursuer of natural philosophy or justice, for example! His wife tries to tell him about the bodily basis for his passions and moods: 'you are altogether governed by humours', she says (III, i, 230). Hotspur cannot 'hear' this, because he thinks he is driven by honour. He mistakes the effect for the cause, in other words. Falstaff, by contrast, never loses sight of his body and he therefore never loses sight of his identity. He is Falstaff wherever he goes, on the battlefield, at court or in the tavern.

I Henry IV is concerned with what 'weighs' people down and gives them substance and solidity in a world which simultaneously promotes, or at least represents, a certain 'lightness of being'. Honour comes and goes, and turns out to be more like a commodity than a 'characteristic' and subject to the system of exchange which is presided over by Hal. Hotspur's use of the word 'robbed' in reference to Hal, as in 'thou hast robbed me of my youth', is apt because Hal has proved himself to be the most efficient robber or usurper of identities in the play. Ironically, Falstaff is afraid of robbing, though he pretends otherwise. On the symbolic level – the level at which the play also invites us to think about robbery – we might say that Hal robs easily because there is little or nothing in his character to prevent him from adopting one or another identity, whereas Falstaff robs with difficulty because of what is already in him. 'Coward' is what Hal calls this 'inside' (II, iii, 64), but there are other, more creditable names for it, which *dis*credit the 'insensibility' of male bravado.

Falstaff can also only superficially play at reforming, as when he promises to 'repent' and blames the 'villainous company' he keeps for his dissolute ways (III, iii, 4; 10). Hal is the better actor, who can adopt the role of the repentant son and make it seem realistic, while at the same time maintaining an awareness of himself as a projector of roles and images for strategic purposes.[48] His 'I know you all' speech anticipates the cold instrumentalism of Iago. It is an instrumentalism which leaves behind notions of grounded identity and substantive humanity in the name of calculated 'subjectivity effects' designed to impress and manipulate:

> I know you all, and will a while uphold
> The unyoked humour of your idleness.
> Yet herein will I imitate the sun,
> To smother up his beauty from the world,
> That when he please again to be himself,
> Being wanted he may be more wondered at
> By breaking through the foul and ugly mists
> Of vapours that did seem to strangle him.
> (I, ii, 192–200)

'I know you all' is addressed to his recently departed tavern companions, but as Hal is now alone on stage it seems also to incorporate the playhouse audience. What is the nature of this knowledge? Along with his later assertion, 'I am now of all humours that have showed themselves humours since the days of goodman Adam' (II, v, 93–5), Hal seems to be claiming an expansive, 'myriad-minded' knowledge of human nature and its various humours on a par with the bard himself.[49] But the knowledge is the knowledge of the passer-by or tourist who 'samples' but does not fully enter into the 'sensate life' of the people he claims to know. He does not, according to my reading, fully 'know' Falstaff, but only those all too obvious parts of Falstaff which will act as a foil to his own wondrous reformation. He cannot have 'full', sensate knowledge because the demands of political utility allow Hal to know 'humours' only well enough to be able to manipulate them.

Hal is nevertheless still sufficiently human to be drawn to Falstaff and to Eastcheap because they have what he is in danger of losing: sentiment, humanity, solidity, roots. When Falstaff asks Hal whether he is not 'horribly afraid' at having such enemies as 'that fiend Douglas, that spirit Percy, and that devil Glyndwr' (II, v, 371–2), Hal answers: 'Not a whit, i'faith. I lack some of thy instinct' (II, v, 374–5). The word 'instinct' has been used several times already in this scene. In Falstaff's initial, expansive use, in which he claims that he knew by 'instinct' that Hal was one of the robbers in disguise at Gads Hill, it means something like intuition or feeling. However, Hal tries to narrow it with every subsequent use to refer once again to Falstaff's cowardice. Nevertheless, the more expansive meaning persists, so that when Hal tells Falstaff that he lacks some of his 'instinct', we read into the comment a Hal who is aware or semi-aware of his emotionally atrophied state.

It is the 'body and not the mind that remembers pain and pleasure', writes Wesley Morris in 'Of Wisdom and Competence' (2000). Morris is commenting on the ruminations on the nature of remembering in William Faulkner's *Absalom, Absalom!* (1936), but because they are so apposite to the themes of this chapter, they are worth quoting more fully:

> It is the body and not the mind that remembers pain and pleasure. The mind can only warp experience into myth, dreams, mere ideas or stories "*for which*, as Rosa says, '*three words are three too many, and three thousand that many words too less*'. Everything that is or has been or will be *can* be told, but life is remembered as pleasure and pain, not as event or tale. Memory is empty, but remembering is the lingering of experience, the tempering of sense as though pleasure and pain have written a message in a script burned into flesh. We say something is beautiful or ugly, kind or careless, good or evil as we say something is hot or cold, soft or harsh. Whatever stories we tell of good or evil, with whatever words we name specific differences, there is always the sense of pleasures and pains, the remembering of sensations which give corporeal foundations to our thoughts and expressions.[50]

Will Hal remember Falstaff in the manner described here, in an emotional, sensory, 'aesthetic' way, a way that, to recall Eagleton's expression, takes account of 'how the world strikes the body on its sensory surfaces'? Or will Hal only remember Falstaff within the coolly moralising language he uses during the play-acting scenes as 'that villainous, abominable misleader of youth . . . that old white-bearded Satan' (II, v, 467–8)? We always know how history is striking Falstaff on the senses: 'I would 'twere bed-time, Hal, and all well' (V, i, 125); 'God keep lead out of me; I need no more weight than my own bowels' (V, iv, 34–5); 'Well, to the latter end of a fray / And the beginning of a feast' (IV, ii, 79–8). Falstaff, the 'greatest vitalist in Shakespeare' according to Harold Bloom,[51] is the playwright's shorthand for embodied history, animated history, history with the flesh and blood, pain and pleasure left in rather than excised, as Hal promises to excise them when in banishing Falstaff he banishes 'the world'.

Did the characteristics I have been associating via Eagleton with the aesthetic always exist or were they invented? Eagleton's use of the term 'discourse', as in 'discourse of the body', to describe the aesthetic raises some intriguing questions about origins and the nature of historical change.[52] Given the recent theoretical lineage of the term 'discourse', there is the implication that 'the body' in question may be a linguistic and ideological construction and not 'the thing itself'. This corresponds with the overall emphasis of Eagleton's book upon the aesthetic as an ideology, a bourgeois ideology whose appeal to the 'realm of sentiments, affections and spontaneous bodily habits' assumed significance in the eighteenth century (and beyond) because it was the glue which held together an increasingly atomised society otherwise bound together only by abstract rights.[53] The body-based materialism of the aesthetic in other words compensates for the other side of bourgeois society: its cold, mechanistic instrumentalism and object-based materialism, as described by Douglas Bruster in *Drama and the Market in the Age of Shakespeare* (1992).[54] One way of thinking about the 'discourse of the body' described by Eagleton is thus to say that while it might look as though this discourse has a timeless material support, its materialism is as socially specific as the materialism investigated by Bruster. The extreme version of this kind of view is to hold bourgeois society almost single-handedly responsible for the invention of sentiment and affect, and to make the 'preposterous claim', as Charles Taylor puts it in *Sources of the Self* (1989), that 'before modern times, people didn't really love their children and never married for love'. What changes, continues Taylor, is 'not that people begin loving their children or feeling affection for their spouses, but that these dispositions come to be seen as a crucial part of what makes life worthy and significant'.[55] The similar argument proposed in this book, which will be further advanced in Chapter 8, is that as modernity takes hold, affect is exiled from the public into the private world where it takes on special significance precisely because it is endangered: the private sphere might become a haven in a heartless world, but the heartless world does not always conveniently stop on the threshold of the haven.

The idea of human dispositions being exiled from one place to another suggests a model of historical change which preserves a place for 'ordinary' human nature. According to this model, human beings have identifiable needs and dispositions, but these needs and dispositions are transposed, displaced, reconfigured, accommodated or negated within different social formations. Bourgeois society according to this view does not 'invent' ordinary, sensate life, but displaces it into the private sphere. We have seen this displacement occurring or starting to occur in some of Shakespeare's plays: in *The Merchant of Venice*, for example, where the attempt to maintain affective ties within the public domain of capitalist transaction is strained, in *Hamlet* where meaning and authenticity are transferred from outer to inner worlds, and in *I Henry IV* where feeling is expunged from the public domain of history. This model of history – as displacement – allows for the fact that, 'of course', human life changes, but it also enables us to identify the deeper continuities which survive in attenuated or reconfigured forms.

Part II

How to Live

Chapter 5

Ethics: *Macbeth*

Part I examined different forms of scepticism about human nature as a foundational principle and the extent to which these scepticisms simultaneously imply the need for foundations. Part II will explore more concertedly the nature of Shakespeare's affirmations of the human and the ethics of how to live which arises from them. Another way of describing Part II is to say that it will try to deepen the descriptions of the human already given, in accordance with the way Shakespeare himself deepens them. Such descriptions have to some extent already been provided: characterisations of the likes of Hal as 'heartless' or Iago as 'inhuman' have presupposed concepts of the human/humane which have been examined in some detail. Part II, however, will further advance the deep or thick description of a 'common humanity' that Shakespeare gives. However, it will also be mindful of what might be called Shakespeare's practical optimism: human nature, as represented in particular by the emotions, is not so 'deep' as to become unfathomable. Human beings are complicated, but not so complicated as to make imponderable the issue of how to live. Concurring with some of the 'Victorian' (as he refers to them) principles of A. C. Bradley, Adrian Poole in 'A. C. Bradley's Shakespearean Tragedy' (2005) writes: 'People are not *that* strange. He [Bradley] would have been perplexed by our absorption with "otherness", let alone "the Other" . . . The idea that we are all strangers to each other is no more a fiction than the idea that we can reach fair understandings'.[1]

Poole's sentiment is echoed by Dominic Rainsford and Tim Woods in *Critical Ethics* (1999) as they summarise the contrasting trajectories within the recent turn or return of literary studies to ethics. The tension, they suggest, is between:

> an ethics that is designed to further the good through consensus or commensurability (which requires that we are not all, ultimately, entirely 'other'), and an ethics that hesitates to say what someone else's good might be, for fear of misconstruing and oppressing them.[2]

The emphasis of this chapter, and of the book overall, on what we have in common, as opposed to what differentiates us, places it more on the side of 'consensus and commensurability' than on difference. However, it does not ignore pressures on consensus and commensurability, which in the case of *Macbeth* come not so much from divergent ethical standpoints as from the assertion of individuality through the individual's transgression of ethical limits. Difference, as we shall see, is granted an ethical dimension in Shakespearean comedy, but in tragedy, difference tends to take the form of a hubristic individualism and be placed in opposition to ethics.

The broad concern of this chapter with how to live ethically will be examined via two specific and closely connected sets of ideas. One, already registered, is the tension evident in *Macbeth* (1606) between the impulse to transgress and the need for ethical boundaries. The second is the importance of the emotions, and in particular fear, in establishing an affectively oriented psychological dimension to the need for ethical limits. The derivation of ethics from emotions has already been partly examined via Falstaff in Chapter 4. In *Macbeth*, however, ethics are rooted even more deeply in sensate and psychological life. The 'psychologising' of ethical principles thickens and deepens their existential significance by showing that ethical limits are not merely external impositions foisted on reluctant individuals naturally prone to excess, but come from 'within'. How to live ethically consequently involves recognising certain psychological and emotional truths. This at least is the play's counter-perspective to the quasi-Nietzschean view, also expressed by the play, that excess is inherent in human beings.

In *Humoring the Body* (2004), Gail Kern Paster examines the ways in which ancient Greek and early modern understandings of the emotions formed what she calls an 'ecology'.[3] By this, she means that macrocosm and microcosm, world and body, 'outer' conditions (such as changes in climate) and inner emotional states, were thought about in terms of each other. 'In both epochs', she writes, 'passion is a change of inner state knowable *as* and *by means of* changes, defined as broadly as possible, in the outer world'.[4] Paster's exploration of the passions is historically specific, but the historically specific ideas she examines credit the emotions with universal significance. There are three ways in which the concept of an ecology of the emotions relates to my own concern with the importance of the emotions for an understanding of human nature. First, emotions are knowable rather than, according to quasi-Romantic representations of them, mysteriously unknowable ('passion is a change of inner state knowable *as* and *by means of* changes, defined as broadly as possible, in the outer world'). Second, the close relationship of inner and outer states can be seen as an example of an enchanted or, in Jürgen Habermas's terms, a 'mythical' view of nature, because nature is animated and anthropomorphicised rather than inert.[5] Since nature is suffused with human significance and mirrors human passions, the human seems to have a settled place in the scheme of things. If emotional turbulence is reflected in such natural phenomena as the blowing of the wind, then human emotions look as though they have the same kind of permanence as natural phenomena. This leads to my third point, which is that the ecology Paster examines indicates the general importance attached to the emotions in ancient Greece and the Renaissance. Emotions have not withdrawn from the world into a self in whom they are locked away more or less accessibly. Emotions are in the world; they are literally 'in the air'; they are part of the world's fabric.[6]

These three points about the emotions – their intelligibility, universality and non-private nature – are encapsulated in Thomas Wright's claim in *The Passions of the Minde* (1601) that the passions are God-given:

> An other difference . . . there is, [i.e., between humans and beasts, on the one hand, and 'inanimate creatures', on the other] because men and beasts, in their appetites, have a certaine pleasure and delectation, paine or griefe, the which affections, cannot be found in any inanimate creatures. This delight or payne God imparted vnto vs, that we might thereby be stirred vp to attempt those actions which were necessary for vs, or flee those inconuences or harmes which might annoy vs: for who would attend to eating or drinking, to the act of generation, if Nature had not ioyned thereunto some delectation?[7]

God imprints upon us the primary emotions of pleasure and pain, writes these into nature and thereby provides us with a reliable means of distinguishing harm from good. It needs a Shakespeare, however, to make these ideas come alive.

Correspondences between what is happening in the human world and what is happening in nature are insisted upon throughout *Macbeth* and support the notion that the killing of the king is a social violation as well as a violation of creation. The king's 'gashed stabs', as Macbeth himself puts it, 'looked like a breach in nature / For ruin's wasteful entrance'.[8] The night of the murder is described by Lennox as 'unruly' (II, iii, 53): 'lamentings' are 'heard i'th' air' and the earth is 'feverous' (II, iii, 55; 59). The political interpretation is that regicide is against the natural order, but a more expansive, existentially oriented interpretation is that it is the death of human cooperation at the hands of human excess which is the cause of the breach in nature. It is this which has made both the natural order and human order afraid. *Macbeth* is a play largely about fear. Fear is at the centre of its 'ecology'. It is a word which appears in virtually every speech of Macbeth's after he has murdered Duncan. Fear is something he cannot rid himself of, he cannot cast out, he cannot 'alienate' from himself. Fear in *Macbeth* also begets fear. Like the 'two truths' told by the witches, it doubles and multiplies (I, iii, 126). It is not just Macbeth who fears. Macbeth is also the object of fear, and fear is general. It is indeed 'in the air'. This viral conception of fear accords with the humoral theory of the emotions described by Katherine Rowe in 'Humoral Knowledge and Liberal Cognition in Davenant's *Macbeth*' (2004) when she describes the fears of Ross and Lady Macduff in Act IV as 'less internal mysteries' than contagious 'inter-subjective fits'.[9] The idea of emotions happening between people rather than inside them, and mirrored, also, by nature, makes collective touchstones of the emotions which in the case of the contagion of fear in *Macbeth* indicate that something is deeply amiss in the human world. In Wright's terms, fear is like 'paine or griefe' and tells us what 'inconuences or harmes' we should 'flee'.

Fear, of course, can be directed at any number of socially specific phenomena, from witchcraft to unemployment. Fear may also be embraced to radically different extents within different belief-systems: fear for a God-fearing religious person may be a virtue, but a vice for a risk-taking entrepreneur. Some of these socially specific manifestations of fear may have, or may be attributed with, universal significance. As I have already argued in previous chapters and will continue to argue in subsequent ones, Shakespeare himself consistently pushes ideas and emotions to the point where they make some kind of existential statement about who we are, what we need and how we should live. That there are many different kinds of existential statement in Shakespeare's plays is what gives his descriptions of human beings a degree of complexity. Fear, as I have already indicated, takes different forms in *Macbeth*, each of which makes its own kind of existential claim. I want to identify some of these and, in the spirit of the play's own literary humanist aspirations, evaluate their claims on us.

First, there is the fear that surrounds not being in control. Macbeth becomes fearful that events will exceed his ability to control them, resolving by way of an antidote to being overwhelmed by events that 'The very firstlings of my heart shall be / The firstlings of my hand' (IV, i, 163–4). This fear arguably has its roots in an albeit distorted human urge: human beings, it might be suggested, have always tried to exert a degree of control over their social and natural environment, either through their own efforts or by petitioning some higher force, although in some religious cultures, such as Buddhism, the desire to control is regarded as an unwanted aspect of a possessive ego. This qualification aside, the fear of being overwhelmed by larger forces (fate, fortune, the gods, nature, social circumstances or other people) may be credited with some kind of universal significance. However, as a Renaissance over-reacher, fearful that he might not be the master of his own destiny that he wants to be, Macbeth with his fear of losing control can be seen in more socially specific terms as the product of an overweening humanism which amplifies the human desire for control. Once this particular fear is 'placed' both historically (as the by-product of a socially specific ideology) and ethically (as a fear which stems from *too much* will to power), it loses some, though not all, of its existential clout.

A second fear takes the form of paranoia. By killing Duncan, the Macbeths create an atmosphere in which friends and allies are no longer reliable. Having betrayed trust, Macbeth is prey to fears that others cannot be trusted. They must therefore be eliminated before they eliminate him. He fears Banquo on these grounds: 'Our fears in Banquo / Stick deep' (III, i, 50–1). And he fears the consequences of Fleance having escaped his plan to have him murdered: 'now I am cabined, cribbed, confined, bound in / To saucy doubts and fears' (III, iv, 23–4). Ethically speaking, the cause of these fears, in the murder of someone who *did* trust, is reprehensible in a probably universal sense, but the list of evocative terms given by Macbeth -'cabined, cribbed, confined, bound in' – adds a psychological dimension to this particular manifestation of fear. Such fear is represented as taking over the psyche. There is nothing else but this fear. Macbeth is reduced to it. I would argue that this expression of fear has a greater existential claim on us than the first, because the collapse of trust on which it is based is unethical, psychologically damaging and destructive of human cooperation. Of cooperation, Terry Eagleton in *Sweet Violence* (2003) writes:

> W. H. Auden's rather too grandiloquent line 'We must love one another or we die', which he was later to reject, nevertheless captures the political truth that unless we cooperate we are unlikely to survive. Philosophers have sometimes puzzled over whether one can progress from a fact to a value; but here, perhaps, is an unexpected example of just such a shift.[10]

A third, equally debilitating, form of fear is the fear of being unprotected. There are no physical or emotional shelters in *Macbeth* because the Macbeths have removed them. The Macbeths' castle may look safe and hospitable to Duncan – a 'pleasant seat' (I, vi, 1) as he calls it – but it is the opposite. The banquet may offer 'hearty welcome' (III, iv, 2) and the promise of warmth and comfort, but the ghost of Banquo which brings on Macbeth's temporary 'fit' (III, iv, 54) makes it a discomforting experience. There is a desperate need for security, peace and predictability, but none can be found, not even in sleep, because Macbeth has murdered sleep:

> Methought I heard a voice cry 'Sleep no more,
> Macbeth does murder sleep' – the innocent sleep,
> Sleep that knits up the ravelled sleave of care,
> The death of each day's life, sore labour's bath
> Balm of hurt minds, great nature's second course,
> Chief nourisher in life's feast.
>
> (II, ii, 33–8)

It is easy to be affected by these images of sleep as 'sore labour's bath', 'balm of hurt minds', 'chief nourisher in life's feast'. One doesn't have to have murdered anyone to experience the precariousness of sleep. The images are especially potent because they capture the value of sleep retrospectively, once the capacity for sleep has gone. Sleeping is 'just' sleeping until the time when it is no longer a given. Then it becomes 'balm' and testimony to the need for places free from the debilitating effects of fear. There are no such places in *Macbeth*.

The irony of all this is that Macbeth was originally the provider of protection and comfort. In the second scene of the play, where the image of Macbeth as war hero dominates, the word 'comfort' is also, rather surprisingly, used to describe Macbeth's initial victory:

> As whence the sun 'gins his reflection
> Shipwrecking storms and direful thunders break,
> So from that spring whence comfort seemed to come
> Discomfort swells. Mark, King of Scotland, mark.
> No sooner justice had, with valour armed,
> Compelled these skipping kerns to trust their heels
> But the Norwegian lord . . .
> Began a fresh assault.
>
> (I, ii, 25–33)

Shakespeare might easily have treated winning and losing as a moral issue only, as a matter, that is, of at least perceived 'justice', but he adds the words 'comfort' and 'discomfort', not just as a *supplement* to the moral language but as a *preface* to it. Macbeth is a comforter, albeit one who uses violent means.[11] This is another example of ethical language being supplemented by emotional and psychological language in such a way as to thicken the existential significance of moral vocabulary. What ensues in the play is a matter of basic (some would say) 'good' versus 'evil', but it is also to do with the contagious fear aroused by the destruction of comfort by the man who was originally its source.

The self thus also becomes 'dangerous' and a source of anxiety. As in *Othello* and *The Merchant of Venice*, 'others' are or become part of the self, and the boundaries separating outsiders from insiders are fragile. This means that the 'self' is itself not a safe place and that interiors, such as the castle, are not immune from the wildness and instability associated with the heath and witches. Macbeth's first encounter with the witches provokes 'thought' which 'shakes so my single state of man' that 'function / Is smothered in surmise, and nothing is / But what is not' (I, iii, 138–41). This is a typical Shakespearean moment, a moment, that is, when a central character's sense of unity is put at risk. Fear always accompanies such disintegration, but in *Macbeth* the images of fear are especially intense and insistent: the idea of assassinating Duncan conjures up a 'horrid image' that 'doth unfix my hair' and 'make my seated heart knock at the ribs'; it produces 'horrible imaginings' (I, iii, 134–7). The political message is that the prospect of regicide is so horrific that it should induce mighty dread. Regicide, however, is one politically charged component of a murder which is again loaded with more broadly human significance: Macbeth will kill a king who was also a guest in his household and someone who trusted him. That Duncan is killed in his sleep adds to the sense that the murder crosses a line which is not only social and political. Macbeth's 'horrible imaginings' of such a transgression make him unsafe to himself. He is turning into someone upon whom he cannot rely. He is becoming a stranger to himself, a microcosm that is 'out of joint'. He is his own worst enemy. All of these formulations are variations on the theme of the horror of disintegration. Taken together, they themselves constitute another variation on the fear of being unprotected. The effect of these multiple images of unsafe places is to push us towards the existential conclusion that human beings need places of safety, even as they often put these places of safety in jeopardy.

The fear of the self, as a place of unpredictable danger, is also evident in Macbeth's belated discovery of conscience. It has taken murder, it seems, to discover or rediscover the supposedly inalienable part of Macbeth. Does it take the extreme action of killing someone to bring a self back to itself? That a 'good' man can become a murderer suggests that conscience *is* alienable, that human beings can lose their conscience and their humanity as defined by their conscience. However, if humanity can be lost, it can be found again, as the conscience-stricken Macbeth shows. Even so, it has still taken murder to discover this. Surely, there might have been less extreme ways of proving the existence of a 'basic' humanity? The fear of the self and the self's loss of ethical orientation means that the anxiety in the play about unprotected places not only comes from 'without' (from the witches, from Macbeth as far as other characters are concerned) but also from 'within'. This fear – the fear of the self and what the self may be capable of – has a powerful existential charge, although like some of the sceptical views considered in previous chapters, the charge is based on the notion that human beings are vacuous and suggestible.

A fourth kind of fear is paradoxically the fear of being unable to fear. Macbeth's response in Act V to the '*cry within of women*' is that he has become blunted to fear: 'I have almost forgot the taste of fears' (V, v, 9). His total desensitisation to fear verges on becoming the occasion for fear: 'I have supped full with horrors. / Direness, familiar to my slaughterous thoughts, / Cannot once start me' (V, v, 13–15). The fear of fearlessness is the fear of being hardened against human suffering and of no longer being able to experience the anguish of serious transgression. The representation of this type of fear is a further example of the way that Shakespeare, by adding psychology to ethics, deepens the existential significance of ethical boundaries. Ashley Tauchert in 'Among the Dark Satanic Wheels: Transgressing Transgression' (2005) asks: 'Is it that when we stop transgressing that thing we call "the law", it reveals itself as something other than simply a mode of oppression?'[12] The notion that taboos are not always or only external to us is also one of the principal concerns of Georges Bataille's *Eroticism* (1957). There he argues:

> We must know, we can know that prohibitions are not imposed from without. This is clear to us in the anguish we feel when we are violating the taboo, especially at that moment when our feelings hang in the balance, when the taboo still holds good and yet we are yielding to the impulsion it forbids. If we observe the taboo, if we submit to it, we are no longer conscious of it. But in the act of violating it we feel the anguish of mind without which the taboo could not exist: that is the experience of sin . . . The inner experience of eroticism demands from the subject a sensitiveness to the anguish at the heart of the taboo no less great than the desire which leads him to infringe it.[13]

For Bataille, the taboo becomes an inner experience at the moment when it is violated (or just about to be). The Macbeths, from this perspective, have to transgress so that they know and we know, experientially or through vicarious experience, what it means to transgress. Of course, not all taboos and moral sanctions are rooted in human nature. They are cultural, rather than natural. Shakespearean tragedy is an attempt to differentiate between those taboos which ultimately 'matter' to us as human beings and those which are externally imposed. Whereas a villain such as Iago tends to homogenise morality by treating all moral codes as external, the tragedies encourage us to differentiate between what 'is' and 'what is not' truly transgressive of human norms by placing characters in extreme situations. Macbeth's fear that he may have become immune to the anguish of serious transgression implies that he is no longer fully human.

After Duncan's murder, the play focuses on what it might feel like to have murdered someone. The Macbeths become increasingly isolated both from other people and from each other. Lady Macbeth becomes fixated by the real or illusory stain on her hand which cannot be washed away, and Macbeth drifts into a kind of numbness. The numbness comes from the realisation that there is nothing left to the Macbeths but the unending aftermath of a moment – the killing of the king – which has indelibly marked their lives. They are now only murderers, nothing else. There is no ordinary future and there are no ordinary feelings available to them:

> I have lived long enough. My way of life
> Is fall'n into the sere, the yellow leaf,
> And that which should accompany old age,
> As honour, love, obedience, troops of friends,
> I must not look to have, but in their stead
> Curses, not loud, but deep.
>
> (V, iii, 24–9)

Anguish of the kind described by Bataille is present here, but the presiding feeling is the emotional void feared by Macbeth when he says that he has 'almost forgot the taste of fears'. This finds its most powerful expression in the nihilism of Macbeth's 'Tomorrow, and tomorrow, and tomorrow' speech, which follows the news of the death of Lady Macbeth:

> Tomorrow, and tomorrow, and tomorrow
> Creeps in this petty pace from day to day
> To the last syllable of recorded time,
> And all our yesterdays have lighted fools
> The way to dusty death. Out, out, brief candle.
> Life's but a walking shadow, a poor player
> That struts and frets his hour upon the stage,
> And then is heard no more. It is a tale
> Told by an idiot, full of sound and fury,
> Signifying nothing.
>
> (V, v, 18–27)

For Macbeth, there are no more feelings to be experienced except for the feeling of emptiness. The meaning of life is that there is no meaning. Macbeth's fear of becoming insensitive to suffering and transgression is fully realised here. Once again the existential significance of moral vocabulary is deepened.

I emphasise this point because although Shakespeare sometimes shows that it is possible to lead a rich and interesting moral life, Hamlet being one example, morality is also often depicted, from the perspective of the villain, as stupid, dull, irrelevant or a means of social control. For Iago, for example, morality, like human nature, is for other people and a mark of their gullibility. To become one's own authority involves treating external moral and other types of authority precisely as 'external'. The process of externalisation is also a process which reinforces the banality of morality as compared with the more interesting and adventurous life led by the villain. The villain who sees morality as so much external constraint upon a human nature thereby cut off from a vast panoply of emotions and instincts anticipates the Nietzschean perspective that morality, especially post-pagan, Christian morality, is basically life-denying. Writing, in *Twilight of the Idols* (1889), about his 'favourite' Greek god, Dionysius, the god of intoxication and wild abandonment, Nietzsche claims that:

> In the Dionysian state . . . the entire emotional system is alerted and intensified: so that it discharges all its powers of representation, imitation, transfiguration, transformation, transmutation, every kind of mimicry and play-acting, conjointly. The essential thing remains the facility of the metamorphosis, the incapacity *not* to react . . . It is impossible for the Dionysian man not to understand any suggestion of whatever kind, he ignores no signal from the emotions, he possesses to the highest degree the instinct for understanding and divining . . . He enters into every skin, into every emotion; he is continually transforming himself.[14]

This description leads to my fifth and final example of the existential claims made by fear in *Macbeth*. This is the 'good' – from a Nietzschean perspective – fear which accompanies exhilaration, risk and experiment. This is the fear that comes with living life to the full or to excess. Fear here almost translates as excitement, but fear is still the appropriate term to use because living dangerously relies upon an element of fear. Tauchert writes that the 'thrill and triumph of transgression . . . testifies to a something *there* that has been shown to be transgress-able, or a something *resistant* to transgression'.[15] An aspect of the 'something' that is resistant to transgression is fear. For the daredevilry of the transgressor to be perceived as such, transgression has to induce fear.

Nietzsche's representation of a Dionysian openness to experience is not a bad way of describing Macbeth's initial reaction to the witches. Twice Banquo describes Macbeth as 'rapt' (I, iii, 55; 142) by the weird sisters. He is transported, suggestible, emotionally alert and open to transformation in the way described by Nietzsche. Where Macbeth is excited by the danger of the witches, Banquo, by contrast, keeps his distance and offers a piece of conventional moral wisdom, which from a Nietzschean perspective is life-denying and dull:

> oftentimes to win us to our harm
> The instruments of darkness tell us truths,
> Win us with honest trifles to betray's
> In deepest consequence.
> (I, iii, 121–4)

Morality as represented here by Banquo cannot compete with the Dionysian allure of the witches, an allure that is intimately connected to their capacity to arouse fear. In *Beyond Good and Evil* (1886), Nietzsche makes a joke at the expense of moral philosophers by claiming that one of the few useful services they have performed is to make sure that morality remains 'boring and a soporific'. He continues, in the same vein: 'It is important that as few people as possible should think about morality – consequently it is *very* important that morality should not one day become interesting!'[16] Banquo, we might say, fails to make morality interesting. If morality is going to be able to compete with excess, then the language of morality will need to be thickened and deepened. This, I have argued, is precisely what Shakespeare does in *Macbeth*.

The attitude to morality of some recent influential theorists, such as the early Foucault, for example, is often broadly Nietzschean, this despite the fact that moral perspectives are still implied.[17] For Nietzsche, albeit playing devil's advocate, morality is dull. He compensates for its dullness by thinking about it in terms of displacement. Morality is thereby emptied of its own substance and treated as a symptom of 'something else' (which tends to vary from book to book). In *Beyond Good and Evil*, for example, Nietzsche prophesies that psychology 'shall again be recognised as the queen of sciences', and morality understood as a symptom of such emotions as 'hatred, envy, covetousness, and lust for domination'.[18] By contrast, in *On the Genealogy of Morals* (1887), history and linguistics are granted the power to disturb the special status of morality as a transcendent, truth-bearing discourse, by refuting the universality of moral codes. Nietzsche's dethroning of morality is repeated by numerous postmodern sceptics whose own turn to history and/or linguistics has had the effect of re-conceiving morality as social morality, which is in turn conceived, in Foucauldian (as well as Nietzschean) terms, as power. Foucault's account of the substitution of spectacular for more discrete mechanisms of social control has been widely used and the new historicist preoccupation with power equally widely documented as well as criticised.[19] Given the social prejudices which masquerade as morality or humanity, there are good reasons for scepticism. However, emphasis on power and the social construction of morality can become a shibboleth which makes it difficult for sceptics either to address moral issues outside of a broadly social constructionist framework or to make explicit their own ethical positions.

Ewan Fernie's introduction to *Spiritual Shakespeares* (2005) is one counter-example, again reflecting the turn or return to ethics within literary studies. Fernie suggests that if 'the spirituality of [Shakespeare's] plays has scandalised the materialism of contemporary thought, it has also often been depreciated or ignored because the truth-claims it involves are presumed to be at odds with Shakespeare's theatrical polyphony'.[20] Theatrical polyphony means or is taken to mean that ethical truth-claims are ironised, but, says Fernie, 'the ironic power of spiritual truth itself has been underestimated in recent criticism'.[21] In *Macbeth* the theatrical polyphony which complicates morality and pits morality against the allure of transgression has the effect of weakening ethical truth-claims, as represented by Banquo, for example, but in the spirit of Fernie's general argument we could also say that morality is in turn strengthened by its psychological intensification. Contra Nietzsche, who in *Beyond Good and Evil* suggests that psychology will displace morality as a master-narrative, morality and psychology are shown in *Macbeth* to be mutually reinforcing. Ethical boundaries exist because without them we become damaged by paranoia and destructively uncooperative. The fear we have of spectacular transgression is psychologically motivated as well as necessary to survival. Fear, from this perspective, is useful. There are various Renaissance equivalents to the notion that emotions, such as fear, are educative rather than, as in some post-Romantic accounts, ineffable. Commenting on Edward Reynolds's *Treatise of the Passions and Faculties of the Soule of Man* (1640), Rowe writes that 'fearful prospects . . . open a channel for external as well as internal redirection of the passions, a process often figured as receptiveness to counsel'.[22] The passion of fearfulness counsels the 'rapt' Macbeth at the beginning of the play against courting the discomfort that will be simultaneously moral, physical, psychological and linguistic. He ignores these warning signals, because fear, understood from a contrasting Nietzschean perspective, also tells him to experience that which is forbidden.

Several existential truths are told in the play about fear, then, but two stand out. One is that the fear of transgressing certain boundaries is a psychological and ethical necessity. The other is that fear activates a desire for transgressive experience. One affirms human beings' need for ethical and psychological limits, the other their thirst for experiment and excess. The important ethical and psychological dimensions of the concepts of limit and excess do not themselves 'limit' the nature of Shakespeare's preoccupation with these concepts, and, before returning the chapter, by way of conclusion, to the issue of ethics, I want briefly to try to capture something of the dizzying richness and versatility of Shakespeare's preoccupation with them. Robert Watson's broad characterisation in 'Tragedies of Revenge and Ambition' (2002) of medieval and Renaissance understandings of desire is a useful starting point:

> this period seems to have invented a new and inexhaustible kind of ambition – and defined it as fundamental to human nature. Against a classical and medieval notion of desire as finite, seeking its own end in satisfaction, Renaissance culture came to advocate a Romantic and modern notion of desire as infinite regress, willing to invent further goals in order perpetually to forestall its own demise in stasis.[23]

The tensions I have been examining, between foundationalist and antifoundationalist concepts of the human, or between limits and excess, or between the fear *of* transgression and fear *as* transgressive, can be recast as the twinned oppositions that Watson uses, between stasis and dynamism, or desire as finite versus desire as 'infinite regress'. Or they can be recast as a dialogue between 'enough' and 'more' (of which 'more' will be said below and in Chapter 8), or as the tension within mainstream humanism between its essentialism, on the one hand, and its celebration of infinite capability and possibility, on the other (see Introduction). These different inflections of similar ideas are an attempt to draw out the full implications, the richness – the atmosphere even – of the existential dilemmas in Shakespeare's work and to do justice to his own inordinate ability to play variations on them. We can express one aspect of this variation in broadly generic terms by suggesting that whereas in comedy 'excess' is represented via carnival in mainly positive terms as liberating and playful, in tragedy excess is exhilarating but ultimately destructive of self and society. Excess is in other words subject to the different normative evaluations which are implicit in comedy and tragedy: in tragedy, the norm is that transgression (of non-arbitrary ethical limits) is 'bad', whereas in comedy, the norm is that transgression (of arbitrary social boundaries) is 'good' and even necessary for the health of the human community. As well as these generic inflections, excess can also take such different forms as: excess of language (*Love's Labour's Lost*), economic excess (*The Merchant of Venice*, *The Comedy of Errors*), excess of generosity (*Timon of Athens*), emotional excess (*King Lear*), excess of thinking (*Hamlet*). Likewise, limits can be a combination and/or confusion of patriarchal, ethical, social, emotional, psychological, linguistic and existential limits.

Listing variations in this way might lead to a meta-commentary on excess whose starting point would be to say that these variations on the themes of excess and limits of course constitute their own kind of excess. However, as a kind of warning against going down the route (or abyss) of stockpiling concepts for concepts' sake, and of thereby losing sight of the 'life-issues' I want them to keep in contact with, my list reminds me of Polonius's in *Hamlet* when he acclaims the players' competence in the genres and sub-genres of 'tragedy, comedy, history, pastoral, pastoral-comical, historical-pastoral, tragical-historical, tragical-comical-historical-pastoral' (II, ii, 398–401). This is lifeless. The life that is in plays is sucked out of them. And there is too much. Or at least too much of the wrong kind of thing: labels deprived of meaning, quantity rather than quality, arid technical terms which miss the existential point.

The existential point might be: when is more (more variations of the theme of limits and excess, for example) too much? At what point does 'the brain', by which I mean, at the risk of subdividing, Polonius-style, when does my brain or your brain or Shakespeare's brain or, if there is such a thing, the 'postmodern brain' or 'Renaissance brain', or my brain – or yours – when it is fresh as opposed to tired, or the trained as compared with the untrained brain, say . . . 'enough'? When *is* enough enough? Is Macbeth's '*single* state of man' (I, iii, 139) [my italics] too parsimonious, too austere? Does he need to be shaken up a little but not too much, by his and human nature's own doubleness, as represented by the 'two truths' spoken by the witches? Two is more interesting than one, but still manageable, still congenial to cognitive mapping. Binary thinking is popular, universal even, if Ferdinand de Saussure is to be believed.[24] Tripartite thinking is also popular, and again, perhaps even universal; there are three witches in *Macbeth*, after all. However, set against the limited conceptual liability and even safety of the twos and the threes in the play is the dangerous allure – or so it is represented in *Macbeth* – of a numberless excess.

When Lady Macbeth is attempting to persuade Macbeth to lay aside his moral qualms, she appeals to the idea that the two of them are all-powerful and that anything – any number of things – is possible. 'What cannot you and I perform', she says, 'upon / The unguarded Duncan? What not put upon / His spongy officers, who shall bear the guilt / Of our great quell? (I, vii, 69–72). For the 'masculinised' Lady Macbeth, who has opened herself to the Dionysian ecstasy of transformation by asking 'the spirits' to 'unsex me here' (I, v, 39–40), obstacles, moral or otherwise, exist to be overcome and prove one's mettle. Accordingly, her definition of what it means to be a man is based on excess. In response to Macbeth's definition of a 'man' in terms of a limit – 'I dare do all that may become a man; / Who dares do more is none' (I, vii, 46–7) – Lady Macbeth answers:

> What beast was't then
> That made you break this enterprise to me?
> When you durst do it, then you were a man;
> And to be more than what you were, you would
> Be so much more the man.
> (I, vii, 48–51)

This is the language of the overreacher, the language spoken by such spectacular individualists as Marlowe's Tamburlaine and Dr Faustus.[25] It corresponds with that aspect of mainstream humanism based on an inflated image of human beings and their infinite capabilities. Alongside the emphasis upon the traditional coordinates of good/bad, heaven/hell, it is the kind of boundary-negating humanism which Pico's *Oration* presents.[26]

Inflation, excess and multiplication are the way of the play. Enough, it seems, is never enough. When Duncan early on says to Macbeth 'I have begun to plant thee, and will labour / To make thee full of growing' (I, iv, 28–9), the spur to excessive ambition is 'more or less' contained by a metaphor from nature suggesting that growth is something that should be organic and gradual. However, in his very next speech Duncan describes his own 'plenteous joys' as being 'wanton in fullness' (I, iv, 33–4), as though he, too, has caught the virus whereby 'more' is always infecting 'enough'. From the combined point of view of the dramatic momentum of the play and the allure attached to going beyond a limit, Macbeth's 'pre-murder' resolution to 'proceed no further in this business' (I, vii, 31) is an impossible statement, a statement that goes against the play's drive towards excess. From the point of view of 'more', 'enough' is the coward's way and the way of 'miserable ease', as Nietzsche's Zarathustra puts it.[27]

An excess of thought, reflecting psychological and emotional turmoil, can also overwhelm the apparent simplicity of ethical positions. There are lines – memorable lines – in *Macbeth* which stake out ethical positions, such as Lady's Macbeth's recognition that her husband is 'too full o' th' milk of human kindness' for the 'illness' required to realise his desires (I, v, 16; 19). However, these markers can become obscured by the convolutions of a speech which mirror the convolutions of mental processes:

> I fear thy nature
> It is too full o' th' milk of human kindness
> To catch the nearest way. Thou wouldst be great,
> Art not without ambition, but without

> The illness should attend it. What thou wouldst highly,
> That wouldst holily; wouldst not play false,
> And yet wouldst wrongly win. Thou'dst have, great Glamis,
> That which cries 'Thus thou must do' if thou have it,
> And that which rather thou dost fear to do
> Than wishest should be undone.
>
> (I, v, 15–24)

Stephen Greenblatt says that this speech becomes 'queasily complicated'.[28] There is, in Shakespeare, a tendency to take thought or language (or both) to the point of no return, to the point, that is, where the simplicity or apparent simplicity of opening pronouncements, ethical or otherwise, cannot be easily recovered. This is notoriously Hamlet's problem, but not only Hamlet's, as the capacity to re-describe – and in re-describing, complicate – ethical, emotional and existential realities is everywhere apparent in Shakespeare's work. Thus limits can be constraining as well as vital. Excess can be exhilarating as well as debilitating. The impasse to which such endless re-description can lead is encapsulated in the insight of Macbeth's that 'nothing is / But what is not' (I, iii, 140–1). The guidelines and the markers are still there, however, and seem all the more important in the face of the obscurity and complexity which threaten to engulf them. The psychological make-up of Macbeth as represented by Lady Macbeth might seem to move out of the orbit of straightforward ethical perspectives, but, as I argued earlier, ethics and psyche are not irredeemably opposed.

Neither is it the case that the life of Nietzschean excess is simply opposed to an enfeebled discourse of ethical limits, for limits are affirmed and strengthened even as they are being recklessly abandoned. Limits may be dismissed as lacklustre by one of the apostles of excess, Lady Macbeth, but her allusion to a past child puts her ruthlessness in a context:

> I have given suck, and know
> How tender 'tis to love the babe that milks me.
> I would, while it was smiling in my face,
> Have plucked my nipple from his boneless gums
> And dashed the brains out, had I so sworn as you
> Have done to this.
>
> (I, vii, 54–9)

In the 1997 television production of *Macbeth* set on the Ladybird housing estate in Birmingham, the motif of the lost child is made explicit by having a clearly distressed Lady Macbeth visit a room in her flat which has been kept intact as an infant's room. The passing allusion in the original play has been hardened into a definite interpretation, but the original play nevertheless gestures towards the idea that Lady Macbeth's ruthless repudiation of compassion might be the result of past trauma. Having loved only to have lost, she now hardens herself against tenderness. The excess that she encourages Macbeth into is therefore 'placed'; it has a history behind it. If human nature is defined or redefined by Lady Macbeth and the play more generally in terms of the 'infinite regress' of desire, as Watson puts it, then we are simultaneously made aware that excess might not be the touchstone for humanity but a kind of displacement that masks damage. Limits, therefore, aren't only for the dull and unadventurous. They are the markers of a compassionate humanity which get transgressed not simply because they represent a challenge, but as the result of past suffering.

Jonathan Dollimore, himself making use of Nietzsche, describes the tragedy of *Macbeth* as 'the recalcitrant conflict between the daemonic and the humane, between the Macbeths' "black and deep desires" and the "milk of human kindness"'. However, this 'recalcitrant conflict' seems to be weighted, as far as Dollimore is concerned, in favour of the daemonic. Nietzsche's 'view of the artist and philosopher', writes Dollimore, is based on them 'knowing too much, of seeing through, demystifying and maybe undermining the ideological, religious and cultural "fictions" of society'.[29] This is a disenchanted sceptic's view of morality based on seeing morality as 'merely' external. Dollimore comes close to suggesting that the daemonic is the real and morality the appearance, but the social constructionist in him draws him back from making such essentialist claims about human nature: '*Macbeth* shows how the threat of the daemonic derives not from a pure, pre-social nature or instinct, clearly distinct from the culture it threatens, but from the return of repressed desire so inextricably bound up with culture'.[30] The daemonic is nevertheless located as the product of artistic demystification which exposes what lies beyond or beneath the 'cultural "fictions" of society'. Morality according to this perspective is external and the daemonic is, if not internal, then destructive of external appearances.

I have tried in this chapter to show how Shakespeare makes morality more robust than this, with the effect that it cannot be easily externalised. Moral roles aren't merely 'roles', but selves or possible selves. These selves come into conflict with other selves, because life in the Shakespearean world is densely complicated. However, it is not so complicated as to prevent albeit belated recognition of psychological and emotional truths which are also ethical truths. The 'more' of excess thus turns out to be 'less', and, conversely, the 'less' of limits, 'more'.

Chapter 6

Only Human: *Coriolanus*

Chapter 4 (on *I Henry IV*) built upon the evolving emphasis of previous chapters on the importance of the emotions for an understanding of human nature. It did so by showing how Falstaff's morality is rooted in the body, conceived of as an emotional rather than purely physical entity. Chapter 5 consolidated this by showing how Shakespeare in *Macbeth* charges ethical limits with psychological/affective significance, thereby deepening their existential import. Such perspectives contribute to the sense that there is such an egalitarian concept as a 'common humanity'. Human nature may be questioned (Chapter 1), emptied (Chapter 2), ironised (Chapter 3), historicised (Chapter 4), or exceeded (Chapter 5), but there is something recalcitrant about it. This recalcitrance is registered in the use of such proverbial phrases as 'only human' and 'all too human'. Of course, reverting for a moment to a sceptical perspective, it is possible to suggest that what is 'only human' about humanity is paradoxically its difference from itself: its mutability, its tendency to become 'more' (superhuman) or 'less' (subhuman) than itself. Concepts of the 'only human' are also unstably plural rather than stably singular: the frailty of the flesh implied by the idea of the 'only human' can refer, as it does in Emilia's speech in *Othello* (IV, iii, 95–102), and almost routinely in Shakespeare's comedies (see Chapter 8 on *As You Like It*), to the impermanence of human affections and desires, or in a religious sense to the fallen and therefore corruptible nature of humanity; or it can suggest the vulnerabilities and weaknesses to which mortal existence is subject. These (sceptical) qualifications notwithstanding, the 'only human' will be taken in this chapter to refer to limits and finite needs of the kind already examined: the frailty of the flesh understood in terms of need and vulnerability; the limits of physical and emotional existence grounded in the ordinary sensate evidence of pleasure and pain; and the need to belong.

The recognition of limits is also levelling. *Coriolanus* (1608) will be discussed in this light, as a levelling play, in which the 'more than human' Coriolanus is brought down to earth and obliged to recognise his 'only human' humanity. The 'only human' here acts as an antidote both to the hauteur of the aristocrat and the 'narcissistically overinflated autonomy' (Habermas) of mainstream humanism.[1] Humility is initially not a word in Coriolanus's vocabulary, for humility would involve acceptance of the ordinary aspects of his humanity. Chapter 7 will examine in some depth the understanding expressed in Shakespearean comedy of what it is to live humbly, with a sense of one's own folly. In *Coriolanus*, the humility to which Coriolanus is eventually subject involves a Falstaff-like acceptance of the fact of human vulnerability. However, where vulnerability is expressed by Falstaff as a 'natural' reaction to the prospect of being killed in battle, and is in a sense what we expect from Falstaff, in *Coriolanus* the scope of vulnerability is broadened. One way it is broadened is through the play's focus on a man who at first sets himself way above ordinary human frailties, only to reveal his mortality. The play in other words seems to go out of its way to make vulnerable someone who seems impervious to vulnerability. This has a universalising effect: if the 'more than human' Coriolanus turns out to be 'only human' after all, then this shows that the 'truism' that we are all only human might have some 'truth' in it. A second way in which vulnerability is broadened is through the association of vulnerability with infantile dependency. Coriolanus has a mother! And he had a childhood. Both are represented in the play. We see how the child grew into the man, but how the child is still in the man. This is everyone's history. I shall initially make use of some insights from psychoanalysis to support this.

The overall aim of this chapter is to do with vulnerability what the last chapter did with fear, which is via *Coriolanus* and a selective use of psychoanalytic theory to draw out its existential significance. That *Coriolanus* lends itself to psychoanalytic interpretation, such as Janet Adelman's in *Suffocating Mothers: Fantasies of Maternal Origin in Shakespeare's Plays* (1992), is unsurprising, for as I have already suggested, the play conspicuously negates heroic self-sufficiency by representing its central figure as having both a mother and a childhood, both of which are grist to the mill of psychoanalysis. This chapter, which is generally informed by Adelman's interpretation of the play, will also broaden out into a discussion of the emotions in general, by considering their transactional nature and the implications of this for ideas of human nature and human well-being.

What is common to the many different kinds of psychoanalytic theory which have developed since Freud is the fact of infantile dependency.

This is the foundation upon which many different psychoanalytic theories are raised. Freud's theory of the Oedipus complex is one notorious example. In *The Interpretation of Dreams* (1900), Freud uses *Hamlet* to develop some of his ideas about the Oedipus complex. Freud's Hamlet cannot take vengeance on his father's murderer, Claudius, because Claudius, writes Freud, 'shows him the repressed wishes of his own childhood', namely to keep his mother for himself.[2] For a post-structuralist variation on the drama of separation played out through the Oedipus complex, a drama which again takes infantile dependency for granted, we can turn to Julia Kristeva's evocative description in *Black Sun* (1989) of the illusion that the lost union with the maternal body might be adequately recovered in word and symbol:

> Signs are arbitrary because language starts with a *negation (Verneinung)* of loss, along with the depression occasioned by mourning. 'I have lost an essential object that happens to be, in the final analysis, my mother,' is what the speaking subject seems to be saying. 'But no, I have found her again in signs, or rather since I consent to lose her I have not lost her (that is the negation), I can recover her in language.'[3]

For Kristeva, the attempt to restore the sense of plenitude, oneness and continuity associated with infantile dependency is accompanied by a sense of exile and division. The infant can 'make do' with surrogate, symbolic versions of the maternal body but loss of the real thing is nevertheless apparent, for, as Kristeva implies, to *consent* to lose something is to acknowledge the loss involved in the act of a metonymic or metaphoric substitution of it.

Kristeva focuses on the desire to return to a state of infantile dependency. But the desire or need to escape is also part of the Oedipus complex, especially for boys, who, according to Freudian psychoanalysis, have to repress the mother in order to establish separate identity. The contrasting experience of girls is described by Nancy Chodorow in *The Reproduction of Mothering* (1978). As the result of a different series of attachments and detachments, 'girls', writes Chodorow, 'come to experience themselves as less separate than boys, as having more permeable ego boundaries. Girls come to define themselves more in relation to others'.[4] The gender issues surrounding the Oedipus complex are ramified and contentious, but the core idea, that we begin our lives in a state of dependency, is still the significant given which drives these various ideas about the ensuing oscillations that take place in our lives between relating and separating, connecting and disconnecting, merging and dividing.[5] To become *totally* disconnected, to 'stand', as Coriolanus puts it, 'as if a man were author of himself / And knew no other kin',[6] is from the perspective of a psychoanalytically inflected variation on the 'only human', to deny our ordinary human need for others, a need which can of course also make us vulnerable to them. Burton Hatlen in 'The "Noble Thing" and the "Boy of Tears": Coriolanus and the Embarrassments of Identity' (1997) describes Coriolanus as an 'absolutist' who 'insists upon absolute separation'. This, Hatlen continues, 'marks him as psychologically flawed, for he is denying the deepest level of his experience', which is 'the primordial experience of unity with the mother'.[7]

Adelman's illuminating book, *Suffocating Mothers*, will help to bring psychoanalytic theory in still closer relation to the Renaissance and Shakespeare. The simultaneously psychoanalytic, feminist and historicist thrust of Adelman's book makes it a mixture of trans-historical and historical perspectives. Infantile dependency and ordinary human vulnerability are again taken for granted, as the material facts about human nature upon which psychoanalytic insights are founded, but Adelman also contextualises vulnerability by examining the 'actual conditions of infancy' which shaped 'infantile fantasy' in the Renaissance:

> If the infant survived, the period of infancy was both dangerous and long: poor nutrition and perhaps rickets sometimes delayed the appearance of teeth – and hence weaning and the routine eating of solid food – until the child was two or three; similar conditions sometimes restricted the child's mobility, delaying the onset of walking also until two or three. What we know of the actual conditions that shape infantile fantasy suggests, that is, that many would have experienced a prolonged period of infantile dependency, during which they were subject to pleasures and dangers especially associated with nursing and the maternal body.[8]

The belief that 'mothers' milk' was 'unwholesome during the period immediately after childbirth' and the notion that 'the mother could literally deform fetuses through her excessive imagination, her uncontrollable longings, her unnatural lusts' are amongst the culturally specific perceptions about the dangers of the maternal body examined by Adelman.[9] She goes on to invoke contemporary object-relations psychoanalysis in order to emphasise the increased anxiety that these beliefs, combined with prolonged infantile dependency, might have provoked in male children and adults:

> Contemporary object-relations psychoanalysis locates differentiation from the mother as a special site of anxiety for the boy-child, who must form his specifically masculine selfhood against the matrix of her overwhelming femaleness; how much more difficult and anxiety-ridden must this process have been if the period of infantile dependency – with all its pleasures and dangers – was prolonged, and if the body itself, in all its vulnerability, could later be understood as the inheritance from her contaminating female matter.[10]

Vulnerability, in other words, is seen to be the mother's fault. She is the scapegoat. In *Coriolanus*, however, Shakespeare turns this around and makes the seemingly invulnerable Coriolanus recognise his 'only human' needs.

Early on in *Coriolanus*, the citizens frame their complaint against the aristocratic ruling class of Rome by appealing to what is humane:

> We are accounted poor citizens, the patricians good. What authority surfeits on would relieve us. If they would yield us but the superfluity while it were wholesome we might guess they relieved us humanely but they think we are too dear. (I, i, 14–18)

The humane operates here as a normative concept, the implication being that any ordinary mortal should recognise any other ordinary mortal's bodily need and react accordingly. But Coriolanus, who is their especial source of grievance, does not recognise ordinariness. He is, according to one of the citizens, a 'dog to the commonality' (I, i, 27). Brimful of aristocratic hauteur and disdainful of the 'vulgar wisdoms' of the citizens (I, i, 213), Coriolanus is offended by ordinariness. For him, citizen life is banal and petty. It is sustained by gossip about the high and mighty, and such ordinary creaturely comforts as a decent fire:

> They'll sit by th' fire and presume to know
> What's done i'th' Capitol, who's like to rise,
> Who thrives and who declines; side factions and give out
> Conjectural marriages, making parties strong
> And feebling such as stand not in their liking
> Below their cobbled shoes.
>
> (I, i, 189–94)

Gossip about who is in and out of favour makes ordinary what should as far as Coriolanus is concerned be seen as extraordinary, for such gossip makes the aristocratic class seem as small-minded as the citizens. It is not surprising that Coriolanus ends this diatribe by reasserting his special vocation as a warrior and disdaining another sign of ordinary human solidarity, namely 'ruth' or compassion:

> Would the nobility lay aside their ruth
> And let me use my sword, I'd make a quarry
> With thousands of these quartered slaves as high
> As I could pitch my lance.
>
> (I, i, 195–8)

Ironically, Coriolanus keeps invoking a sense of the ordinary (sitting by the fire, gossip, ruth) in order to establish his difference from it and make his extraordinariness appear all the more extraordinary. He in other words needs ordinariness as his foil but cannot admit this because 'need' would itself be a sign of belonging to the common stream of humanity.

The spurning of emotional vulnerability is mirrored by Coriolanus's spurning of physical vulnerability. Not only does he make light of his wounds (I, vi), but he refers to them in the third person as though they are not his: 'I have some wounds upon me, and they smart / To hear themselves remembered' (I, x, 27–8). Vulnerability is in this way exported by Coriolanus, treated as though not part of him. He also refuses to perform the public ritual of showing his wounds to the people (II, ii). Of the shame involved in showing his wounds, Hatlen asks: 'what is it he fears, if not the revelation that he too is human, a creature of flesh and blood, sharing a common destiny with the ordinary people that he so disdains'?[11] Ewan Fernie in *Shame in Shakespeare* (2002) concurs, suggesting that 'revelation of his wounds would . . . expose his fleshly vulnerability, mutability, and mortality'.[12]

However, it is worth complicating these views slightly, for the public spectacle would draw attention to his 'fleshly vulnerability' in both a simple and extended sense: simple, in that showing his wounds would, as Fernie suggests, demonstrate his 'mutability and mortality'; extended, because in drawing attention to his overcoming of the ordinary human emotion of fear and the ordinary human sensation of pain, he would be highlighting that which has been overcome. We marvel at heroes because they surpass recognisable limits which are thereby reinforced. The public ritual of showing wounds to the people, accompanied by official praise for military prowess, is, amongst other things, testimony to the 'reality' of ordinary human feelings and bodily experiences, which the hero has succeeded in subduing. Cominius, in the typical manner of an encomium, focuses on the heroic feat of converting 'only human' flesh and blood into 'more than human' strength of body and mind: 'When by and by the din of war gan pierce / His ready sense, then straight his doubled spirit / Requickened what in flesh was fatigate' (II, ii, 115–17). In one sense, this confirms what I have already suggested about Coriolanus, that he needs a sense of the ordinary as a foil to his extraordinariness. However, the difference between Cominius and Coriolanus is that where Cominius empathises with the reality of ordinary 'sensate life', Coriolanus utterly disdains this reality. Cominius in other words understands that bodies get tired, whereas Coriolanus can only be frustrated by such bodily weaknesses and pretend that they do not happen. This might be one of the reasons why Coriolanus is so addicted to anger. Anger provides the emotional energy which gives the body its seemingly 'more than human' stamina. In humours theory, anger gives the body 'heat'. In one of the several attempts to calm Coriolanus down, a senator advises him not to deliver a speech to the people 'in this heat' (III, i, 67). Fiery, hot-blooded anger is what keeps Coriolanus going and drives him to extremes.

Anger is Coriolanus's chief emotion not only because it energises him, but because it also separates him from others, so much so that Brutus identifies Coriolanus's vindictive anger as a sign of his desire to be at a godlike distance from mere mortals: 'You speak o'th' people as if you were a god / To punish, not a man of their infirmity' (III, i, 85–6). The reference to 'infirmity' is another of the play's reminders of the reality of the common human nature which Coriolanus spurns. Here, as elsewhere in the play, the 'more than human' state to which Coriolanus aspires is implicitly identified as something which paradoxically also marks Coriolanus as 'less than human'.[13] So impervious is he to ordinary human needs, failings and affections that he seems almost inhuman, like 'an engine', as Menenius describes him following his unsuccessful attempt to persuade Coriolanus to spare Rome (V, iv, 19). Although anger is an ordinary enough human emotion, its single-minded pursuit seems mechanistic and as though Coriolanus has lost touch with other emotions, expressing dependence, which would humanise him. As Katharine Eisaman Maus suggests, anger is an emotion that marks off boundaries between self and other:

> Contempt and anger, like aggression, reinforce and clarify the boundaries of the self, marking it vividly off from those whom one hates, despises, or conquers. Coriolanus does not merely happen to be inflexible and narrow-minded; too much tolerance, too much sensitivity, would endanger him to the core.[14]

Anger also marks Coriolanus off not just in a general way from other human beings, but in terms of class. Writing of the impact of humours theory on the work of Francis Bacon, Gail Kern Paster in *Humoring the Body* (2004) suggests that Bacon invokes a broad cultural narrative in which 'high . . . value is assigned to aristocratic spiritedness, courage, and impulsivity'. She cites Hotspur in *I Henry IV* as an example of the 'vigorous strength, athleticism' and 'spontaneity' that were thought to be the 'behavioral products' of aristocratic 'hot-bloodedness' (see Chapter 4).[15] Anger, then, is the property of the aristocrat which in the case of Coriolanus says 'do not touch'.

Adelman offers a specifically psychoanalytic reading of Coriolanus's anger when she suggests that:

> His whole life becomes a kind of phallic exhibitionism, devoted to disproving the possibility that he is vulnerable. In the transformation from oral neediness to phallic aggression, anger becomes his meat . . . Fighting . . . is a poorly concealed substitute for feeding . . . and the unsatisfied ravenous attack of the infant upon the breast provides the motive force for warfare.[16]

We should take, as Freud does, 'oral neediness' not just in a physical sense but in sexual and emotional senses as well. The translation of needs of these various kinds into aggression and aristocratic aloofness reaches its apotheosis towards the end of the play, when in exile Coriolanus disowns 'Wife, mother, child' (V, ii, 82) and proclaims, in the quotation already referred to, that he will 'stand / As if a man were author of himself / And knew no other kin'. This is the kind of (unbridled) humanism, glorifying the sovereignty and autonomy of the self, which as I argued in the Introduction has often been taken to represent humanism in its entirety. In the context of *Coriolanus*, where sovereignty amounts to a repudiation of all human ties and affections, it is a humanism lacking in any ordinary sense of humanity. From the perspective of a normative psychoanalysis, the imbalance in Coriolanus, caused by the urge to disconnect overwhelming the urge to connect, is unhealthy and constitutes a denial of primary human experience.[17]

There is, however, as ever with Shakespeare, another story to tell, for the play keeps reminding us of Coriolanus's ordinary humanity even as he repudiates it. The hero is, after all, of this world. He has a mother and he had a childhood, and both of these ordinary facts, which are given some prominence in the play, domesticate Coriolanus and bring him down to earth. A tale of autonomous, superhuman heroism is thus converted little by little into an ordinary, human family saga. Early on in the play, one of the citizens makes a reference to the common perception amongst 'soft-conscienced men' that Coriolanus's heroism is at least partly driven by his desire to 'please his mother' (I, i, 35–7). The maternal influence upon Coriolanus is corroborated a few scenes later in Volumnia's account of how she brought up her son:

> When yet he was but tender-bodied and the only son of my womb, when youth with comeliness plucked all gaze his way, when for a day of kings' entreaties a mother should not sell him an hour from her beholding, I, considering how honour would become such a person – that it was no better than, picture-like, to hang by th' wall if renown made it not stir – was pleased to let him seek danger where he was like to find fame. To a cruel war I sent him, from whence he returned his brows bound with oak. I tell thee, daughter, I sprang not more in joy at first hearing he was a man-child than now in first seeing he had proved himself a man. (I, iii, 5–17)

Coriolanus is a Freudian everyman. As a child he was physically and emotionally dependent, as we all are, on another human being or other human beings. This ordinary dependency was, however, cut short by a mother keen to make him a man. What it means to be a man, though, is paradoxical, because it combines heroic self-sufficiency with the need to win fame and so be recognised. Manly heroism thus replays the family saga which preceded it, in that it affirms the ordinary human need for affection and recognition at the same time as it denies this need. This psychology works for Volumnia as well. Undervalued and under-recognised as a woman in a male-dominated world, she gains recognition not only by living vicariously through her son, but by making herself known in her own right as the mother who produced and moulded Coriolanus.

Behind the 'more than human' story of autonomous heroism, then, are 'only human' stories about ordinary needs which have been thwarted. For all his talk of self-sufficiency, Coriolanus cannot disengage himself from such stories. This is partly because Volumnia is a forceful character who does not embody the stereotypically female attributes of silence and passivity to which Valeria, Coriolanus's wife, conforms, and partly because Coriolanus is still in many ways a boy seeking his mother's approval. He cannot expunge his mother. He cannot separate himself from what his mother represents, which is the human desire for affection and recognition. His vaunted invulnerability might turn him into a machine but the depth psychology of the play – its existential thickness – encourages us to see this as a defensive mask. Because the mask is an obvious sign of denial, there is actually more traffic between Coriolanus's public and private selves than is sometimes the case with the other characters, whose public roles seem more instrumentalised. In an effort to persuade Coriolanus to bend a little to the will of the people, some members of the Roman aristocracy, including his mother, Volumnia, attempt to steer politics in an instrumental direction by equating politics with policy. Policy is anathema to Coriolanus because he sees it as a betrayal of the person he thinks his mother wants him to be. 'Why did you wish me milder?' he asks Volumnia in the public forum of the Capitol. He continues: 'Would you have me / False to my nature? / Rather say I play the man I am' (III, ii, 13–15).

Policy is also anathema to Coriolanus because it requires a cooler, more rationalised approach to politics than the affectively charged version of it that he practices. Where others are thinking tactically and expediently about how to pacify an inflamed populace, Coriolanus brings (albeit displaced) affairs of the heart to bear upon affairs of state. Volumnia tries to justify the use of policy to her son by speaking in terms that she hopes he will understand about the compatibility between the cool, rationalised exercise of policy and the affectively charged (because maternally inspired) demands of honour. Drawing an analogy between the legitimate use of policy in battle and the use of policy in peacetime, she says to her son: 'I have heard you say / Honour and policy, like unsevered friends, / I'th' war do grow together (III, ii, 42–4). 'Grant that', she continues, 'and tell me / In peace what each of them by th' other lose / That they combine not there' (III, ii, 44–6). She is appealing here to the war hero, but also to the child who in chasing honour has been chasing her affection. That she is obliged to frame her appeal in these terms speaks to Coriolanus's inability to separate off policy from passion.

For Coriolanus, then, including the Coriolanus addressed in Volumnia's justification of policy, neither policy nor autonomous heroism can free themselves from ordinary human needs. Where policy brackets off issues of need and neediness as irrelevant to affairs of state, and autonomous heroism is in (obvious) denial of them, the play itself endorses ordinariness. One of its most compelling and moving moments is the quasi-Aristotelian 'recognition scene' in which Coriolanus, following his mother's example, affirms affection and tenderness. Yielding to his mother's passionate entreaty to spare the people of Rome, Coriolanus's vengeful wrath subsides to reveal what was there all along: 'compassion' (V, iii, 197). In the familial terms in which the play encourages us to think, it is as if the mother has finally allowed the son to express the tenderness that she previously suppressed in him. And the broader human story which these family matters describe is one about human affections and needs being thwarted but finally acknowledged in a scene whose extraordinariness, in terms of its emotional intensity, constitutes a strong affirmation of ordinary life. Stephen Greenblatt in *Will in the World* (2005) writes that 'Shakespeare loved to reveal the presence of ordinariness in the midst of the extraordinary', but the opposite is also true, that he sometimes finds something extraordinary in the ordinary, if only because the ordinary is so often forgotten by characters that its recovery seems momentous.[18] In the case of Coriolanus, the way back to a sense of human vulnerability involves recognising the mask of invulnerability precisely as a mask.

Coriolanus also has to unlearn some of his ideas about the nature of emotion. Coriolanus the military hero seems for most of the play to have a fairly straightforward understanding of emotion, based on a version of humours theory. Coriolanus's (aristocratic) blood is hot and it is this 'heat' (III, i, 67) or 'choler' (III, i, 88), as other characters in the play themselves refer to it, which generates his martial strength and vigour. On this model of humoral theory, 'character is destiny' and emotions are the result of people's humoral constitution. When Brutus is plotting the overthrow of Coriolanus, he relies on this understanding of Coriolanus's character:

> Put him to choler straight. He hath been used
> Ever to conquer and to have his worth
> Of contradiction. Being once chafed, he cannot
> Be reined in again to temperance. Then he speaks
> What's in his heart, and that is there which looks
> With us to break his neck.
>
> (III, iii, 25–30)

Coriolanus's own self-conception makes it easy for Brutus to predict the future, for Coriolanus insists on always being himself, telling those he leaves behind in Rome that they will never 'hear . . . of me aught / But what is like me formerly' (IV, i, 53–4). Coriolanus's insistence upon fixed disposition is a reduced, individualistic version of humours theory which ignores the way that humours also formed an inter-subjective 'ecology', to recall Paster's term from Chapter 5.[19] From an ecological perspective, emotions are contagious. They happen between people as well as between human and natural worlds.

For an updated, psychoanalytic perspective on the notion that emotions are intrinsically interactive, we can again turn to object-relations theory, as employed by Martha Nussbaum in *Upheavals of Thought: The Intelligence of the Emotions* (2001). Nussbaum characterises feelings in general 'as complex object relations'.[20] By this she means that they are intimately linked to 'our urgent need for and attachment to things outside ourselves that we do not control'.[21] Broadly understood, in object-relations psychoanalytic theory the need we have of 'things outside ourselves' is born once again of our early infantile dependence on another or others for survival. We learn independence – because the carer is not always there for us and is therefore someone whom 'we do not control'– but the need for, and attachment to, others remain.[22] Emotions express this need. Despite Coriolanus's short-lived determination to stand as though 'a man were author of himself / And knew no other kin', his emotions, including his anger, show otherwise, because emotions are not only internal states, but directed outwards to other people and/or objects. Anger from this perspective is a controlling emotion born of the frustration that the world does not immediately or completely meet our needs. As Nussbaum puts it:

> the process of development entails many moments of discomfort and frustration. Indeed, some frustration of the infant's wants by the caretaker's separate comings and goings is essential to development – for if everything were always simply given in advance of discomfort, the child would never try out its own projects of control.
>
> On the other hand, the infant can hardly be in a position to comprehend this grand design. Its posture is one of infantile omnipotence, in which the entire world revolves around its wants. Any failure on the part of the caretaker to fulfil those wants will lead to reactive anger.[23]

Coriolanus may think that choler and hot-bloodedness are 'inside' him as part of his special aristocratic disposition, but the more 'ordinary' human reality is that Coriolanus has temper tantrums. These temper tantrums are directed at the failure of others and the world in general to meet his demands. The recognition scene can from this perspective be seen as an acknowledgement of his need of others, as well as a recognition of others' needs. Tenderness and affection make this need explicit, while anger masks it because it seems to be asserting the opposite of need. To recall Maus: 'Contempt and anger, like aggression, reinforce and clarify the boundaries of the self, marking it vividly off from those whom one hates, despises, or conquers.' Anger appears to assert the independence of self from others, but the reality is that, as with emotions in general, it expresses interdependence. Emotions tell Coriolanus things which are not just about him, but about how he is with others.

Coriolanus can mostly think about human nature only in terms of what is in him, rather than in terms of what is shared. Any deviation from this individualised notion of nature constitutes a dilution of the aristocratic essentialism that he lives by. His rigid views, however, do not go unchallenged and a degree of complexity is introduced about who or what is responsible for which of his characteristics. Volumnia initiates this kind of complexity when she is trying to persuade Coriolanus to placate the people:

> I prithee now, sweet son, as thou hast said
> My praises made thee first a soldier, so,
> To have my praise for this, perform a part
> Thou hast not done before.
>
> (III, ii, 107–10)

We learn from Volumnia that the aggression required of a soldier was learned rather than innate and that it was the desire for his mother's praise which was the prior driving force behind his character. She goes on to add further twists to the conundrum of where Coriolanus derived his character:

> Do as thou list.
> Thy valiantness was mine, thou sucked'st it from me,
> But owe thy pride thyself.
>
> (III, ii, 128–30)

'Sucked'st' suggests humours passing from one body to another and to some extent undermines Volumnia's emphasis elsewhere on nurture rather than nature as the basis of character, though the idea that her praise for Coriolanus made him a soldier could be seen as an encouragement of what was already there 'in' Coriolanus. She introduces a further question about origins when she tells him that his pride is not a biological inheritance from her to him but exclusively his. So is Coriolanus Coriolanus as a result of nurture, the nature he inherited from his mother, the nature that alone is 'his', or an untidy combination of these?

Coriolanus's reaction at this stage of the play to these questions and complications is basically to ignore them and cling to the idea of possessing an irreducible, aristocratic disposition:

> Well, I must do't.
> Away, my disposition; and possess me
> Some harlot's spirit! . . .
> . . . The smiles of knaves
> Tent in my cheeks, and schoolboys' tears take up
> The glasses of my sight! A beggar's tongue
> Make motion through my lips, and my armed knees,
> Who bowed but in my stirrup, bend like his
> That hath received an alms! I will not do't,
> Lest I surcease to honour mine own truth,
> And by my body's action teach my mind
> A most inherent baseness.
>
> (III, ii, 110–23)

Here, as elsewhere in Coriolanus's angry diatribes, the concept of innate disposition supports class difference and a sense of aristocratic superiority. Bending to the will of another is a sign of whorish, knavish or beggarly conduct which he, as aristocrat, cannot countenance because his superior disposition gives him the right to mould rather than be moulded. In other of Shakespeare's plays, such as *Othello*, it becomes clear that aristocrats do not have a monopoly on autonomy and that autonomy is an achievable condition rather than the outcome of a fixed humoral disposition. In a sense this supports Volumnia's position (or one of them) that self-sufficient men are made rather than born. Coriolanus fights against such perspectives, because they threaten the only kind of essentialism he understands, which is a class-based essentialism, an essentialism which carves out a special, extraordinary place for him within a naturalised hierarchy.

However, the choice in the play is not just the limited choice set out by Coriolanus in the above speech between an essentialism conceived of in aristocratic, hierarchical terms as special disposition and an anti-essentialism understood, again from Coriolanus's aristocratic perspective, as the betrayal of aristocratic identity. The choice or debate which emerges is instead a choice between two different kinds of essentialism: between Coriolanus's divisive, hierarchical concept of natural difference and a more levelling, democratising notion of a shared human nature. As I have already argued, contrasting attitudes towards the emotions are central to these different essentialisms: for Coriolanus, emotions are 'inside' the individual and the product of a special humoral constitution, whereas in the more democratic concept of human nature, emotions happen 'between' people and express need.

It is tempting to argue as a consequence of the idea that emotions take place 'between' people that emotions only reinforce the fact that we are social beings. Isobel Armstrong in *The Radical Aesthetic* (2000), paraphrasing the insights of the Russian thinker Lev Semenovich Vygotsky, writes: 'Emotion is always social'.[24] Such a perspective might in turn be used to support a social constructionist insistence upon the ways that societies produce different kinds of emotional transaction between people. While this is undoubtedly true, this and the previous chapter have explored what kinds of existential statement feelings such as fear and vulnerability make beyond and above the statement that we are social beings. The normative psychology which I have been invoking via selective use of psychoanalytic theory pushes us towards the conclusion that human beings are not only social beings whose 'emotion scripts' – as discussed by Gail Kern Paster, Katherine Rowe and Mary Floyd-Wilson in *Reading the Early Modern Passions* (2004) – are shaped by society, but emotional beings whose affective needs can be more or less met by their societies.[25] Using *Coriolanus* for the emotional wisdom that it imparts, we might say that too much fostering of autonomy and detachment can lead to feelings of disconnection, while too much dependence can generate feelings of helplessness. These are normative statements which have implications for how we might live and which enable us to make judgements about the nature of Coriolanus's socialisation into a rigid and emotionally damaging form of heroic self-assertion.

Chapter 7

Humility: *Love's Labour's Lost*

I suggested in the previous chapter that *Coriolanus* is a levelling play, a play that brings Coriolanus down to earth and forces him to recognise his 'only human' needs and vulnerabilities. This chapter will take up the theme of levelling and direct it towards the matter of living humbly, with a healthy sense of one's own folly. As the chapter proceeds, it will draw connections between humility, folly and the conditions for being taken seriously as a lover. This will prepare the way for Chapter 8, which will examine the intimate connection in *As You Like It* between living well and loving well.

The natural home for the 'only human' is comedy, for comedy routinely substitutes elevated human realities for ordinary or base ones.[1] A classic comic moment, from this point of view, is the Eastcheap tavern scene in *I Henry IV* in which Falstaff and Hal engage in role-play and improvise by using the objects around them:

> *Prince Harry*: Do thou stand for my father, and examine me upon the particulars of my life.
> *Sir John*: Shall I? Content. This chair shall be my state, this dagger my sceptre, and this cushion my crown.
> *He sits*
> *Prince Harry*: Thy state is taken for a joint-stool, thy golden sceptre for a leaden dagger, and thy precious rich crown for a pitiful bald crown.
> (II, v, 379–85)

The irreverent use of a cushion to represent a crown has the effect of deconsecrating kingship and of implying that monarchs are ordinary human beings rather than 'more than human' individuals. According to the levelling principles of comedy, the elevated status of the monarch is neither God-given nor the result of natural aristocratic superiority, but a theatrical performance which depends on an audience's acceptance of an illusion. Comedy of this sort is almost synonymous with carnival. In *Carnival and Theater* (1985), Michael Bristol writes that 'in Carnival a crown *is* just a funny hat, and a funny hat, or some even more inappropriate object, is a crown'.[2] Carnival, for Bristol, involves 'a comprehensive rethinking of the social world in terms of common, everyday material and physical experience'; it 'brings all knowledge of social reality down to earth and places the body, its needs and its capabilities, at the center of the social process'.[3]

Bristol concentrates more on the social implications of carnival than on the nature of the common humanity that it putatively expresses. However, the irreverence which is at the heart not just of carnival, but of many different kinds of comedy, gives rise to the belittling, humbling perspective that human existence is cause for laughter, mirth and ridicule. As Simon Critchley argues in *On Humour* (2002): 'humour recalls us to the modesty and limitedness of the human condition, a limitedness that calls not for tragic-heroic affirmation but comic *acknowledgement*, not Promethean authenticity but a laughable inauthenticity'.[4] The irreverence of comedy means that the 'ordinary' is not sanctified in the way that it often is in tragedy. The natural *gravitas* of tragedy confers upon virtually everything it touches a certain reverence, such that the eventual recognition by Coriolanus of ordinary human emotions can be described in quasi-religious language as a kind of redemptive moment. Shakespearean comedy, as I shall later argue in more detail, *does* also dignify and solemnise the human, but the starting point of comedy – in irreverence rather than reverence – means that humanity's indignities and foibles are a major object of attention. Comedy neither swerves away from this errant humanity to a higher being thought of as being able to save us from ourselves, nor does it borrow from the language of religion in order to consecrate the human or at the very least to take it seriously. Shakespearean comedy does not banish seriousness and elevation, but these are hard-won and pitted against the comic injunction *not* to take ourselves too seriously.

Comedy, of course, comes in various shapes and sizes, and not all of them have the effect of belittling human beings en masse and as a species. Comedy is often social comedy, the purpose of which is not necessarily to hold up a mirror to (human) nature but to 'the times'. The follies targeted in *Love's Labour's Lost* (1594–5) are from this perspective the socially specific ones of rhetorical excess, and its corollaries, verbal vacuity and an obsession with fashion. The 'illustrious wight' Armado is the first but not the last figure in the play to be ridiculed for these characteristics.[5] He is, according to the King:

> A man in all the world's new fashion planted,
> That hath a mint of phrases in his brain.
> One who the music of his own vain tongue

> Doth ravish the enchanting harmony;
> A man of complements, whom right and wrong
> Have chose as umpire of their mutiny.
> (I, i, 162–7)

The follies represented by Armado, of course, turn out to be general rather than particular, for the courtiers of Navarre are themselves guilty of privileging style over substance, manner over matter, eloquence over wisdom. On one, important, level, 'comedy' in *Love's Labour's Lost* is therefore social comedy, its target being Renaissance rhetoric and the exhilarating possibilities as well as dangers inherent in the encouragement of rhetorical fluency. The 'sweet smoke of rhetoric' (III, i, 61) is the object of the play's socially specific satire, in which the likes of Armado, Holofernes the schoolmaster and the courtiers of Navarre are all implicated. I noted in the Introduction that rhetoric in the Renaissance could become its own end, rather than a means to the end of wisdom; the characters in *Love's Labour's Lost* – comic versions of the likes of Iago and Richard III – show the direction in which the rhetorical culture of the sixteenth and seventeenth centuries could go. Lynne Magnusson further highlights the social specificity of the play by linking its concern with eloquence to the gradual acceptance in the latter part of the sixteenth century of the English language as a viable medium for learning:

> When Shakespeare made eloquence his chief object of attention in *Love's Labour's Lost*, he was not merely indulging a seemingly unstoppable showmanship in words that was fostered by his interest in rhetoric. He was also at once celebrating and critiquing – even if he did set this play of eloquence in France – what contemporaries saw as the triumphant coming of age of English. Indeed, in making his vernacular play an exhibit in rhetoric, showing that English could do as much with words as Latin, he was helping to make it happen.[6]

Important as the social dimension of comedy in *Love's Labour's Lost* is, it is not the only level, as the objects of ridicule broaden to such an extent that virtually nothing or no one is exempt from it. Thus ridicule is itself ridiculed, and the mockers who think they are immune from the ridiculous are in turn mocked. The scene which demonstrates this general folly and therefore pushes the comedy towards existential statement is the one in which one courtier after another achieves comic ascendancy only for his position of superiority to be immediately overturned. Having collectively foresworn love, each courtier (predictably) falls in love and is (equally predictably) found out. The (unpredictable) method of finding out nicely ridicules the ridiculer and turns the one-upmanship of 'ego humour' into a shared recognition of folly. First the King comes onstage to read his love sonnet alone – or so he thinks – and then stands aside to overhear Longueville do exactly the same. This pattern is repeated and so, too, is the subsequent exposure of one courtier by another. Longueville steps forward to tell Dumaine that 'I should blush, I know, / To be o'erheard and taken napping so' (IV, iii, 127–8), only for the King to use Longueville's own words to shame Longueville himself: 'Come sir, you blush. As his, your case is such. / You chide at him, offending twice as much' (IV, iii, 129–30).

The figure who has overseen and overheard everything without yet being exposed is Biron, whose scorn is significantly more vitriolic than the previous two exposers of folly. Where Longueville and the King talk about being shamed in terms of blushing, Biron talks about whipping and hypocrisy: 'Now step I forth to whip hypocrisy' (IV, iii, 149). In another dramatic life, Biron might have been Coriolanus, but in *Love's Labour's Lost*, where wit and words rather than weapons are a sign of the aristocrat's 'more than human' status, words are used, here at least, as weapons. Humour, here, is ego humour, humour designed to bolster the self at the expense of another. Biron's aggressive Juvenalian satire also makes a proverbial mountain out of a molehill. It makes a catastrophe of folly. By contrast, the thought that the appropriate response to being found out is 'merely' to blush normalises folly. Folly is cause for 'only human' comic embarrassment rather than tragedy. Biron, as the King points out, has struck the wrong tone; his 'jest' is too 'bitter' (IV, iii, 172).

Blushing also feminises the courtiers, because blushing has conventionally been associated with femininity.[7] The levelling principle of comedy applies to gender identities, and perhaps especially to gender identities, because, as I shall argue in Chapter 8, gender hierarchies are overturned by virtue of women being designated as *custodians* of the human. Women are in other words placed in important roles above men as salvagers of threatened human values. It seems that men, for example, cannot be entrusted with such a precious human commodity as love. The same could be said of folly and the recognition of folly. The courtiers need to recognise that folly is normal, that they are foolish to think that they are immune from it, and that folly is not cause for the kind of moral panic that the scourge Biron thinks it is. Biron's moment of triumph is in any case short-lived as his love is in turn exposed and he is himself levelled by folly: 'I confess, I confess . . . That you three fools lacked me fool to make up the mess' (IV, iii, 203–5). Folly is fast becoming the existential norm rather than exception, such that, as C. L. Barber puts it in *Shakespeare's Festive Comedy* (1959): 'in the classic manner of Erasmus in his *Praise of Folly*, it becomes folly not to be a fool'.[8]

But what kind of fool? As both Erasmus's *Praise of Folly* (1509) and Shakespeare's plays demonstrate, there are fools and fools, wise and otherwise.[9] Following the lead of the aphorism quoted by Touchstone in *As You Like It* that 'The fool doth think he is wise, but the wise man knows himself to be a fool',[10] we could say the wise fool knows that humans are prone to folly, is able to laugh at him- or herself, recognises his or her own limits (and the limits of human beings in general) and is aware that claims to authenticity, longevity or knowledge can be, at best, premature, and at worst, permanently unrealistic. The wise fool is another variation on the disengaged scepticism discussed in Chapters 1 and 2, but with the difference that where Hamlet questions human nature and Iago disbelieves in it, the wise fool knows and accepts what it is, namely that human beings are inherently flawed. The answer of the wise fool to the question of 'how to live' is therefore to live humbly. To quote Critchley again: 'humour recalls us to the modesty and limitedness of the human condition, a limitedness that calls not for tragic-heroic affirmation but comic *acknowledgement*'. Wise folly makes a 'serious' existential statement about the need for humility and modesty even as it warns against taking oneself too seriously. Not taking oneself too seriously is in other words the basis of a serious 'life' message.

In contrast to the figure of the wise fool, is the foolish fool, such as Armado in *Love's Labour's Lost*, who is everything that the wise fool is not. That is, he does not recognise his own folly and lives in the delusional world that he is in fact wise. Not only this, but he does not recognise his own limits and limitations. The pedant Holofernes is another example of a foolish fool. In calling himself 'foolish', Holofernes displays a mock humility which disguises (but only barely disguises) his inflated sense of his own linguistic and imaginative capabilities:

> This is a gift that I have, simple, simple – a foolish extravagant spirit, full of forms, figures, shapes, objects, ideas, apprehensions, motions, revolutions. These are begot in the ventricle of memory, nourished in the womb of *pia mater*, and delivered upon the mellowing of occasion. But the gift is good in those in whom it is acute, and I am thankful for it. (IV, ii, 66–72)

To the figures of the wise fool and the foolish fool, we can add another category of folly relevant to Shakespeare in general and *Love's Labour's Lost* in particular, which is the sophisticated fool. Sophisticated fools are wise to the extent that they acknowledge their own folly, but they do so in a smugly self-congratulatory way through their promotion of a sense of knowing irony. The courtiers in some ways exemplify this sophisticated form of folly. For example, Biron's sudden turnaround from scourge to self-acknowledged fool suggests that the 'scourge' role was only skin-deep, that he was, perhaps consciously, playing a part (like the protean Iago) rather than seriously affirming a self. Having foresworn their devotion to celibate study, the courtiers then make Biron their spokesperson for their next 'project', which is love. There is a certain amount of knowingness here as well, as the courtiers seem to be only 'performing' repentance for their broken vows and fickleness, and congratulating themselves instead on the verbal and psychological flexibility which enables them to swap roles (from scholars to lovers) and to justify that swap. 'Now prove / Our loving lawful', says the King 'and our faith not torn' (IV, iii, 282–3). Dumaine follows suit: 'Ay, marry there, some flattery for this evil' (IV, iii, 284), and Longueville in similar vein pleads for 'some authority how to proceed, / Some tricks, some quillets how to cheat the devil' (IV, iii, 285–6). The courtiers are registering the fact that they are trying to legitimise their own folly and give themselves respectable-looking reasons for switching from one sworn identity to another. But the *ability* to refashion themselves and carry it off seems more important to them than the ethical issue, which seems therefore only to be a mock-ethical issue. Verbal ingenuity is more important than real or perceived vice. And verbal ingenuity is more important, at the moment, than the opportunity for self-discovery provided by 'wise folly'. Sophisticated fools are addicted to their own sophistication. They do not want to be 'weighed down' by an existentially charged form of folly.

The courtiers, however, are a mixture of wise, foolish and sophisticated folly. Their sophistication, in registering their folly but then using it to emphasise their dexterity, recalls the 'foolish folly' of Holofernes and his belief in his own limitless capabilities. The courtiers express faith in Biron's way with words and their ability to transform an unpromising situation into a promising one. Biron does not disappoint. He manages to turn the situation around and ingeniously 'prove' that to keep their original oaths would be sacrilegious:

> Then fools you were these women to foreswear,
> Or keeping what is sworn, you will prove fools.
> For wisdom's sake – a word that all men love –
> Or for love's sake – a word that loves all men –
> Or for men's sake – the authors of these women –
> Or women's sake – by whom we men are men –
> Let us once lose our oaths to find ourselves,
> Or else we lose ourselves to keep our oaths.
> It is religion to be thus foresworn,
> For charity itself fulfils the law,
> And who can sever love from charity?
> (IV, iii, 331–41)

The verbal sophisticate is foolish, in the sense of immodest, for thinking that his verbal skills enable him to do and be anything, because according to the logic of the play, words are 'merely' words until they have been put to the test of experience. Biron's 'For charity itself fulfils the law, / And who can sever love from charity?' is a glib saw which we suspect is a purely intellectual rather than a tried and tested observation. Love, that is, is a word rather than a felt experience. It is a word that can be moved around highly skilfully by Biron, but it thereby lacks roots. The literary humanist principle of *embodiment*, discussed in the Introduction, is again pertinent here, for in *Love's Labour's Lost* one of the conditions for being taken seriously as a lover is that love should be something substantially more than a sophisticated textual game. If, as Eagleton suggests, the aesthetic is about the business 'of how the world strikes the body on its sensory surfaces, of that which takes root in the gaze and the guts', then these cloistered young men of the court, whose first ambition was to remove themselves from the world and from all sensory contact with women, are merely repeating their disdain for ordinary experiential reality in their highly textual, linguistic 'inscription' of love.[11] The wise fool in Biron might be able to recognise the immodest folly of this and not take himself or his specious logic too seriously, but the foolish fool, buoyed by his sophisticated verbal powers, only sees the world bending to his linguistic will.

It would be a mistake to be too po-faced about the verbal inflation in the play, for its linguistic excess – its 'great feast of languages' (V, i, 36–7) – is part of its festive, holiday mood. As I suggested earlier, however, comedy comes in different shapes and sizes, and part of the mix of Shakespearean comedy is to combine the 'light' with the 'heavy', release with a sense that comedy has something serious to say, even if its serious message is about the pitfalls of egocentric seriousness and the need to be able to laugh at ourselves. An irreverent sense of the ridiculousness of all human aspirations and endeavours is not, however, where Shakespearean comedy leaves us, because out of such inauthentic plans and claims as the courtiers' comes at least a degree of greater awareness and wisdom. So far, I have talked about comedy only really in terms of the dynamics of ridicule and folly, but comedy, as Barber, Northrop Frye and others have recognised, is also a plot structure and a ritualistic patterning of experience, leading from confusion to clarification, or from the destruction of selves via ridicule and mayhem to the tentative renewal of them.[12] To talk about Shakespearean comedy in terms of rites of passage, comings of age and collective journeys of self-discovery therefore seems appropriate.

Biron's own use of the language of self-loss and self-renewal – 'Let us lose our oaths to find ourselves, / Or else we lose ourselves to keep our oaths' – itself nudges the play into becoming an existential quest-narrative, whereby an inauthentic self is shed in favour of a more authentic one. For all Biron's verbal showmanship, which in carnivalesque style releases language from the necessity of 'meaning', another comedic register makes its presence felt in this semi-serious quest for renewal and rebirth. At the heart of this quest are love and the question, revisited again and again by Shakespeare, of whether love is the gateway to authenticity or further proof of human folly. Biron's grandiose elevation of love can be simultaneously read as a mock-elevation and a serious one, a speech that on the one hand disproves his eligibility for love and on the other treats the courtiers' new vocation, as lovers, as the 'real thing' (in contrast with their previous vocation as celibate scholars):

> [Love] adds a precious seeing to the eye –
> A lover's eyes will gaze an eagle blind.
> A lover's ear will hear the lowest sound
> When the suspicious head of theft is stopped.
> Love's feeling is more soft and sensible
> Than are the tender horns of cockled snails.
> . . .
> And when love speaks, the voice of all the gods
> Make heaven drowsy with the harmony.
> Never durst poet touch a pen to write
> Until his ink were tempered with love's sighs.
> O, then his lines would ravish savage ears,
> And plant in tyrants mild humility.
> From women's eyes this doctrine I derive.
> They sparkle still the right Promethean fire.
> They are the books, the arts, the academes
> That show, contain, and nourish all the world,
> Else none at all in aught proves excellent.
> (IV, iii, 309–30)

If we take this seriously, as opposed to a playful display (only) of rhetorical ability, then one aspect of its seriousness is its attempt to give a counter-perspective to the notion that is ubiquitous in Shakespeare's comedies that love is folly: love is foolish and proves the 'only human' ridiculousness of human beings for a variety of reasons, which will be examined in detail in Chapter 8. Suffice it to say for the moment that Biron at the beginning of this scene has already declared 'his love' to be 'mad' (IV, iii, 6) and continues in the same vein from his hidden position as onlooker to identify 'falling in love' precisely as a 'fall' into folly, intoxication or idolatry: 'Now in thy likeness one more fool appear!' (IV, iii, 43); 'One drunkard loves another of the name' (IV, iii, 47); 'This is the liver vein, which makes flesh a deity, / A green goose a goddess, pure, pure idolatry. / God amend us, God amend: we are much out o'th' way' (IV, iii, 71–3). Biron's last aside gives one reason why love is foolish, which is that it worships the false god of human sexuality. The courtly, Neoplatonic counter-perspective subsequently presented by Biron as justification for their sudden turnaround is that love heightens perception (it 'adds a precious seeing to the eye'), sensitises ('Love's feeling is . . . soft and sensitive'), civilises (it ravishes 'savage ears'), humbles (it plants 'in tyrants mild humility') and brings 'harmony'. These serious counter-claims for love are partly ironised (because Biron as verbal trickster may not 'mean' them), but if they are also partly meant, then in the mouth of Biron (or perhaps any mouth) they are themselves 'foolish' because their claims to authenticity are premature, untested and idealistic. They are once again the product of intellect rather than experience and too diametrically opposed to the alternative perspective – of love as folly – which Biron himself has only just been advancing. For love to be taken seriously, its foolish aspects will have to be 'seriously' reckoned with rather than foolishly 'forgotten'.

Nevertheless, Biron's partially serious attempt to take love seriously mirrors Shakespeare's own intense preoccupation with love, not only in the romantic comedies, but across his work. Given that love is the object of sceptical disenchantment, 'light' and 'heavy' ridicule, a sign of inauthenticity not least because it masquerades as authentic, the question of how and when one can take love seriously without appearing foolish is an intriguing one that I would argue intrigued Shakespeare himself. It is a question which is built into the title of the play (the labour of love might always be lost labour because love is folly) and into its ending. As is common in Shakespeare's comedies, the question has a gendered dimension, for the women refuse to take seriously the men's professions of love. Injecting another sombre note into the comedy, the Princess, now Queen because of the recently arrived news of the death of her father, has this blunt message for the men:

> We have received your letters full of love,
> Your favours the ambassadors of love,
> And in our maiden council rated them
> At courtship, pleasant jest, and courtesy,
> As bombast and as lining to the time.
> But more devout than this in our respects
> Have we not been, and therefore met your loves
> In their own fashion, like a merriment.
> (V, ii, 769–76)

From the perspective of a Lent/carnival dynamic, it is tempting to see this and the other sombre notes struck at the end of the play in terms of the return of a Lenten seriousness to a play whose carnivalesque spirit has been embodied in the courtiers' linguistic misrule and excess. This, however, is to ignore the specifically female appropriation of a carnivalesque voice by the Queen, for the invocation of a 'maiden council' inverts gender hierarchies and places women in judgement of men. Here and elsewhere in Shakespeare's plays (Rosalind in *As You Like It*, Paulina in *The Winter's Tale*, Cordelia as the albeit initially ignored spokeswoman for love in *King Lear*), women are empowered in relation to love and men disempowered. Women are educators, sages and judges, and men, novices. While this might be read as reinforcing gender stereotypes by 'relegating' women to a private rather than public sphere of influence, such is the importance of love to worlds that are often presented in Shakespeare's plays as heartless, that to be an arbiter of love is to be significantly empowered. Moreover, love is not just a private matter between two people, for as Biron suggests in his encomium or mock-encomium, love's ability to ravish 'savage ears' and plant 'in tyrants mild humility' attributes to love a significance which reaches far beyond the private sphere.[13] As we have seen in the case of *Hamlet, The Merchant of Venice* and *Othello*, affect and affection are in danger of being permanently exiled from the public domains represented in these plays, but in comedy that danger, while present, is eventually averted.

The carnivalesque, or a version of it, is also evident in the prolongation by the women of the love plot. Insofar as carnival in Shakespeare's romantic comedies revolves around love and the topsy-turvy complications of love, it makes of love a primary rather than secondary discourse. Where love is initially downgraded by the courtiers in favour of scholarship, this hierarchy of priorities is subsequently inverted. When it is inverted, 'love' comes increasingly into its own as a multifaceted phenomenon which is both worthy and demanding of a complex kind of attention. Rather than closing down the space which carnival opens up for dialogue about the authenticity or inauthenticity of love, the ending of the play keeps the dialogue going. As Biron puts it, 'Our wooing doth not end like an old play. / Jack hath not Jill. These ladies' courtesy / Might well have made our sport a comedy' (V, ii, 860–3). The men may have had their sport and now want the closure of a conventional comedy, but the women are now negotiating their own version of carnival, by refusing to settle the *question* of love in favour of the men's professions of serious intention. To Dumaine's claim that 'Our letters . . . showed much more than jest' and Longueville's supporting 'So did our looks', Rosaline simply replies: 'We did not quote them so' (V, ii, 777–8).

Of course, those arguably carnivalesque aspects of the play's ending, which involve the inversion of gender hierarchies and the refusal to accept male professions of seriousness on their own terms, are also accompanied by a Lenten seriousness on the part of the women. A key aspect of this is their setting of a love test to prove the men's constancy. Suspicious of the courtiers' propensity to make and break oaths – 'swear not, lest ye be forsworn again' (V, ii, 818) – and suspicious, too, of offers made 'in heat of blood' (V, ii, 792), the women put love's Lenten seriousness to the test by requiring the men to stay faithful to their promises for one year. The severest test, however, is reserved for the wittiest of the courtiers, Biron. The task Rosaline sets him, to 'visit the speechless sick', 'converse / with groaning wretches' and 'with all the fierce endeavour of your wit / To enforce the painèd impotent to smile' (V, ii, 837–40), is one that makes a mockery of the courtiers' glorious sense of limitlessness. For the accomplished wit, it has seemed that anything and everything can be done in language. As Rosaline remarks of Biron early on in the play: 'His eye begets occasion for his wit, / For every object that the one doth catch / The other turns to a mirth-moving jest' (II, i, 69–71). But the task that Rosaline sets Biron at the end of the play challenges the heady sense that 'words' can transform any 'matter' into an occasion for wit. Biron's response to his task is that it will be impossible to convert suffering into mirth:

> To move wild laughter in the throat of death? –
> It cannot be, it is impossible.
> Mirth cannot move a soul in agony.
> (V, ii, 841–3)

Any kind of mirth might be difficult under such circumstances, but the kind of wit practised by Biron seems particularly ineffectual and empty, for his wit has been more 'wounding' (V, ii, 830) than to help the wounded. The fate of Biron, which is to confront his own impotence, is the basis of a humiliation that goes deeper than any of the other, more superficial, humiliations which he and his fellow courtiers have so far experienced. Used to discountenancing others, Biron must himself be thoroughly discountenanced for any kind of renewal to take place.

An acknowledgement of human limitations which, in Biron's case, involves an acknowledgement of his inability to perform or transform any identity through language is thus one aspect of the love test. Paradoxically, however, another aspect of it is the test of Biron's ability to surpass himself and the limits of ego humour. The witty performance of a variety of linguistically constructed roles serves to flatter the ego. If he is to travel the romantic comic route from an 'inauthentic' to a 'more authentic' self which will make him in Rosaline's eyes a more acceptable lover, then he will have to learn attentiveness. Attention to the needs of the sick and dying will put a stop to his habit of using others as grist for the mill of his ego humour and force him to be responsive. Such, at least, is Rosaline's hope and the lesson which she expresses in one of the most memorable and often quoted *sententiae* in the play: 'A jest's prosperity lies in the ear / Of him that hears it, never in the tongue / Of him that makes it' (V, ii, 847–9). Rosaline's emphasis on reception rather than production instructs Biron that the tellers of jokes are dependent on their listeners, that listeners should be regarded as more than a pair of admiring ears and that this should be reflected in a more intimate knowledge of one's audience(s). Transferred to the domain of love, this means that Biron will need to learn the relatively simple, but so far unlearned, lesson that love is a two-way process.

One further aspect of the love test is endurance. The staying power of the silver-tongued Biron is also to be tested. Words come easily to Biron, but the actions they promise do not necessarily follow. 'Bombast' needs to be ballasted by long-term commitment (in comic terms, a year is long-term), and the bearable lightness of being enjoyed in the cloistered world of courtly wit weighed down by experience in the 'real' world of human suffering.

If it is wit rather than the weapons of a Coriolanus which elevates Biron above the common stream of humanity, then the levelling impetus of comedy makes it folly to consider oneself a cut above the rest. Comedy brings down the high and mighty to the level of the 'only human' and does not compensate by sanctifying or dignifying ordinary human emotions such as compassion. Love seems only to reinforce the folly of human beings. The existential message of comedy therefore seems to be to live humbly and with a healthy sense of one's own limitations. To recall Touchstone: 'The fool doth think he is wise, but the wise man knows himself to be a fool.' However, Shakespearean comedy has another existential dimension to it in the ritualistic narrative that it plots from destruction to renewal. In explicitly psychological terms, this involves shedding inauthentic for more authentic selves, but with the wise fool's understanding that claims to authenticity may make one look even more foolish. This raises the question of when, how and if one can ever talk seriously about love. This question is built into the ending of *Love's Labour's Lost*, where the women lay down conditions for being taking seriously a lover.

Chapter 8

Love: *As You Like It*

As I argued in the Introduction, humanism has frequently been represented by anti-humanists as a mainstream affair, the lynchpin of western or bourgeois ideology or ideology in general (and sometimes all three at once). This is true of the three probably most influential anti-humanist critics who in the 1980s – the heyday of anti-humanist theory and criticism – produced books on the emergence of humanism in the Renaissance: Catherine Belsey, Jonathan Dollimore and Francis Barker. I have already discussed features of Belsey's and Dollimore's version of humanism in the Introduction, but, given one of the purposes of this chapter, to wrest humanism away from the mainstream, it is worth briefly rehearsing the opposite, anti-humanist perception of humanism as a dominant ideology. In *The Subject of Tragedy* (1985), Belsey claims that: 'Liberal humanism, locating agency and meaning in the unified human subject, becomes an orthodoxy at the moment when the bourgeoisie is installed as the ruling class'.[1] Meanwhile, Dollimore in *Radical Tragedy* (1984) writes of the 'essentialist humanism which has pervaded English studies and carried within it a residual metaphysic, one which makes for the ideological effacement of socio-cultural difference and historical context'. The source of the 'residual metaphysic' present in English studies is 'western metaphysics' in general, with its 'three indissociable categories' of 'the universal (or absolute), essence, and teleology'.[2] Finally, in *The Tremulous Private Body* (1984), Francis Barker suggests that the influential modern equation of 'literary greatness' with 'universality', embodied in the '"broad humanism"' of Shakespeare's texts, masks 'historical difference' and the historically specific nature of bourgeois subjectivity.[3] Humanism in all of these accounts is identified as the massively influential weapon of bourgeois ideology. More than this, humanism is by definition implicated in all would-be dominant ideologies, by virtue of the fact that it is in the nature of ideology to pass off particular, historically specific, beliefs and values as universal truths about the human condition. There is no recognition, here, of humanism as a potential source of resistance to dominant ideologies and the dehumanising effects of ideologies. Moreover, because humanism is regarded as mainstream, it is represented by such canonical figures as Pepys, Shakespeare and Descartes (in Barker), Bacon, Descartes and Locke (in Belsey) and Descartes, Locke and Kant (in Dollimore).[4]

The question that needs asking here is: who gets to represent what kind of humanism? In the context of Shakespeare, if the definition of humanism follows Barker's, Belsey's and Dollimore's, and associates essentialism with a belief in the supreme autonomy of the individual (the 'unified human subject', as Belsey puts it), then it is likely to be represented by such spectacular individualists as Coriolanus or the Macbeths. As discussed in Chapters 5 and 6, there is a significant amount of internal dramatic questioning of such humanism, but this only makes Shakespeare an anti-humanist if we continue to think of humanism as a singular, uncontested phenomenon. Shakespeare's humanism, I have been insisting, is different from what I have been referring to as mainstream humanism. This different kind of humanism – literary humanism – has a greater variety of spokesmen and spokeswomen than the kind of humanism represented by, say, Coriolanus. This, I would argue, is because it mirrors Shakespeare's own (literary humanist) inclinations, which are always returning him via different characters to the question of how to live. Answers to this broad question come from different quarters within Shakespeare's plays. They are not the sole preserve of men, for example, or of upper class individuals. Men who move in high circles, like Polonius, may think they have the authority to tell others how to live, but Polonius is an object of ridicule. Literary humanist wisdom often comes from below rather than from above, in the shape of women or wise fools or denigrated individuals, such as Shylock in *The Merchant of Venice*, who speak back to the dominant culture about its inhumanity, its dehumanising instrumentalism or its deficient version(s) of humanism.

As You Like It (1599–1600) presents a variety of subaltern custodians of the human. The loyalty and love of the feudal retainer, Adam, for example, are nostalgically inscribed by Orlando as one kind of literary humanist lesson in how to live. In Adam, according to Orlando, 'appears / The constant service of the antique world'.[5] Adam keeps intact the affective ties between master and servant which are sundered by those 'who sweat but for promotion' (II, iii, 61). He is the embodiment of 'pure love' (II, vii, 131). Adam's loyalty to Orlando is reciprocated by Orlando in an iconic scene in which Orlando carries the exhausted Adam to the food and safety provided by the exiled Duke Senior and his entourage (II, vii). Duke Senior's hospitality, simply expressed in his 'Welcome. Set down your venerable burden / And let him feed' (II, vii, 167–8), is itself an example of the survival (in the forest of Arden) of human values in a world from which they have been (literally) banished. While in the context of the forest this lesson in exemplary living comes from above rather than from below, in the broader context depicted in the play of one ruling class representative (Duke Frederick) having ostracised another (Duke Senior), it is one which takes on some of the characteristics of a subaltern humanism, for, according to the simplified historical narrative of the play, the values of Duke Senior are on the wane.

This simplified historical narrative, in which the antique world is preferred to the new world on the basis that it treats human ties as sacrosanct, is complicated by the influential presence of other 'custodians' of the human, Celia and Rosalind. However, to see how they fit into the play's schemes of value, it is first necessary to say more about the conflict between the old and the new. One of the distinguishing traits of the new court, headed by Duke Frederick, is the expectation of a continuous production of the new. 'What's the new news at the new court?' (I, i, 92–3), asks Oliver of the wrestler Charles in expectation that the decisive innovation which resulted in the banishment of Duke Senior by his younger brother will be repeated in further innovations, such as shifts, for example, in who is in and out of favour at the new court. The new court, then, represents change, innovation and a certain dynamism, which from the perspective of the 'antique world' is a bad dynamism. I qualify the new court's dynamism as a 'certain dynamism', because the 'new news at the new court' is in fact always driven by the 'same old story', or at least a story that was becoming an increasingly visible one in Shakespeare's world, of acquisition:[6]

> There's no news at the court, sir, but the old news: that is, the old Duke is banished by his younger brother, the new Duke, and three or four loving lords have put themselves into voluntary exile with him, whose lands and revenues enrich the new Duke; therefore he gives them good leave to wander. (I, i, 94–9)

As in *Macbeth*, the desire for 'more' is in tension with the principle of 'enough'. In *As You Like It*, the dynamism of the new court, which is paradoxically fuelled by the same desire for 'more', stands in continual contrast with the values of the antique world where 'less is more'. Alongside Adam, who labours for love not money, the pastoral simplicity of the shepherd Corin, although he expresses anti-pastoral sentiments or at least sentiments that indicate a gap between pastoral ideals and reality (II, iv, 74–86), also represents the principle of 'enough':

> I am a true labourer. I earn that I eat, get that I wear; owe no man hate, envy no man's happiness; glad of other men's good, content with my harm; and the greatest of my pride is to see my ewes graze and my lambs suck. (III, ii, 71–5)

In the post-lapsarian world of the new court, change driven by acquisition leads to the treatment of people as assets, whereas in the prelapsarian world of Arden/Eden, enough *is* enough and other people are therefore not objects of envy, but love and respect.

The difference between the old and the new which underlies all the other differences, however, centres upon the issue of kinship. The revolution in the state which has taken place before the play begins is a decidedly family affair, a matter of brothers behaving badly. Not only has Duke Frederick banished his elder brother, Duke Senior, but Oliver has reneged on the will of his father, Rowland de Bois, which made provision for the education of the youngest son, Orlando. Oliver's disregard for the bonds of kinship is therefore twofold: he 'bars' Orlando from 'the place of a brother' (I, i, 18) and ignores the father's wishes.[7] As Orlando complains, 'My father charged you in his will to give me good education' (I, i, 62–3). Orlando, at the beginning of the play, is bereft and full of the injustice of his situation because he can think about identity only in terms of (biological) kinship. He constantly reiterates the sacrosanct nature of the father/son bond and refutes the idea that terms of kinship are transferable: 'I am', he says, 'more proud to be Sir Rowland's son, / His youngest son, and would not change that calling / To be adopted heir to Frederick' (I, ii, 221–3). Orlando probably has his brother Oliver in mind here, because Oliver is intent on currying favour at the new court of Duke Frederick, despite the fact that Frederick has declared Rowland de Bois to have been 'mine enemy' (I, ii, 215). Oliver's disowning, to Duke Frederick's face, of his brother – 'I never loved my brother in my life (III, i, 14) – is therefore compounded by his disloyalty to his father. Oliver's family allegiances are frangible, it seems, while Orlando's sense of his familial origins is that these origins are irreplaceable and continue to shape his sense of who he is: 'I am the youngest son of Sir Rowland de Bois' (I, i, 53–4); 'The spirit of my father grows strong in me' (I, i, 66).

So important and so sacrosanct to the 'antique world' are kinship ties that a person, such as Oliver, who breaks them becomes almost impossible to name. This is how Adam falteringly informs Orlando of his brother's latest plot against him:

> O, unhappy youth,
> Come not within these doors. Within this roof
> The enemy of all your graces lives,

> Your brother – no, no brother – yet the son –
> Yet not the son, I will not call him son –
> Of him I was about to call his father,
> Hath heard your praises, and this night he means
> To burn the lodging where you use to lie,
> And you within it.
>
> (II, iii, 17–25)

Oliver's Cain-like breach of the bonds of kinship, for which the antique world represented by Adam holds such reverence, means that Oliver cannot be identified within its system of representation or scheme of values.

According to the play's simplified and nostalgia-driven historical narrative, then, characters belong to either the 'good old days' or the 'bad new ones' and are judged accordingly. That is to say, they are either acquisitive or loyal; destroyers of the bonds of kinship or guardians of them; innovators or traditionalists; selfish or selfless; driven by the desire for 'more' or happy with 'enough'; dismantlers of foundations or observers of them. If literary humanism involves judging social systems on the humanity of their ways of life, then the ruling judgments seem in *As You Like It* to be exclusively expressed by representatives from the top (Duke Senior and Orlando) and bottom (Adam) of the exiled 'antique world'. However, there are other custodians of the human, in the shape of Celia and Rosalind, who taken together do not fit very easily into the play's old/new binary. As daughter of the banished Duke Senior, Rosalind, for example, initially expresses sentiments which are similar to Orlando's. Distraught because of her father's exile and consequently stuck in an affective rut, she resists the idea that a banished father could ever be forgotten, let alone replaced: 'Unless you could teach me to forget my banished father', she tells her friend Celia, 'you must not learn me how to remember any extraordinary pleasure' (I, ii, 3–6). Celia's response, however, is precisely to suggest that Rosalind substitutes Rosalind's father for Celia's:

> Herein I see thou lovest me not with the full weight that I love thee. If my uncle, thy banished father, had banished thy uncle, the Duke my father, so thou hadst been still with me I could have taught my love to take thy father for mine. So wouldst thou, if the truth of thy love to me were so righteously tempered as mine is to thee. (I, ii, 7–13)

Celia's advice, like Claudius's similar advice to Hamlet to 'think of us [Claudius] / As of a father', might be considered tactless to someone for whom ties of kinship and the affections they are supposed to express are all-important. Just as the 'new world' Oliver seems to have shifted his allegiance, so Celia seems to be recommending a certain mobility in terms of allegiance and affection. For Celia, kinship is less a biological given than a moveable feast. And not only is she offering her father as a surrogate father for Rosalind, but as a consequence of this, she is offering herself as sister instead of cousin.

Family for Celia thus lacks the finality which Orlando and initially Rosalind attach to it. For Celia, kinship terms and the true and lasting affections which they should ideally denote are transferable. They can be recreated, relocated, re-imagined. Celia *mobilises* Rosalind. She encourages Rosalind to think in terms of transfers of familial and other kinds of affection. She is also implicitly dissuading Rosalind from the backward-looking nostalgia expressed elsewhere in the play by representatives of the antique world which associates 'real', true, lasting affections with the past. Celia is asking Rosalind to recognise those people in the present to whom she might transfer her affections. This being a Shakespearean romantic comedy, in which desires and affections are typically volatile, Rosalind is quick to learn from Celia, for she immediately mimics Celia's principle of transferring emotional focus from one object to another: 'Well, I will forget the condition of my estate to rejoice in yours' (I, ii, 14–15). Rosalind is becoming emotionally mobile. She is learning some of the ways of the new court (which are also some of the ways of carnivalesque comedy). As a further indication of Rosalind's partial acceptance of (aspects of) the new world, she tacitly accedes to a plan of Celia's, to become Duke Frederick's quasi-heir, an idea which the staunchly 'old-world' Orlando unconditionally rejects. 'When he [Duke Frederick] dies', Celia tells Rosalind, 'thou shalt be his heir; for what he hath taken away from thy father perforce, I will render thee again in affection' (I, ii, 17–19).

In the mental and emotional mobility which she both demonstrates and encourages, and in her casual attitude towards the 'natural' family, Celia is in some ways like her father. As Duke Frederick has shown no respect for his natural brother, and has introduced the principles of radical instability and change into the 'new' court, so Celia is likewise irreverent and innovative. When Celia and Rosalind, on Celia's initiative, make plans to flee the new court together, Celia's flippant attitude towards the natural family mirrors the father's casualness: 'Shall we be sundered? Shall we part, sweet girl? / No. Let my father seek another heir' (I, iii, 97–8). She will be as apparently unconcerned to abandon her father as her father was to abandon his brother. There, though, the similarity ends, for whereas the 'tyrant Duke' (I, ii, 278) seems intent on destroying the bonds of kinship, Celia is intent on reconstructing them. Her family – her adopted family – is Rosalind. Sharing love which is, as the new courtier Le Beau recognises, 'dearer than the natural bond of sisters' (I, ii, 266), Celia and Rosalind create their own surrogate family.

It is worth elaborating further on the difference between father and daughter, as this holds the key to the play's preoccupation with the emotions. Where Duke Frederick seems to be affectively dead, Celia compensates or even overcompensates by speaking the language of love from the moment she first appears. The first action we hear Duke Frederick perform is to trade in the love of others (the 'loving lords' who follow Duke Senior into exile) for money and land (their 'lands and revenues enrich the new Duke, therefore he gives them good leave to wander'). By contrast, Celia's first words are an expression of affection: 'I pray thee Rosalind, sweet my coz, be merry' (I, ii, 1). Celia, like everyone who loves, whether the love is sisterly, feudal, quasi-familial, romantic, erotic or some combination of these, ends up in the forest of Arden. This suggests that the disenchanted world they leave behind is loveless and represents the 'death of affect'. However, what follows at least some of the exiles into the wood is the sense, which is intensified by carnival, of the impermanence of affective ties. Perhaps because Celia has witnessed her father's aggression towards members of the natural family, she attaches considerable significance to the surrogate family and wants Rosalind to do likewise. She worries on several occasions that her love for Rosalind is not reciprocated: 'I see thou lovest me not with the full weight that I love thee' (I, ii, 7–8); 'Rosalind, lack'st thou then the love / Which teacheth thee that thou and I am one?' (I, iii, 95–6). If affections and terms of kinship are transferable, then where and how does this process stop? Might the bond which is 'dearer than the natural bond of sisters' itself be broken or transferred? Celia advises Rosalind to 'love no man in good earnest' (I, ii, 25–6), as though this might pose a threat to their relationship. She wants to have Rosalind to herself, it seems, to compensate for the destructions of affection which she has witnessed at her father's court.

Celia's dilemma, which is not an uncommon one in Shakespearean drama, can be connected to that aspect of modernity, closely related to the phenomena of disengagement, disenchantment and scepticism discussed in the Introduction (and in subsequent chapters), which Zygmunt Bauman calls 'liquid modernity'.[8] In *Liquid Love* (2003), Bauman describes the difference between 'kinship' and 'affinity' as follows:

> 'Affinity' is kinship *qualified* . . . Choice is the qualifying factor: it transforms kinship into affinity. It also, however, betrays affinity's ambition: its intention to be *like* kinship, as unconditional, irrevocable and unbreakable as kinship is (eventually, affinity will weave into the lineage and become indistinguishable from the rest of the kinship network; the affinity of one generation will turn into the kinship of the next). But even

> marriages, contrary to priestly insistence, are not made in heaven – and what has been tied together by humans, humans may, and can, and given a chance will untie.[9]

Celia wants friendship and the diluted kinship bond of cousin to solidify into the firmer tie of sisterhood, in order to counteract the 'liquid' bonds of the new court. However, the recognition in the last sentence of the quotation from Bauman that nothing 'human' is forever implies that modernity (represented in *As You Like It* by the 'new court') cannot be held entirely responsible for the dissolution of bonds. Modernity may take advantage of the natural human phenomenon of impermanence, but it is not the sole cause of it. Celia's anxieties are in other words overdetermined, for if they are partly the product of the new court's disregard for family ties, then they are also part of the play's more general preoccupation with the complicated and unguaranteed nature of human affection. The new court from this perspective is only a reflection of the deeper, 'only human' reality (or one version of it), that, 'of course', human affections are uncertain, brothers can all too easily envy or dislike each other, love can turn to hate and so on. The complication in Celia's case seems to be that affection is morphing into the possessiveness of erotic and/or romantic love. Thus not only are affections transferable from one person to another, but the nature of affection itself seems to be sliding about. This, of course, is the cue for romantic comedy and the representation of love in all its labyrinthine confusion and variety.

Where does this leave Rosalind and Celia as 'custodians' of the human? If affective ties are located in this play (and others) as the benchmark for a humane society and affection then turns out to be intrinsically unstable rather than unstable as a result of an 'emotionally mobile' society, then 'loving well' cannot be the basis for 'living well' because love just does not provide that kind of basis. Love is instead once again proof of human folly and the volatility and unpredictability of human passions. As the refrain in the song sung by Amiens has it: 'Most friendship is feigning, most loving, mere folly' (II, vii, 182). I am not suggesting that Celia's affection for Rosalind is inconstant just because she might love her in more than one way, but that the 'truism' that erotic/romantic love adds a degree of complication to friendship has some 'truth' in it. Erotic/romantic love is often presented by Shakespeare (in *A Midsummer Night's Dream*, *King Lear* and the sonnets, as well as in *Love's Labour's Lost* and *As You Like It*) as all-consuming, obsessive and, perhaps most importantly, annihilating of the other. In *Love's Labour's Lost*, when the men find out that they have been tricked by the women into wooing the wrong partners, Biron responds by saying that they 'wooed but the sign of she'

(V, ii, 469). Biron is referring to a particular incident, but it may have always been the case that the men were pursuing 'signs' rather than realities, romantic projections of their supposed loved ones rather than the real thing. Orlando, as we shall see, is this kind of lover, at least to begin with. Celia's love for Rosalind is ostensibly different, because the solid ground of friendship is based not on projection, but on the mutual knowledge born of 'being ever from their cradles bred together' (I, i, 103). Nevertheless, Celia's 'thou lovest me not with the full weight that I love thee' pushes the circumscribed insecurities that can occupy friendship in the direction of the obsessive narcissistic frustration which characterises romantic/erotic love. Celia wants Rosalind to be exclusively 'her' Rosalind, and she wants a Rosalind who is 'more than' Rosalind, a Rosalind who can answer to all her needs. Friends can be needy, but Celia's romantic/erotic neediness seems to be in danger of overwhelming her ability to recognise Rosalind and Rosalind's own emotional quandaries, for on virtually every occasion that Rosalind mentions the loss of her father, Celia turns this into the accusation that Rosalind does not adequately love her friend.

When Orlando describes Adam in the forest of Arden as limping after him in 'pure love', the term 'love' is used in an uncomplicated way. In the pastoral world, life is simple, love is simple and Adam can function in a straightforward way as a lesson in how to live an authentically humane life. As central or near-central characters, Celia and Rosalind, unlike Adam, bear the brunt of the play's plot complications which with Shakespeare are often simultaneously emotional, psychological, existential and linguistic complications. If in romantic comedy the question of how to live becomes intensely focused on the question of how to love, then Celia and Rosalind expose those risky, uncertain as well as playful aspects of love which do not easily lend themselves as foundational principles. Often the opposite seems to be the case, that love lacks firm foundations. When friends who have been 'bred together' and whose friendship is 'dearer than the natural bond of sisters' feel, on one side at least, threatened by rejection, then friendship begins to appear – in the mind if not in reality – chancy and without absolute guarantees. In the forest of Arden, however, the lack of absolute guarantees is the occasion for recreation, not mourning. One answer – but not *the* answer – that emerges from Celia and Rosalind to the question of how to live is to embrace, and in fact to celebrate, the 'messiness' of affection as variety.

In the world of festive, carnivalesque comedy, which alongside pastoral is also what the green world of Arden sets in motion, love's uncertainty is the source of exuberant play. If Celia and especially Rosalind are 'custodians' of the human, then the humanity they represent is from this perspective an unbridled humanity, released from a variety of constraints, including gender, mono-sexuality and the limited canivalesque world, which always returns to acquisition, of the new court. Love's variety is the driver of the 'good' excess of comedy (as opposed to the 'bad' excess of tragedy), an excess which is communal rather than individualistic, which liquefies all that is solid in order to release unrealised erotic and emotional possibilities, and one where arbitrary social boundaries and barriers, rather than non-arbitrary ethical boundaries, seem mainly to be traversed. If the icon for the pastoral simplicity of love is the image of Orlando bearing the faithful Adam on his back, then the icon for the infinite variety of love and desire is the scenario of a boy actor playing the part of a woman (Rosalind), who then disguises herself as a boy (Ganymede), who in turn pretends to be Rosalind, so that Orlando can practise wooing her. Love is a game, one with few rules and many surprises. Rosalind-as-Ganymede-as-Rosalind can pretend to be a number of different Rosalinds, unrestrained by the need to confirm any of them as the 'real' thing, and love-as-desire can be permuted in a number of ways, to include the possibility of Orlando desiring not only the various Rosalinds played by Ganymede, but Ganymede as well.

As Jean Howard points out, Ganymede was a 'name that had longstanding and unmistakable associations with homoerotic love', which originated in Greek mythology and Jove's desire for a young boy called Ganymede, and 'in Shakespeare's day commonly signified a young boy who was the lover of another (usually older) man'.[10] As Celia's love for Rosalind thus contains within it the possibility of female–female desire, so Orlando's wooing of Rosalind-as-Ganymede-as-Rosalind has a homoerotic component, while maintaining a heterosexual dimension.[11] This exhilarating array of erotic possibilities is a concrete example of the conversion of the 'bad' excess of tragedy (present at the beginning of *As You Like It*) into its 'good' comic counterpart, for where the transgression of limits heads inexorably in tragedy towards death and destruction, limitlessness in comedy is so much holiday sport and carnivalesque freedom. Converting positives into negatives – 'banishment', for example, into 'liberty' (I, iii, 137) – we almost forget that emotional and now erotic mobility can be, and has been, the cause of unhappiness and insecurity. What characters seem to be required to do in Arden is to learn the 'good' mobility of desire and let go of any overly fixed idea of whom and how to love. As in *Love's Labour's Lost*, lovers (usually male) who take themselves too seriously and do not recognise the folly of love are liable to be mocked by (usually their) female counterparts. This is the fate of Orlando, who, in response to his claim that he will 'die' (IV, i, 87) for the lack of Rosalind, is subjected by Rosalind (playing Ganymede playing Rosalind) to yet another manifestation of the disenchanted scepticism which is never very far away in Shakespeare's plays. 'Men', he/she says, 'have died from time to time, and worms have eaten them, but not for love' (IV, i, 99–101). 'Love is merely a madness' (III, ii, 386), declares Rosalind-as-Ganymede on a previous occasion. To love without a healthy sense of scepticism, which in carnival translates as 'play', is to risk being ridiculed.

Despite the mockery of seriousness that goes on in the play, there are still serious undertones in its representation of love. Playful disenchantment, for example, is only one of Rosalind's roles, for with Orlando gone, she herself professes a 'deep' love of 'unknown bottom' (IV, i, 196–8) for him, only to be mocked in turn by Celia: 'Or rather bottomless, that as fast as you pour affection in, it runs out' (IV, i, 199–200). Everyone, it seems, or virtually everyone, is prey to the 'madness' of love. Everyone is liable to claim that his or her love is the 'real' thing, only for the humbling 'carnivalesque' counter-perspective to be almost immediately advanced that humans are as prone to waywardness in love as they are in everything else. To try to 'fix' love is therefore folly.

However, this is not the final perspective, as beneath the play, banter and frivolity that rob would-be lovers of the authenticity they claim, the play worries away at the 'problem of knowledge' which love becomes as a result of the distrust that is expressed towards it: 'I would', says Orlando to Rosalind-as-Ganymede, 'I could make thee believe I love' (III, ii, 372–3). How can you know, for certain, when someone is 'truly' in love? And how do you know with whom or what they are in love? On the subject of Rosalind's uncertainty about the object of Orlando's love, Mario Digangi in *The Homoerotics of Early Modern Drama* (1997) asks: 'Whom or what does Orlando really love: Rosalind? the idea of marrying Rosalind? the public pose of the Petrarchan lover? himself? Ganymede? Ganymede's impersonation of Rosalind? the company of other men?'[12] Rosalind-as-Ganymede has already cast doubt, or mock-doubt (because everyone knows that in Shakespeare's world appearances are often deceptive), on the authenticity of Orlando's appearance: he does not have 'the lean cheek', 'blue eye and sunken', 'beard neglected' (III, ii, 361–3) and so on of a lover. At the end of this speech, he/she casts further and more telling doubt on Orlando's authenticity by wondering whether his 'point-device' appearance is more an indication of 'loving yourself than seeming the lover of any other' (III, ii, 370–1). As Digangi indicates, amongst the variety of loves and ways of loving that are evident in Arden, from feudal to female–female, self-love is also an option. The ability to perceive extreme self-love goes at least some way towards resolving the conundrum of telling whether someone 'really' loves you.

One tell-tale sign of self-love is the substitution within the lover's poetic discourse of a real object for an imaginary one. As further evidence of Orlando's possible inauthenticity, Rosalind-as-Ganymede targets the Petrarchan rhymes with which he has been plastering the trees of the forest. 'Are you so much in love', he/she asks, 'as your rhymes speak?' (III, ii, 382–3). This goes to the heart of the matter, for the 'Rosalind' of Orlando's verses could be any Rosalind:

> From the east to western Ind
> No jewel is like Rosalind.
> Her worth being mounted on the wind
> Through all the world bears Rosalind.
> All the pictures fairest lined
> Are but black to Rosalind.
> Let no face be kept in mind
> But the fair of Rosalind.
> (III, ii, 86–93)

The 'berhymed' Rosalind (III, ii, 172) is the Rosalind of Orlando's not very fertile romantic imagination. That we are so obviously intended to find Orlando ridiculous, not just for his lack of literary skill, but for the 'category mistake' whereby his 'berhymed' Rosalind is confused with the real thing, helps to bring at least some solidity to the otherwise unsolid, 'carnivalised' discourses of love and desire in the play. Rosalind *knows* that she is not the same as the 'berhymed' version of her, that the berhymed version says more about Orlando than it does about Rosalind, namely that Orlando may be in love with the idea of love or the idea of Rosalind. Whatever 'love' is, it does not or should not involve the narcissistic absorption of the 'other' into a lover's text that has little or nothing to do with the actual other and everything to do with the poetic creator. In the Petrarchan tradition, represented by Orlando, the mistress is usually inaccessible. Her absence means that she is available to the poet for projection and that the poet can therefore do what he will with her. Echoing the title of the play, or an aspect of it, Orlando takes advantage of Rosalind's absence by constructing her 'as he likes her'.

Unlike *Love's Labour's Lost*, where the love test is projected into the future, after the actual play is done, in *As You Like It* the love test is a main part of the play and takes the form of the conversations that take place between Orlando and the disguised Rosalind. That they are conversations is significant in itself, for instead of writing love poems in isolation from the real Rosalind, Orlando is obliged to enter into dialogue with someone (Rosalind-as-Ganymede) who promises to project Rosalinds far different from the one he has so far imagined. This is the way Rosalind-as-Ganymede describes to Orlando how she cured someone of lovesickness in the past:

> *Orlando*: Did you ever cure any so?
> *Rosalind*: Yes, one; and in this manner. He was to imagine me his love, his mistress; and I set him every day to woo me. At which time would I, being but a moonish youth, grieve, be effeminate, changeable, longing and liking, proud, fantastical, apish, shallow, inconstant, full of tears, full of smiles; for every passion something, and for no passion truly anything, as boys and women are for the most part cattle of this colour – would now like him, now loathe him; then entertain him, then forswear him; now weep for him, then spit at him, that I drave my suitor from his mad humour of love to a living humour of madness, which was to forswear the full stream of the world and to live in a nook merely monastic.
>
> (III, ii, 391–405)

The aim, of course, is not to cure but to test Orlando, and to do so by drawing him out of his poetic world where his mistress is as he likes her, and therefore his to control, into a world where the opposite is the case. This mistress will instead be uncontrollable and volatile. On one level, Rosalind is offering Orlando a crash-course in the unpredictability and chanciness of 'real-life' human emotions, such as are represented elsewhere in the play in its carnivalesque depiction of the impermanence of love and desire. On another level, however, Rosalind is testing Orlando's capacity to be *attentive* to another and keep on being attentive in the face of the severe challenge of a mistress who is no longer the passive and silent mistress inscribed in Orlando's verses, but the difficult partner imagined here by Rosalind-as-Ganymede. The inconstant, 'only human' mistress is an antidote to Orlando's idealised, 'more than human' one, because the 'only human' version will require Orlando to attend on a moment-by-moment basis to a living, breathing presence, as opposed to revelling in an absence.

The question Orlando asks midway through one of his conversations with Rosalind-as-Ganymede – 'But will my Rosalind do so?' (IV, i, 149) – betrays his lack of knowledge of the 'real' Rosalind. The response which comes back – 'By my life, she will do as I do' (IV, i, 150) – is as far as Orlando is concerned the claim of a stranger to know Rosalind better than he does. Orlando's ignorance means that he has no way of telling how the reality of Rosalind might compare with the Rosalinds presented by Rosalind-as-Ganymede. The disguised Rosalind on several occasions appeals to the authenticity of her impersonation of Rosalind and/or to the illusionist fantasy (again as far as Orlando knows) that Rosalind is actually present: 'I am your Rosalind' (IV, i, 61); 'What would you say to me now an I were your very, very Rosalind?' (IV, i, 65–7). Orlando willingly accedes to the illusion that Ganymede is Rosalind when he says that he will keep his promise to return to her/him on time 'with no less religion than if thou wert indeed my Rosalind' (IV, i, 187–8).

However, at the same time as Rosalind closes the gap between reality and performance by insisting on the credibility of her impersonation, she puts doubt in Orlando's mind about whom he is talking to, and opens rather than closes the gap between reality and illusion: 'Am not I your Rosalind?' (IV, i, 83); 'in her person I say I will not have you' (IV, i, 86); 'now I will be your Rosalind in a more coming-on disposition' (IV, i, 105–6). The doubt about who Rosalind 'really' is, and whether the Rosalind repeatedly referred to by Orlando as 'my Rosalind' (IV, i, 59; 149; 187) in any way matches up with the Rosalinds presented by Rosalind-as-Ganymede, has the effect of making Orlando curious ('will my Rosalind do so?'). He realises the need to find out more! This need is not always in as much evidence as Rosalind would like it to be, as not knowing creates space for romantic projection. To some of the questions put to Orlando, such as 'Now tell me how long you would have her after you have possessed her' (IV, i, 135–6), Orlando gives stock romantic answers: 'For ever and a day' (IV, i, 137). This is a romantic ideal which resists knowledge of the other as human being in favour of an abstraction. Orlando has a plentiful supply of these romantic abstractions which he clings to despite the anti-romantic reality of the person he is currently talking to:

> *Rosalind*: . . . Men have died from time to time, and worms have eaten them, but not for love.
> *Orlando*: I would not have my right Rosalind of this mind, for I protest her frown might kill me.
> *Rosalind*: By this hand, it will not kill a fly. But come, now I will be your Rosalind in a more coming-on disposition; and ask me what you will, I will grant it.
> *Orlando*: Then love me, Rosalind.
> *Rosalind*: Yes, faith, will I, Fridays and Saturdays and all.
> *Orlando*: And wilt thou have me?
> *Rosalind*: Ay, and twenty such.
> *Orlando*: What sayst thou?
> *Rosalind*: Are you not good?
> *Orlando*: I hope so.
> *Rosalind*: Why then, can one desire too much of a good thing?
> (IV, i, 99–116)

Orlando is trying to have a conversation with his romantic idealisation of Rosalind, while the disguised Rosalind is trying to get him to have a conversation with her impersonation of an anti-romantic Rosalind. The conversation Orlando wants to have is not a real conversation (because it is with someone who only exists in his head), whereas the conversation Rosalind playing Rosalind wants to have is with an Orlando who is able to recognise the difference between an imaginary conversation and a real one. With the stock romantic phrases which he continues to use, Orlando is trying to superimpose his own idealised reality onto the much bawdier one that is taking place. The more romantically 'removed' Orlando threatens to become, the more iconoclastically anti-romantic Rosalind becomes. Orlando's shocked 'What sayst thou?' snaps him out of the imaginary conversation and draws him into the real one. And this is what is needed if Orlando is to begin to question his own assumed knowledge of Rosalind, recognise that this knowledge is slight and realise that he may need to find out more. This attentiveness is what we might, despite the insolidity, chanciness and mobility of affection in the play, call 'love'.

I may again have constructed something 'heavy' (a message about how to love) out of something 'light' (flirtatious banter), but as in *Love's Labour's Lost* stark oppositions between heavy and light tend to falter. Characters are themselves mocked for 'getting serious' about love, but they do it anyway and with such frequency that the 'serious' issue of when and under what conditions lovers should be taken seriously once again presses upon them (and us). Moreover, if the disguised Rosalind is really Shakespeare in disguise, a Shakespeare himself torn between anti-romantic scepticism and a desire to take love seriously enough for it to be an antidote to the loveless instrumentality represented at the beginning of *As You Like It* (and elsewhere), then mockery of love will inevitably be combined with a 'serious' quest for knowledge of its stable core.

One 'non-answer' to the problem of knowledge that love is in *As You Like It* is that love is in fact not a matter of 'knowledge' but 'faith'. The beautifully evocative religious language used of human love in the play – such as Rosalind's 'his kissing is as full of sanctity as the touch of holy bread' (III, iv, 12–13) – treats love as a holy mystery. Yet just as the idea of incarnation present in this image of the Eucharist brings religion into human focus, so, love, too, is not always a matter of blind faith to be either revered or ridiculed, but something that can be humanly 'known' and experienced. The love test in romantic comedy can come across as a lottery or a foolish attempt to fathom the unfathomable, but it can also be the source of quasi-Aristotelian moments of recognition, such as Orlando encounters. Orlando needs to find out more about a Rosalind who is not the same as his projection of her. He needs to be attentive because attentiveness to another is what love might be.

Towards the end of the play, Orlando seems to have learned at least something from his mentor Rosalind about the art of loving well, which in romantic comedy is the basis of living well, for the questions he asks of his erstwhile estranged brother, Oliver, about the suddenness of his love for Celia (disguised as Aliena) are about Oliver's own level of knowledge and attentiveness: 'Is't possible that on so little acquaintance you should like her? That but seeing, you should love her? And loving, woo? And wooing, she should grant? And will you persevere to enjoy her?' (V, ii, 1–4). 'Falling in love' has often been represented as a speedy process, but Celia/Aliena and Oliver possibly break the record. The suddenness of Oliver's falling in love is in a way predictable, because it is merely the reverse of the suddenness of his 'falling into hate' at the beginning of the play with his niece, Rosalind. Just as Oliver's 'malice 'gainst the lady [Rosalind]' will as predicted by Le Beau 'suddenly break forth' (I, ii, 272–3), so Celia's and Oliver's 'wrath of love' (V, ii, 38–9), as Rosalind describes it, is equally hasty and misses out the training in the art of intimacy undertaken by Orlando under Rosalind's tutelage. If, to recall Bauman, affinity strives for the (supposed) solidity of kinship in order to compensate for the liquidity of human ties exacerbated by modernity, then falling in or out of love at such speed renders affinity and kinship permanent strangers to one another. Although Orlando's use of the word 'acquaintance' offers a bridge between affinity and kinship which might remedy the suddenness of the making and breaking of ties, Oliver will brook no questioning of his love:

> Neither call the giddiness of it in question, the poverty of her, the small acquaintance, my sudden wooing, nor her sudden consenting; but say with me, 'I love Aliena'; say with her, that she loves me; consent with both that we may enjoy each other. (V, ii, 5–9)

Significantly, Oliver does not refute the 'giddiness' of his love, but asks Orlando not to question it, as if to imply that love just is naturally giddy.

Despite their suspicion of all things supposedly natural, theory-influenced perspectives on love and desire within literary studies over the last thirty years have tended to concur with Oliver's view. Roland Barthes's entertaining *A Lover's Discourse* (1977), for example, deliberately eschews narrative in order to represent love, in post-structuralist style, as a heterogeneous collection of 'fragments of discourse' or '*figures*'.[13] 'Throughout any love life', writes Barthes, 'figures occur to the lover without any order, for on each occasion they depend on an (internal or external) accident'.[14] Taking a similarly post-structuralist approach, Catherine Belsey in *Desire: Love Stories in Western Culture* (1994) writes:

> Desire is in the end a question of writing; at the same time, desire is writing in question. The human being in love necessarily writes, inscribes desire in the hollows of enunciation, means passion in the physiology of sex. Nevertheless, desire remains finally uninscribed, in excess of its own performance.[15]

This is a new variation on the old theme of love and desire as naturally 'giddy', excessive, unpredictable and liquid. In the context of Shakespearean comedy and the spirit of holiday release which informs it, Catherine Bates likewise emphasises the 'unregularized state' in which desire and sexuality typically exist before institutionalised desire arrives in the shape of marriage to impose order upon this disorder.[16]

Given, however, that the world from which the lovers escape bears some resemblance by virtue of its 'liquid' state to the world they escape to, the need to rescue and strengthen affective ties seems pressing. For what if the status quo itself were a 'bad' version of the carnivalesque which involved the continual making and breaking of bonds at the whim of a ruling class given over to the values of acquisition? What if affection in such a world were to become so lacking in foundations as to become meaningless? In stark contrast to Oliver's foundation-less love, Rosalind emphasises almost to the point of parody her position as a 'knowing' subject, whose love is built if not on certain then on surer knowledge than Oliver's. In her reassurance to Orlando that he will have 'his' Rosalind, the words 'know' or 'knowledge' are repeated several times in quick succession:

> Know of me then – for now I speak to some purpose – that I know you are a gentleman of good conceit. I speak not this that you should bear a good opinion of my knowledge, insomuch I say I know you are. (V, ii, 50–4).

Nothing in love, of course, is certain, but Rosalind has tried to become at least a little less uncertain.

Orlando consents to Oliver's sudden love, but not without reservation. Rosalind likewise expresses similar reservations in her mockery of its 'incontinent' haste:

> There was never anything so sudden but the fight of two rams, and Caesar's thrasonical brag of 'I came, saw, and overcame', for your brother and my sister no sooner met but they looked; no sooner looked but they loved; no sooner loved but they sighed; no sooner sighed but they asked one another the reason; no sooner knew the reason but they sought the remedy; and in these degrees have made a pair of stairs to marriage, which they will climb incontinent, or else be incontinent before marriage. They are in the very wrath of love, and they will together. (V, ii, 28–39)

For the dalliance of Orlando and Rosalind's courtship, designed, amongst other things, to confront Orlando with the mismatch between reality and romantic projection, Oliver and Celia substitute the rush of impatient desire, represented in the bestial as well as militaristic language of the Petrarchan tradition, in terms of conflict and conquest. In Oliver and Celia's courtship, the other is not so much a human being to get to know, but an object to be overcome. Such, at any rate, is the kind of humane perspective that comes from the sentimental education Rosalind has offered Orlando.

Chapter 9

Hope: *The Winter's Tale*

In Samuel Beckett's *Endgame* (1958), Clov claims – provisionally – that 'There's no more nature':

> *Hamm*: Nature has forgotten us.
> *Clov*: There's no more nature.
> *Hamm*: No more nature! You exaggerate.
> *Clov*: In the vicinity.
> *Hamm*: But we breathe, we change! We lose our hair, our teeth! Our bloom! Our ideals!
> *Clov*: Then she hasn't forgotten us.
> *Hamm*: But you say there is none.
> *Clov*: [*Sadly*.] No one that ever lived ever thought so crooked as we.[1]

The world of *Endgame* is featureless, monotonous and uncertain. These aspects of the play make it difficult to know whether nature has ceased to exist or not. There are no markers, no reference points. To Hamm's repeated question 'What's happening, what's happening?', Clov (repeatedly) answers: 'Something is taking its course'.[2] The 'something' is unspecified. That this something could be anything at all suggests that the claustrophobic world inhabited by the characters in *Endgame* is paradoxically also an unlimited world, a 'grey' world with neither external nor internal landmarks.[3]

If one of the endgames of the 'liquid modern world' (so described by Zygmunt Bauman in *Liquid Love*) is the possible disappearance of nature, including human nature, then some of modernity's opening moves, as played by Shakespeare, are to embrace modernity's positive aspects (the openness of nature and human nature to question and transformation), but to resist the negatives (featurelessness, total plasticity and disintegration) by reorienting characters to human landmarks and connecting these to nature.[4] If, as this book and other critics have argued, Shakespeare is modern or incipiently modern, then an albeit fleeting comparison between *Endgame* as the apotheosis of disintegration and

Shakespeare serves to suggest that 'liquidity' in Shakespeare's work is not the cataclysmic meltdown that it is in Beckett's work. As we have seen, some of the corrosive effects of modernity are present in Shakespeare's work, but they are tempered by sheltering from them a sense of the human.

A way of accounting for the survival, amidst a sense of loss and disorientation, of recognisable human coordinates in *The Winter's Tale* (1609–10) in particular is via the theory of archetypes developed by Northrop Frye in his proto-structuralist *Anatomy of Criticism* (1957). As *The Winter's Tale* is one of the most obviously 'archetypal' of Shakespeare's plays, it makes sense briefly to invoke some of Frye's insights here. However, it is not archetypes in general in which I am interested, but, in line with the emphasis of preceding chapters, archetypal emotional states. I shall discuss these subsequently.

The deeply rooted archetypes identified by Frye, such as the 'green world' of comedy or the 'successful quest' of romance, suggest the existence of perennial if not permanent narrative motifs and patterns which may appear and reappear in different guises, but which nevertheless retain their essential characteristics across time.[5] Thus romance, initially defined by Frye as 'nearest of all literary forms to the wish-fulfilment dream' may be thought of from the perspective of archetypal criticism as common to such disparate texts as Edmund Spenser's *The Faerie Queene* (1596) and Karl Marx and Friedrich Engels's *The Communist Manifesto* (1848), for despite their obviously different historical situations, they both participate in utopian hope.[6] 'No matter how great a change may take place in society', writes Frye, 'romance will turn up again, as hungry as ever, looking for new hopes and desires to feed on'.[7] Frye's perception of sameness-within-difference corresponds in broad terms to the argument pursued in Chapter 4 about the deep continuities of human experience which underlie historical change.

Romance as described by Frye also partitions the world into distinct realms made meaningful once again by the presence of recognisable archetypes. Writing of the difference between romance as defined by Frye and conventional narrative realism, Fredric Jameson in *The Political Unconscious* (1981) offers some fruitful insights into the distinctly segmented realms of romance, as opposed to the indistinct and infinite world of conventional realism:

> events [in conventional narrative realism] take place within the infinite space of sheer Cartesian extension, of the quantification of the market system: a space which like that of film extends indefinitely beyond any particular momentary 'still' or setting or larger vista or panorama, and is incapable of symbolic unification.

> A first specification of romance would then be achieved if we could account for the way in which, in contrast to realism, its inner-worldly objects such as landscape or village, forest or mansion – mere temporary stopping places on the lumbering coach or express-train itinerary of realistic representation – are somehow transformed into folds of space, into discontinuous pockets of homogeneous time and of heightened symbolic closure.[8]

A concrete as well as straightforward example from Frye of the way romance slices up reality and attributes to it the kind of heightened symbolic significance missing, according to Jameson, in the empty, disenchanted space of conventional realism is Frye's description of the association of the hero with spring and hostile forces with winter. 'The enemy', writes Frye, 'is associated with winter, darkness, confusion, sterility, moribund life, and old age, and the hero with spring, dawn, order, fertility, vigor, and youth'.[9]

In Shakespeare's romances, archetypes have a strong emotional content. As Robin Headlam Wells in *Shakespeare's Humanism* (2005) puts it: '*The Winter's Tale* is a play about archetypal passions'.[10] Circumstantial detail is therefore kept to a minimum, and emotions in the romances are even more distilled than they are in Shakespeare's previous work. These emotions are also firmly linked to the seasonal cycle of winter and spring: once again, only more emphatically, what is happening inside human beings mirrors what is happening outside as part of a pattern that is taken to be universal. Thus in the case of *The Winter's Tale*, there *is* an answer to Hamm's question: 'What's happening?' The answer is that 'jealousy is happening' or 'forgiveness is happening', and that these emotions are the perennial causes of human distress or hope. In the romances, characters lose their way both literally and metaphorically and become estranged from themselves, from each other, from their origins and families, but they are never so disoriented (as Beckett's characters are) as to make it impossible for them or us to recognise emotions and *types* of emotion which the romances mark as archetypal. I emphasise 'types' of emotion because it is not just a simple matter of recognising emotions such as jealousy as 'stand-alone' emotions, but of seeing them as a certain category of emotion (wintry and deadening, in the case of jealousy) whose effect and meaning are clarified by their association with the seasons. As argued in previous chapters, emotions are not so intangible or internalised that they become illegible or separable from the larger structures – of nature and human nature – of which they are a part. This is because, to recall the term used by Gail Kern Paster, emotions form part of an 'ecology' (see Chapter 5).[11] Where 'Hamm' as a diminished 'Hamlet' fails to mean anything by his emotions or thoughts – 'We're not beginning to . . . to . . . mean something?'[12] – and fails to connect anything going on inside him to anything going on outside, emotions in *The Winter's Tale* are eloquent and ecological.

It is therefore possible to detect in jealousy, for example, an archetypal pattern or structure which connects it with other emotions on the basis that such emotions: (a) alienate selves from others, and (b) assume a degree of unintelligibility. The contrasting archetype would account for those emotions which: (a) seek redemptive contact with an alienated other or others, and (b) tell us things about ourselves that we can know and act upon. The contrasting views of the emotions implied by these archetypes are similar to the contrast in *Coriolanus* between individualised and transactional models. That they are placed in *The Winter's Tale* in clear contrast to one another through the winter/spring opposition helps to bring their meaning in relation to one another into focus and clarify their archetypal significance. Jealousy, being a 'winter' emotion because of its destructive and isolating qualities, obviously belongs to the first category, while love, forgiveness and sociality belong to the second archetype and are associated with spring and a sense of renewal.

The first movement of the play is dominated by the first archetype by virtue of Leontes's withdrawal into the subjectivist world of 'weak-hinged fancy', as Paulina refers to his causeless jealousy:

> I'll not call you tyrant;
> But this most cruel usage of your queen –
> Not able to produce more accusation
> Than your own weak-hinged fancy – something savours
> Of tyranny, and will ignoble make you,
> Yea, scandalous to the world.[13]

Emotions, as defined by Leontes's jealousy, are volatile, unpredictable and groundless, and they support 'inward' states which disconnect selves from others. 'Affection', says Leontes, 'dost make possible things not so held, / Communicat'st with dreams' (I, ii, 140–2).[14] Leontes is beyond help and cannot or will not listen to those advisers and counsellors, such as Paulina, who try to bring him out of the world of 'fancy', where reality is in the eye of the subjectivist 'emoter', and back into the communal world, where reality is based on long-standing and therefore apparently secure, tried and tested affective ties. The view of emotions as transactional, communal and potentially a stable basis for relationship is not safely protected from the model defined through Leontes's jealousy, but, by the same token, the latter is not the whole truth either. Before the more hopeful picture of the emotions can emerge, characters must experience the dead, but all too plausible, end to which the first view leads them.

The compelling picture of human emotions that the play draws via Leontes in the first movement of the play is that the human reality they define is one of complex overdetermination. As I argued in Chapter 6 using psychoanalytic perspectives, we may identify connecting and disconnecting as primary human urges, and derive from them some normative conclusions about the need to balance independence with interdependence, but a different understanding, focused on the overdetermination of emotions and the restlessness of desire, again gives rise to the view that emotions are incapable of generating norms. Taking a psychoanalytic standpoint different from that used in Chapter 6, one might say that emotions, like love, come with too much baggage from the unconscious. Drawing on the work of Jacques Lacan, Catherine Belsey in *Shakespeare and the Loss of Eden* (1999) writes:

> Jacques Lacan, who reserves his most dismissive moments for the moralizing tendency that masks desire as true love, places aggressivity at the root of psychic life. The tormented space of passion is not in psychoanalytic theory a cosy enclave. Desire, which is absolute, can never believe itself adequately reciprocated. Young children learn this when they discover that they cannot have the ceaseless and undivided attention of their carers.[15]

In her interpretation of *The Winter's Tale* (and *Othello*), Belsey consequently suggests that 'love is the cause of jealous rage and not its cure'.[16] Rather than being a perversion or opposite of love, jealousy is part of love which is itself inseparable from insatiable desire.

From this perspective, Leontes's groundless jealousy is not simply an example of the triumph of illusion over reality, 'weak-hinged fancy' over truth, for Leontes is disclosing the otherwise hidden truth about love: that it is aggressive, jealous and destructive. Belsey, however, is in danger of essentialising love and assimilating it to the anarchy of Eros.[17] This is certainly one version of love in the play, but, as is the case in *Love's Labour's Lost* and *As You Like It*, Shakespeare juxtaposes different versions of love. As the archetypal 'winter king', Leontes – or rather Leontes's version of love – is sacrificed to allow other, more benevolent and hopeful versions of love to emerge. This does not mean that the emotions expressed by Leontes can be simply wished away or treated as aberrant in comparison with their more optimistic counterparts. 'Winter' emotions, by which I mean not just the narcissism of love-as-desire but all emotions that suspect, resent, fear or overwhelm the other, are obviously not 'winter' emotions in a literal sense, for they surface at other times and places. However, their association with winter clarifies the play's distinction between deadening emotions, which kill off meaningful interaction with others, and animating emotions, which bring people back to life through renewed contact and communion. The first two acts compress via Leontes virtually all those emotions which dissolve human contact by finding everything and everyone outside the self cause for despair, anger, resentment, jealousy and suspicion. The outcome of these emotions is Leontes's warped conclusion that 'All's true that is mistrusted' (II, i, 50). The source of mistrust is particularly those who are closest to him: his wife, his son and his best friend from childhood. That his closest others should be the target of his resentment is due to the fact that close others can never be close enough, they can never answer desire, because desire, according to Belsey's Lacanian perspective, 'can never believe itself adequately reciprocated'. Frustration, aggression, restlessness, irritability and disappointment are the rotten fruits of the attempt to close a gap which can never be closed.

These emotions, however, though compelling and plausible, are not the entire story of the emotions, but part of the ritual cycle of death/renewal, winter/spring. We can choose to essentialise one set of emotions (those associated with winter), or the other (those associated with spring), or we can opt for complexity, by suggesting along with Frye that both are part of human experience:

> Participation and detachment, sympathy and ridicule, sociability and isolation, are inseparable in the complex we call comedy, a complex that is begotten by the paradox of life itself, in which to exist is both to be a part of something else and yet never to be a part of it, and in which all freedom and joy are inseparably a belonging and an escape.[18]

But however much critics insist, as they often do, upon the complexity of response which *The Winter's Tale* seems to provoke, and which in Frye's terms mirrors the duality of life itself, critics tend to lean in the direct of either a 'winter' pessimism and irony or a 'spring' optimism.

Frank Kermode in his introduction to the play veers towards the optimistic reading when he describes how 'nature . . . re-establishes love and human continuance and proves that time and change are her servants, agents not only of change but of perpetuity, redeemers as well as destroyers'.[19] By contrast, Belsey's psychoanalytic as well as deconstructive reading is far more sanguine about the possibility of extricating the positively humane from its 'others'. In conclusion to her discussion of Perdita's speech on the power of flowers in Act IV, she argues that the speech

> calls into question any simple polarity between the court and nature, true love and blindness, pathology and health. The desire it invokes is variously exhilarating, frightening, violent, divisive, blatant, thwarted, as well as irresistibly seductive; it is driven by lack and precipitates loss.[20]

Psychoanalysis does not inevitably lead to this kind of conclusion (although deconstructive psychoanalysis probably does), for other psychoanalytically inclined critics, such as Janet Adelman in *Suffocating*

Mothers, tend towards an optimism, based upon the play's recovery of a positive version of the maternal body. According to Adelman, the 'stasis of Leontes's winter's tale' – a stasis in which 'only contamination and dread' can be located 'in the female space outside the female body' – is overcome by the female pastoral of Act IV:

> The pastoral of act 4 acknowledges . . . danger – hence its bear and storm – but it insists on the possibility of hope: here, the mother's body is full of promise. Through its association with the female and its structural position in the play – outside Leontes's control, outside his knowledge – the pastoral can figure this body, the unknown place outside the self where good things come from.[21]

Belsey and Adelman pay roughly equivalent attention to the same scene, the pastoral scene of Act IV, but arrive at strikingly different conclusions. For Belsey, the presence of emotional forces, such as aggression, hate and frustration within the supposedly 'cosy enclave' of love, thwarts any hopeful movement that the play simultaneously seems to chart from a less to a more healthy way of living/loving. By contrast, Adelman sees Leontes's vision of the world and the maternal body which informs that vision as a 'disease' that involves 'reducing [the world] to nothingness in order to stave off its capacity to hurt him'.[22] For Adelman, growth from an 'unhealthy' to a 'healthy' emotional state is the basis of the play's optimistic practical ethics, whereas for Belsey, health and pathology are permanently intertwined.

I have dwelt on Belsey's and Adelman's differing interpretations of the pastoral scene because they lead us to the question of whether a literary humanism, based on the possibility of human beings living better lives, can survive irony, pessimism and disenchantment. The difference between Belsey and Adelman's accounts of pastoral comes down to the simple – or so it appears – question of hope. Adelman's reading is basically a hopeful reading, a reading which takes account of the play's complexity and qualifies its optimism, but which nevertheless finds a hopeful message about gender relations in it (and one which to an extent compensates for the more dismal attitudes towards the maternal body in other plays discussed by Adelman). Perhaps, then, it is necessary to consider hope itself and the conditions for hope, both in the play and as the basis for a literary humanist form of literary criticism committed to the hopeful notion that literature can teach us how to live.

There is considerable encouragement – or even pressure – to read the romances in a spirit of hopefulness. Hope comes from three related sources: romance (already discussed), pastoral (discussed below) and Christianity. The play is, amongst other things, a resurrection narrative in which the apparently dead are brought to life, and a redemption narrative in which everything apparently lost or spoiled is saved. A sceptical reaction towards the religiously inflected romance improbabilities of the play is of course possible and indeed drawn attention to, for when the statuesque Hermione comes to life, Paulina comments: 'That she is living, / Were it but told you, should be hooted at / Like an old tale' (V, iii, 117–19). However, drawing attention to the actual or potential disbelief of both onstage and offstage audiences makes *total* disbelief problematic and once again encourages a scepticism towards scepticism itself. Total disbelief would involve being too coldly remote from the hopeful possibility that 'spring' emotions can be redeemed from their 'winter' counterparts. 'It is required', says Paulina at the moment of Hermione's resurrection, 'You do awake your faith' (V, iii, 94–5), which in the context of the emotional currents and cross-currents of the play can be taken to mean a faith in others as opposed to a desire for their abolition.

More specifically, Paulina's appeal is an appeal for men to trust women. In Act I, Polixenes's fond reminiscences of his boyhood friendship with Leontes – 'We were as twinned lambs that did frisk i'th' sun' (I, ii, 69) – carries the implication, brought out by Hermione, that the women in their lives have corrupted their boyhood innocence. In response to Polixenes's nostalgic evocation of what Adelman refers to as 'male pastoral', Hermione banteringly points to the assumptions made by Polixenes about the women:[23]

> *Hermione*: By this we gather
> You have tripped since.
> *Polixenes*: O my most sacred lady,
> Temptations have since then been born to's; for
> In those unfledged days was my wife a girl.
> Your precious self had then not crossed the eyes
> Of my young playfellow.
> *Hermione*: Grace to boot!
> Of this make no conclusion, lest you say
> Your queen and I are devils. Yet go on.
> Th'offences we have made you do we'll answer,
> If you first sinned with us, and that with us
> You did continue fault, and that you slipped not
> With any but us.
> (I, ii, 78–88)

Like other excluded or scapegoated figures in Shakespeare's plays, Hermione draws attention to the shortcomings of cliques and groups in which human/humane bonds are cosily preserved at the expense of other people. As has been discussed in previous chapters, whenever someone is excluded (or excludes him/herself), whether it is Shylock or Antonio in *The Merchant of Venice*, or Falstaff in *I Henry IV*, the excluded figure is conspicuous to the point of sometimes speaking back to the clique about its biases. However, the emotional needs which the closed circle meets may still be seen as valid and valuable. If they were not, then those outside them would not feel excluded so much as relieved *not* to be part of them. I made the point in the case of *The Merchant of Venice* that Antonio's 'marriage' to his ships at the end of the play is a poor replacement for the more 'authentic', person-to-person coupling which is the basis of a traditional comic ending. The problem with closed circles is not necessarily the values – of 'social warmth', to recall Michael Ferber's phrase from Chapter 3 – that they endorse, but their exclusivity.[24] Social warmth in other words needs to be extended. The infectious hopefulness of *The Winter's Tale* is that it can be extended. Pastoral in the play is reworked to affirm the possibility of widening affective networks where they have been narrowed.

In Act I, male pastoral is an enclave for two: Polixenes and Leontes. By Act IV, it has broadened to include noblemen and noblewomen, shepherds and shepherdesses, a clown, the 'out of service' (IV, iii, 14) Autolycus (now turned petty criminal), and a servant. Hierarchical distinctions are still observed and pastoral idealism is qualified by the reality of unemployment. However, hierarchical principles are themselves qualified by the levelling principle of love endorsed by Florizel when he chooses affection over inheritance: 'From my succession wipe me, father! I / Am heir to my affection' (IV, iv, 480–1). A woman, Perdita, is asked to host the pastoral (IV, iv, 72). And Perdita's adopted father, the 'Old Shepherd', prepares her for the role of hostess at the beginning of the sheep-shearing festival by emphasising the value of hospitality and the importance of welcoming 'unknown friends':

> Fie, daughter, when my old wife lived, upon
> This day she was both pantler, butler, cook,
> Both dame and servant, welcomed all, served all,
> Would sing her song and dance her turn, now here
> At upper end o'th' table, now i'th' middle,
> On his shoulder, and his, her face afire
> With labour, and the thing she took to quench it
> She would to each one sip. You are retired
> As if you were a feasted one and not
> The hostess of the meeting. Pray you bid
> These unknown friends to's welcome, for it is
> A way to make us better friends, more known.
> (IV, iv, 55–66)

The Old Shepherd worries here about losing a tradition and the values of friendship and welcome which it embodies. Pastoral is in this respect an act of preservation. However, the tradition of hospitality which he invokes means that it is by definition an open tradition, a tradition that allows 'unknown friends' to infiltrate it and perhaps even transform it.

Richard Wilson in 'Making Men of Monsters: Shakespeare in the Company of Strangers' (2005) suggests that in echoing '*the* winter's tale' (the Christian winter's tale, in other words), the play promises that 'the advent of *many strangers* means a multitude of gifts'.[25] The principle of grafting the new and strange onto the old and familiar is encouraged by Polixenes in the art versus nature debate that also takes place in Act IV. Although he later contradicts himself in his negative reaction to the relationship between his son, Florizel, and the lowly (or so it seems) Perdita, Polixenes encourages Perdita to embrace hybridity and diversity by making her garden 'rich in gillyvors' (which were thought to be cross-bred). And, he adds, 'do not call them bastards' (IV, iv, 97–8). This echoes the Old Shepherd's insistence on extending hospitality beyond the boundaries of the natural or naturalised community. It contrasts with the 'closed' version of pastoral imagined by Polixenes in Act I in which, as Hermione indicates, contact with the outside world is viewed as contaminating.

Polixenes's encouragement of diversity is part of a debate of the kind which was widespread in Shakespeare's plays and the Renaissance in general about the relative merits of nature as compared with human art and cultivation. In response to Perdita's argument that the products of grafting wrongly confuse the natural with the artificial, Polixenes comes out in support of cultivation, but on the basis that cultivation is itself part of nature:

> *Polixenes*: Wherefore, gentle maiden,
> Do you neglect them [gillyvors]?
> *Perdita*: For I have heard it said that
> There is an art which in their piedness shares
> With great creating nature.
> *Polixenes*: Say there be,
> Yet nature is made better by no mean
> But nature makes that mean. So over that art
> Which you say adds to nature is an art
> That nature makes. You see, sweet maid, we marry
> A gentler scion to the wildest stock,
> And make conceive a bark of baser kind
> By bud of nobler race. This is an art
> Which does mend nature – change it rather; but
> The art itself is nature.
>
> (IV, iv, 85–97)

If value and significance inhere in nature, if there is meaning in the movement of the wind or the cycle of the seasons, then a human art in touch with nature without being enslaved to it (by cultivating new variants from existing stock) is an art which is sensitive to what already exists, but able, at the same time, to transform or renew it. Applied to the ideas of human nature embedded in the artificial world of pastoral that is at the same time thought to reflect aspects of the natural world, we might say that at the heart of pastoral is an emphasis upon the importance of affective ties, idealised as peace and harmonious love, and represented in Act I in the image of Polixenes and Leontes as 'twinned lambs that did frisk i'th' sun'. The reworked pastoral of Act IV respects the core values of pastoral, but combines them with other, equally naturalised traditions (of hospitality and community), thereby making pastoral available for new graftings. In practice, this means that the exclusive, all-male pastoral of Act I is expanded to include women and strangers.

The aesthetic principles of *The Winter's Tale*, that art should be in some sort of contact with nature and/or human nature, are in striking contrast with those expressed by Theseus in *A Midsummer Night's Dream*:

> The lunatic, the lover, and the poet
> Are of imagination all compact.
> One sees more devils than vast hell can hold:
> That is the madman. The lover, all as frantic,
> Sees Helen's beauty in a brow of Egypt.
> The poet's eye, in a fine frenzy rolling,
> Doth glance from heaven to earth, from earth to heaven,
> And as imagination bodies forth
> The forms of things unknown, the poet's pen
> Turns them to shapes, and gives to airy nothing
> A local habitation and a name.
> Such tricks hath strong imagination
> That if it would but apprehend some joy
> It comprehends some bringer of that joy;
> Or in the night, imagining some fear,
> How easy is a bush supposed a bear![26]

The poet is figured here as a visionary, whose proto-Romantic imagination is not confined by what already exists, but who instead makes incredible things seem credible. The something out of nothing which the poet creates is seen by Theseus as both awe-inspiringly miraculous and dangerously ungrounded.[27] While there is obviously something of 'the impossible' (or the possibility of the impossible) at work in *The Winter's Tale*, the aesthetic which it implies is at the same time more grounded because more ostensibly mimetic of nature and human nature. If the impossible is to occur, then it will be based on aspects of human beings which already exist, albeit in subdued or compromised form.

The climax of the play – the resurrection of Hermione – continues with the themes of art and ('pastoralised') nature. What we and the onstage audience are led to believe is Hermione's statue is admired for a lifelikeness that according to the 'Third Gentleman' appropriates the role of nature:

> The Princess, hearing of her mother's statue, which is in the keeping of Paulina, a piece many years in doing, and now newly performed by that rare Italian master Giulio Romano, who, had he himself eternity and could put breath into his work, would beguile nature of her custom, so perfectly he is her ape. He so near to Hermione hath done Hermione that they say one would speak to her and stand in hope of answer. (V, ii, 93–101)

This is an art which is not only faithful to nature, albeit mainly through its technical skill, but an art which threatens to take the place of nature. It is an example, it appears, not just of an art which 'does mend nature', to use Polixenes's phrase, but one which, as Perdita fears, usurps it. This partly mirrors the paradox of pastoral itself, as an art form rooted in nature but one which is so clearly the product of art that there seems to be nothing whatsoever natural about it. However, if art is in danger of displacing nature (either by being too lifelike or too artful), then nature exerts a humbling influence upon the ingenuity of human art when it is discovered that Hermione is actually alive, thanks to 'great creating nature' in conjunction with nature's artistic midwife, Paulina. Nature, including human nature, destroys, but in its hopeful spring guise it restores and renews. Love kills, but it can also bring life. Such is the hope, at any rate, coursing through the play's interpenetrating streams of art and nature.[28]

Paulina, the figure who presides over proceedings at the end, is the catalyst for hope throughout the play. She is the character who breaks the cycle of rejecting others and instead initiates contact with them, even when they seem literally or metaphorically dead and therefore beyond hope of contact. In the context of the emphasis of Chapters 7 and 8 upon the role of women as sages who offer answers to the literary humanist question of how to live, she is a figure who preaches hope where others have abandoned it in their descent into winter archetypes. As in *As You Like It* and *Love's Labour's Lost*, the empowerment of women as sages constitutes a 'holiday' inversion of normal gender roles. In 'Carnival and the Sacred' (1998), Anthony Gash sees Paulina as a carnivalesque figure who is 'related to a long tradition of unruly theatrical women, acted by men, like Lysistrata, Noah's wife and Maid Marion, and to folk-customs which allowed women temporary rule'.[29] The nature of Paulina's rule changes. At first she channels all her energy into humiliating Leontes and castigating him for his tyrannical behaviour. She in other words treats Leontes as Leontes has treated Hermione, as a loathed, unworthy object, with whom there can be no redemptive contact:

> But O thou tyrant,
> Do not repent these things, for they are heavier
> Than all thy woes can stir. Therefore betake thee
> To nothing but despair. A thousand knees,
> Ten thousand years together, naked, fasting,
> Upon a barren mountain, and still winter
> In storm perpetual, could not move the gods
> To look that way thou wert.
> (III, ii, 206–13)

But Paulina, in partial response to the rebuke made by one of Leontes's lords that 'you have made fault / I'th' boldness of your speech' (III, ii, 216–17), then begins to undo the one-way channelling of aggression towards others who have in psychoanalytic terms either failed to meet the infantile desire for total communion (such as Hermione in the eyes of Leontes) or broken the compensatory bonds of friendship and marriage (as has Leontes). Paulina instead seems to promote self-criticism and to turn aggression in upon herself:

> All faults I make, when I shall come to know them
> I do repent. Alas, I have showed too much
> The rashness of a woman. He is touched
> To th' noble heart. What's gone and what's past help
> Should be past grief.
> (*To Leontes*) Do not receive affliction
> At my petition. I beseech you, rather
> Let me be punished, that have minded you
> Of what you should forget. Now, good my liege,
> Sir, royal sir, forgive a foolish woman.
> The love I bore our queen – lo, fool again!
> I'll speak of her no more, nor of your children.
> I'll not remember you of my own lord,
> Who is lost too. Take your patience to you,
> And I'll say nothing.
> (III, ii, 219–31)

This is ambiguous, as the speech of wise fools often is. Paulina rebukes herself for her rashness and her folly only to persist in them, by putting Leontes in mind of people in the very act of promising to forget them: 'I'll not remember you of . . .'. Paulina is not so saintly as to be easily forgiving of Leontes. But neither is she so resentful and lacerating as to preclude various 'hopeful' scenarios: that Leontes might follow her lead and become more self-critical; that forgiveness, though difficult, is not impossible; that a deeper level of self is indeed 'touched' within Leontes that goes beyond 'love-turned-to-hate', as Belsey puts it, to find hate-(re)turned-to-love.[30] This last possibility is only a hopeful possibility, but it is nevertheless grounded, as is Belsey's invocation of love-turned-to-hate, on an account of the human psyche based on our emotional constitution. That it is hopeful perhaps tips the balance in its favour, as hope is also part of that constitution. Without hope, life would be one long winter's tale.

Conclusion

We might live in the way described by Gonzalo in *The Tempest* (1610–11):

> no kind of traffic
> Would I admit, no name of magistrate;
> Letters should not be known; riches, poverty,
> And use of service, none; contract, succession,
> Bourn, bound of land, tilth, vineyard, none;
> No use of metal, corn, or wine, or oil;
> No occupation, all men idle, all;
> And women too – but innocent and pure;
> No sovereignty.[1]

Gonzalo's utopian vision is interrupted by the sceptics, Sebastian and Antonio, but that does not deter him:

> All things in common nature should produce
> Without sweat or endeavour. Treason, felony,
> Sword, pike, knife, gun, or need of any engine,
> Would I not have; but nature should bring forth
> Of it own kind all foison, abundance,
> To feed my innocent people.
> (II, i, 165–70)

I, too, feel the need to interrupt Gonzalo, but not just to puncture his idealism. Hope, to continue the previous chapter's theme, prompts engagement with his utopia to the extent of wondering how his vision might have some sort of practical application or embodiment, to recall the term I have been using to describe one of the features of literary humanism. The natural conclusion to the argument of previous chapters is that we might use literary texts, not only – as sceptics – to interrogate their and our own literary, cultural and historical contexts, and the meanings, values and ideologies that people have lived by, but also – as 'literary humanists' – to talk about the question of how life might be.

I want to end, therefore, not by re-describing the book's intellectual context (its argument with dominant conceptions of humanism, its understanding of modernity, its relation to Shakespeare studies, and to literary criticism and theory in general), but, in the simultaneously idealistic and practical spirit of literary humanism, with a thumbnail sketch, adapted from Gonzalo, of what life might be like.

Gonzalo's Vision Re-visioned

Although we might all benefit from the idleness recommended by Gonzalo – or at least from the kind of 'work', belittlingly referred to as hobbies, which does not feel like work because we derive pleasure from it – it might be difficult, as Thomas More's *Utopia* (1516) indicates, to avoid 'sweat' altogether.[2] Imagine, though, if the use of advanced technology enabled us to perspire lightly for just three and a half days of the week to produce for everyone the essential necessities of life (food, clothing, shelter, basic education, medical care), and the remaining three and a half days were ours to fill according to our diverse other needs, wants, capabilities and temperaments. Gonzalo's idleness might be one option, but not by any means the only one: the 'superfluous' items banned by Gonzalo, such as oil and wine, would be independently or collaboratively produced and bartered, while other, non-material goods, such as 'letters' (education), also deemed superfluous by Gonzalo, would be acquired through voluntary educational associations. For half the week, in other words, we would be absolutely communal, and for the other half, absolutely individualistic, free to cultivate our individual selves and join, form or withdraw from any group activity we chose.

This book has been about the first three and a half days of the week, the communal half, the half in which we live out what it means to share a common humanity, rooted in the basic principle of egalitarianism. Shakespeare gives us strong images of such a common humanity, both in the plays discussed in previous chapters and in those not discussed, such as Gonzalo's utopian vision in *The Tempest*, as well as Lear's famous epiphany on the heath: 'See how yon justice rails upon yon simple thief. Hark in thine ear: change places, and handy-dandy, which is the justice, which is the thief?'[3] As the example of Gonzalo demonstrates, however, these images are not protected against irony, scepticism or other, countervailing images of humanity. Lear may emerge as an egalitarian, but he started out as a narcissist. For every Gonzalo, there is an Iago. Or, to cast individualism in a more positive light, for every Orlando, stuck in the rut of (Petrarchan) convention, there is a Rosalind, who makes him see her difference from his version of her, even as she pushes him towards romantic comedy's egalitarian conclusion that all everyone needs is (the right kind of) love.

It may be that the egalitarian concept of a common humanity, in which women and men are bound together by their recognition of similar emotional needs, is not enough to withstand the pressures and/or pleasures of individuality, diversity, cultural difference and the tendency (also evident in romantic comedy) for people to be explicably or inexplicably drawn to some more than others. This is why only three and a half days a week would be devoted to communal time, time in which we recognise our shared humanity and cooperate accordingly.

Notes

Introduction

1. Philip Yancey, *What's So Amazing about Grace*? (Grand Rapids, MI: Zondervan, 1997), p. 88.
2. Margreta de Grazia, 'The Ideology of Superfluous Things: King Lear as Period Piece', in *Subject and Object in Renaissance Culture*, ed. Margreta de Grazia, Maureen Quilligan and Peter Stallybrass (Cambridge: Cambridge University Press, 1996), p. 19.
3. Simon Barker, 'Introduction', in *New Casebooks: Shakespeare's Problem Plays*, ed. Simon Barker (Basingstoke: Palgrave, 2005), p. 9.
4. Terry Eagleton, *After Theory* (London: Allen Lane, 2003), p. 184.
5. Robert N. Watson, 'Teaching "Shakespeare": Theory versus Practice', in *Teaching Literature: What is Needed Now*, ed. James Engell and David Perkins (Cambridge, MA: Harvard University Press, 1988), p. 123.
6. Ibid., p. 126.
7. Ibid., pp. 124, 121.
8. Timothy Clark describes this division in specifically class terms. 'For most of the twentieth century', he writes, 'literary studies bore the marks of its institutionalisation as part of the nineteenth-century struggle for dominance between two factions of the bourgeoisie – the managerial/technical/utilitarian, and the liberal/humanist. The concept of literature as imaginative writing, a site of humane values and of the creative as a self-evident good, was forged in this struggle': Timothy Clark, 'Literary Force, Institutional Values', in *The Question of Literature*, ed. Elizabeth Beaumont Bissell (Manchester: Manchester University Press, 2002), p. 96.
9. Terry Eagleton, *The Function of Criticism* (London: Verso, 1984), p. 18.
10. Gerald Graff, *Professing Literature* (Chicago: University of Chicago Press, 1987), pp. 3–4.
11. Chris Baldick, *Criticism and Literary Theory: 1890 to the Present* (London: Longman, 1996), p. 15.
12. Ibid., p. 18.
13. Ibid., p. 17.
14. For other histories of literary studies, see John Guillory, 'Literary Study and the Modern System of the Disciplines', in *Disciplinarity at the Fin*

de Siècle, ed. Amanda Anderson and Joseph Valente (Princeton: Princeton University Press, 2002), pp. 19–43; John Guillory, *Cultural Capital* (Chicago: University of Chicago Press, 1993); Brian Doyle, *English and Englishness* (London: Routledge, 1989); Gauri Viswanathan, *Masks of Conquest: Literary Study and British Rule in India* (London: Faber and Faber, [1989] 1990); Ian Hunter, *Culture and Government: The Emergence of Literary Education* (Basingstoke: Macmillan, 1988); Richard Ohmann, *Politics of Letters* (Middletown, CT: Wesleyan University Press, 1987); Michael Warner, 'Professionalization and the Rewards of Literature', *Criticism*, 26 (1985), 1–28; Chris Baldick, *The Social Mission of English Criticism* (Oxford: Clarendon, 1983); Francis Mulhern, *The Moment of 'Scrutiny'* (London: New Left, 1979); John Gross, *The Rise and Fall of the Man of Letters* (London: Weidenfeld and Nicolson, 1969); D. J. Palmer, *The Rise of English Studies* (London: Oxford University Press, 1965). Hunter and Viswanathan are referred to further on in my Introduction. Viswanathan examines some of the issues surrounding the writing of the history of literary studies in 'Subjecting English and the Question of Representation', in *Disciplinarity at the Fin de Siècle*, ed. Anderson and Valente, pp. 177–95. For a history of Shakespearean criticism in the twentieth century, linked to literary critical and broader social and ideological trends, see Hugh Grady, *The Modernist Shakespeare* (Oxford: Clarendon, 1991).

15. See Jean-François Lyotard, *The Postmodern Condition*, trans. Geoffrey Bennington and Brian Massumi (Manchester: Manchester University Press, [1979] 1984).
16. See Max Weber, *General Economic History*, trans. Frank H. Knight (London: George Allen and Unwin, 1927), especially chapter 30, 'Evolution of the Capitalistic Spirit', pp. 352–69; Theodor Adorno and Max Horkheimer, *Dialectic of Enlightenment*, trans. John Cumming (London: Verso, [1944] 1979), pp. 3–42. Habermas and Taylor are discussed further on in my Introduction. For a recent discussion of Adorno and Horkheimer's concept of disenchantment, see Patrice Haynes, ' "To Rescue Means to Love Things": Adorno and the Re-enchantment of Bodies', *Critical Quarterly*, 47 (2005), 64–78, 65–7.
17. Charles Taylor, *Sources of the Self* (Cambridge: Cambridge University Press, 1989), p. 175.
18. John Joughin, 'Philosophical Shakespeares: An Introduction', in *Philosophical Shakespeares*, ed. John Joughin (London: Routledge, 2000), p. 15.
19. Horkheimer and Adorno, *Dialectic of Enlightenment*, p. 19.
20. Ewan Fernie, *Shame in Shakespeare* (London: Routledge, 2002), pp. 1, 21.
21. Paul Hamilton, *Historicism* (London: Routledge, 1996), p. 41.
22. Valentine Cunningham, *Reading after Theory* (Oxford: Blackwell, 2002), p. 147.
23. Robert Eaglestone, 'Critical Knowledge, Scientific Knowledge and the Truth of Literature', in *The New Aestheticism*, ed. John Joughin (Manchester: Manchester University Press, 2003), p. 156.

24. Robert Matz, *Defending Literature in Early Modern England* (Cambridge: Cambridge University Press, 2000), p. 133.
25. Thomas Docherty, 'Aesthetic Education and the Demise of Experience', in *The New Aestheticism*, ed. Joughin, p. 26.
26. Ibid., p. 27.
27. Michael D. Bristol, 'How Many Children Did She Have?', in *Philosophical Shakespeares*, ed. Joughin, p. 30.
28. For further discussion of postmodernism's universalisation of anti-universalism, see Jane Dowson and Steve Earnshaw, 'Preface', in *Postmodern Subjects: Postmodern Texts* (Amsterdam: Rodopi, 1995), p. 7, and, in the same volume, Kate Fullbrook, 'Whose Postmodernism', pp. 71–87, especially p. 76.
29. Matthew Arnold, *Essays in Criticism: First and Second Series* (London: Dent, 1964), p. 302.
30. Classical philosophy was, according to Michel Foucault, 'the art of existence': Michel Foucault, *The Care of the Self*, vol. 3 of *The History of Sexuality*, trans. Robert Hurley (New York: Pantheon, [1986] 1984), p. 44. See also Alexander Nehamas, *The Art of Living: Socratic Reflections from Plato to Foucault* (Berkeley: University of California Press, 2000).
31. Philip Sidney, *A Defence of Poetry*, ed. Jan Van Dorsten (Oxford: Oxford University Press, [1595] 1966), p. 32.
32. F. R. Leavis, *Education and the University*, 2nd edn (Cambridge: Cambridge University Press, [1943] 1979), p. 76.
33. Ibid., p. 77.
34. Theodor Adorno, *Minima Moralia*, trans. E. F. N. Jephcott (London: Verso, [1951] 1974), p. 18. See also 'Always speak of it, never think of it', pp. 65–6.
35. Terry Eagleton, *Criticism and Ideology* (London: Verso, [1976] 1978), p. 147.
36. Ibid., p. 102.
37. Lars Engle, '*Measure for Measure* and Modernity: The Problem of the Sceptic's Authority', in *Shakespeare and Modernity*, ed. Hugh Grady (London: Routledge, 2000), p. 85.
38. Jane Adamson, 'Against Tidiness: Literature and/versus Moral Philosophy', in *Renegotiating Ethics in Literature, Philosophy, and Theory*, ed. Jane Adamson, Richard Freadman and David Parker (Cambridge: Cambridge University Press, 1998), p. 87.
39. Eagleton, *Criticism and Ideology*, p. 101.
40. Leavis, *Education and the University*, p. 75.
41. The same is true of the following sentence of Engle's, in which Shakespeare's 'taste for embeddedness' might be taken as referring to the density of Shakespeare's depiction of either social context or human existence: 'Shakespeare embeds general ideas in their particular enactments with such complexity that his taste for embeddedness itself might be seen as an implicit critique of methodical philosophy and pure science, a critique which arises just before those discourses get started': Engle, '*Measure for Measure* and Modernity', in *Shakespeare and Modernity*, ed. Grady, p. 85.

42. Stephen Toulmin, *Cosmopolis: The Hidden Agenda of Modernity* (Chicago: University of Chicago Press, 1990), p. 26.
43. Ibid., pp. 26–7.
44. Shakespeare, *Hamlet*, in *The Oxford Shakespeare*, 2nd edn, ed. Stanley Wells et al. (Oxford: Clarendon, [1986] 2005), V, ii, 10. All subsequent references in the text are to this edition.
45. Kent Cartwright, *Theatre and Humanism: English Drama in the Sixteenth Century* (Cambridge: Cambridge University Press, 1999), p. 19.
46. Paul Tillich, 'Existential Philosophy', *Journal of the History of Ideas*, 5 (1994), 44–70, 68.
47. Theodor Adorno, *The Jargon of Authenticity*, trans. Knut Tarnowski and Frederic Will (Evanston: Northwestern University Press, [1964] 1973).
48. Andrew Hadfield, Dominic Rainsford and Tim Woods, 'Introduction: Literature and the Return to Ethics', in *The Ethics in Literature*, ed. Andrew Hadfield, Dominic Rainsford and Tim Woods (Basingstoke: Macmillan, 1999), p. 5.
49. Although Adorno inevitably complicates this conception of the work of art, he still sees art as a form of resistance to 'the bidding of the alienated world': Theodor Adorno, 'Reconciliation under Duress' [1961], in *Aesthetics and Politics*, ed. Ernst Bloch et al. (London: Verso, [1977] 1980), p. 160. For a less ramified promotion of literature's utopian possibilities, see Kiernan Ryan, *Shakespeare*, 3rd edn (Basingstoke: Palgrave, [1989] 2002).
50. Robin Headlam Wells, *Shakespeare's Humanism* (Cambridge: Cambridge University Press, 2005), p. ix.
51. Harold Bloom, *Shakespeare: The Invention of the Human* (London: Fourth Estate, [1998] 1999), p. 734. For further discussion of Bloom's book, see *Harold Bloom's Shakespeare*, ed. Christy Desmet and Robert Sawyer (New York: Palgrave, 2001).
52. A. C. Bradley, *Shakespearean Tragedy*, 3rd edn (Basingstoke: Macmillan, [1904] 1992), p. 16.
53. G. Wilson Knight, *The Wheel of Fire* (London: Oxford University Press, 1930); *The Crown of Life* (London: Methuen, [1947] 1948).
54. Harold C. Goddard, *The Meaning of Shakespeare*, vol. 2 (Chicago: University of Chicago Press, [1951] 1960), p. 136.
55. L. C. Knights, 'Historical Scholarship and the Interpretation of Shakespeare' (1955), in his *'Hamlet' and Other Shakespearean Essays* (Cambridge: Cambridge University Press, 1979), p. 236. Another notable example of Shakespeare criticism within this humanist mould is A. P. Rossiter, *Angel with Horns*, ed. Graham Storey (London: Longman, [1961] 1989).
56. Catherine Belsey, *Critical Practice* (London: Methuen, 1980), p. 7.
57. Iain Chambers, *Culture after Humanism* (London: Routledge, 2001), pp. 2–3.
58. Several recent publications, including issues of journals entirely devoted to the topic of humanism, illustrate the variety of humanist traditions. See, as examples: *Diogenes*, 52, Emerging Humanisms (2005); Martin Halliwell and Andy Mousley, *Critical Humanisms: Humanist/Anti-Humanist Dialogues* (Edinburgh: Edinburgh University Press,

2003); *Comparative Criticism*, 23, Humanist Traditions in the Twentieth Century (2001); *The Question of Humanism*, ed. David Goicoechea, John Luik and Tim Madigan (Buffalo, NY: Prometheus, 1991). The diversification of humanism has also brought with it examination of non-western humanist traditions, thereby challenging the common assumption that humanism is an exclusively occidental phenomenon. See, for example: Lenn E. Goodman, *Islamic Humanism* (Oxford: Oxford University Press, 2003); D. M. Praharaj, *Humanism in Contemporary Indian Philosophical Perspectives* (Meerut: Anu, 1995); Mohammed Arkoun, 'From Islamic Humanism to the Ideology of Liberation', in *Humanism toward the Third Millennium*, ed. Fons Elders (Amsterdam: VUB Press, 1993), pp. 13–21.

59. Geoffrey Galt Harpham makes a similar point, arguing that 'the prevailing feeling among advanced theorists has been that the very notions of human being, human nature, and human voice – not to mention the individual human subject – are nothing more than ideologically generated mystifications': Geoffrey Galt Harpham, 'Beneath and Beyond the "Crisis in the Humanities" ', *New Literary History*, 36 (2005), 21–36, 27.
60. Jonathan Dollimore, *Radical Tragedy*, 3rd edn (Basingstoke: Palgrave, [1984] 2004), p. 250.
61. 'Man is nothing else but that which he makes of himself': Jean-Paul Sartre, *Existentialism and Humanism*, trans. Philip Mairet (London: Methuen, [1946] 1948), p. 28.
62. Quoted in Tzvetan Todorov, *On Human Diversity*, trans. Catherine Porter (Cambridge, MA: Harvard University Press, 1993), pp. 66–7.
63. Jacob Burckhardt, *The Civilization of the Renaissance in Italy*, trans. S. G. C. Middlemore (London: Phaidon, [1860] 1950), p. 81.
64. For discussion of the tendency to homogenise (Renaissance) individualism and the need to counteract this by supplying different descriptions of it, see Hugh Grady, 'On the Need for a Differentiated Theory of (Early) Modern Subjects', in *Philosophical Shakespeares*, ed. Joughin, pp. 34–50; Andrew Mousley, 'Hamlet and the Politics of Individualism', in *New Essays on Hamlet*, ed. Mark Thornton Burnett and John Manning (New York: AMS, 1994), pp. 67–82.
65. Catherine Belsey, *The Subject of Tragedy* (London: Methuen, 1985), p. 48.
66. Ronald Knowles, '*Hamlet* and Counter-Humanism', *Renaissance Quarterly*, 52 (1999), 1046–69, 1066.
67. Ibid., 1048.
68. Philip Sidney, *A Defence of Poetry*, p. 25.
69. Thomas Wilson, 'The Preface', *The Arte of Rhetorique, 1553. And Now Newly Set forth Againe, with a Prologue to the Reader, 1567* (London: George Robinson, 1585).
70. Ibid., p. 75.
71. Andrew Hadfield, *The English Renaissance, 1500–1620* (Oxford: Blackwell, 2001), p. 239.
72. Pico della Mirandola, *On the Dignity of Man and Other Works*, trans. Charles Glenn Wallis, Paul J. W. Miller and Douglas Carmichael (Indianapolis: Bobbs-Merrill Educational, 1965), pp. 4–5.

73. For a full-length discussion of the critical reception of Pico's work, see William G. Craven, *Giovanni Pico della Mirandola: Symbol of His Age* (Genève: Droz, 1981).
74. Dollimore, *Radical Tragedy*, p. 155.
75. Ibid., p. 179.
76. Headlam Wells, *Shakespeare's Humanism*, p. 96.
77. James Hankins divides interpreters of Renaissance humanism into 'lumpers and splitters', lumpers being those (like Eugenio Garin) who 'stress genetic *connections* between the literary and moral reform movement of the Renaissance and the philosophical humanism of the moderns', and splitters being critics (such as Paul O. Kristeller) who insist in the name of historical specificity on '*discontinuities* between the two humanisms': James Hankins, 'Two Twentieth-Century Interpreters of Renaissance Humanism: Eugenio Garin and Paul Oskar Kristeller', *Comparative Criticism*, 23 (2001), 3–19, 5.
78. Paul O. Kristeller and John Herman Randall Jr, 'General Introduction', in *The Renaissance Philosophy of Man*, ed. Ernst Cassirer, Paul O. Kristeller and John Herman Randall Jr (Chicago: University of Chicago Press, 1948), pp. 2–3.
79. Isabel Rivers, *Classical and Christian Ideas in English Renaissance Poetry* (London: George Allen and Unwin, 1979), p. 132.
80. Tony Davies, *Humanism* (London: Routledge, 1997), pp. 98–9. Davies wrongly attributes the introduction to *The Renaissance Philosophy of Man* to Cassirer, Kristeller and Randall (Kristeller and Randall wrote the introduction, while all three edited it).
81. Debora Keller Shuger argues that 'the sacramental/analogical character of premodern thought tends to deny rigid boundaries; nothing is simply itself, but things are signs of other things and one thing may be inside another': Debora Keller Shuger, *Habits of Thought in the English Renaissance* (Berkeley: University of California Press, 1990), p. 11.
82. Desiderius Erasmus, *Praise of Folly and Letter to Martin Dorp*, trans. Betty Radice (Harmondsworth: Penguin, [1509 and 1515] 1971), pp. 241–52. For an interesting discussion of Renaissance humanists' critical philology and its contribution to western pragmatism, see Jerry H. Bentley, 'Renaissance Culture and Western Pragmatism', in *Humanity and Divinity in Renaissance and Reformation*, ed. John W. O'Malley, Thomas M. Izbicki and Gerald Christianson (Leiden: E. J. Brill, 1993), pp. 35–52.
83. Erasmus, *Praise of Folly*, p. 156.
84. Martin Andic, 'What is Renaissance Humanism?', in *The Question of Humanism*, ed. Goicoechea et al., p. 92.
85. Mikhail Bakhtin, *Rabelais and His World*, trans. Hélène Iswolsky (Bloomington, IN: Indiana University Press, 1984), p. 364.
86. Rivers, *Classical and Christian Ideas*, p. 132.
87. For further discussions of Renaissance humanism which collectively and often individually show how Renaissance humanism has become almost as diversified a historical phenomenon as humanism in general, see *Reassessing Tudor Humanism*, ed. Jonathan Woolfson (Basingstoke: Palgrave, 2002); Mike Pincombe, *Elizabethan Humanism* (London: Longman, 2001); *Renaissance Civic Humanism: Reappraisals and*

Reflections, ed. James Hankins (Cambridge: Cambridge University Press 2000); *Humanism and Early Modern Philosophy*, ed. Jill Kraye and M. W. F. Stone (London: Routledge, 2000); Cartwright, *Theatre and Humanism*; Markku Peltonen, *Classical Humanism and Republicanism in English Political Thought* (Cambridge: Cambridge University Press, 1995); Rebecca W. Bushnell, *A Culture of Teaching: Early Modern Humanism in Theory and Practice* (Ithaca: Cornell University Press, 1996); *The Cambridge Companion to Renaissance Humanism*, ed. Jill Kraye (Cambridge: Cambridge University Press, 1996); William Bouwsma, 'Two Faces of Humanism: Stoicism and Augustinianism in Renaissance Thought' [1975], in his *A Usable Past* (Berkeley: University of California Press, 1990), pp. 19–73; *Renaissance Humanism: Foundations, Forms and Legacy*, 3 vols, ed. Albert Rabil Jr (Philadelphia: University of Pennsylvania Press, 1988).

88. See Graham Bradshaw, *Shakespeare's Scepticism* (Brighton: Harvester, 1987), and Stanley Cavell, *Disowning Knowledge in Six Plays of Shakespeare* (New York: Cambridge University Press, 1987). For related discussions, see Bentley, 'Renaissance Culture and Western Pragmatism', and Lars Engle, *Shakespearean Pragmatism: Market of his Time* (Chicago: Chicago University Press, 1993). For a discussion of scepticism in the context of Renaissance tragedy and the Renaissance in general, see William M. Hamlin, *Tragedy and Scepticism in Shakespeare's England* (Basingstoke: Palgrave, 2005).
89. Toulmin, *Cosmopolis*, p. 28.
90. Ibid., p. 30.
91. Lars Engle, '*Measure for Measure* and Modernity', p. 85.
92. Ibid., p. 86.
93. Ibid., p. 86.
94. Hunter, *Culture and Government*, p. 7. See also Ian Hunter, 'Aesthetics and Cultural Studies', in *Cultural Studies*, ed. Lawrence Grossberg, Cary Nelson and Paula A. Treichler (New York: Routledge, 1992), pp. 347–72.
95. Hunter, *Culture and Government*, p. 286.
96. Viswanathan, *Masks of Conquest*, p. 18.
97. For a discussion of the various ways in which modernity has been understood and their relevance to Shakespeare, see Grady, 'Introduction: Shakespeare and Modernity', in *Shakespeare and Modernity*, ed. Grady, pp. 1–19. Theodore B. Leinwand identifies those aspects of the transition to modernity commonly associated with the Renaissance as 'status to contract . . . sacred to secular, ascription to achievement, finite to open, fixed to contingent, use to exchange, bounty to profit, feudal to (nascent) capitalist': Theodore B. Leinwand, *Theatre, Finance and Society in Early Modern England* (Cambridge: Cambridge University Press, 1999), p. 1.
98. 'The disenchantment of the world is the extirpation of animism': Adorno and Horkheimer, *Dialectic of Enlightenment*, p. 5.
99. Roger Rosenblatt, 'The Age of Irony Comes to an End', *Time* (24 September 2001). Accessed at www.time.com/time/magazine.
100. Samuel Taylor Coleridge, *Biographia Literaria*, in *The Oxford Authors: Samuel Taylor Coleridge*, ed. H. J. Jackson (Oxford: Oxford University Press, 1985), p. 320.

101. Cavell, *Disowning Knowledge*, p. 3.
102. Karl Marx and Friedrich Engels, *The Communist Manifesto*, trans. Samuel Moore (Harmondsworth: Penguin, [1848] 1967), p. 83.
103. Hugh Grady, *Shakespeare's Universal Wolf* (Oxford: Clarendon, 1996), p. 185.
104. Jürgen Habermas, *The Philosophical Discourse of Modernity*, trans. Frederick Lawrence (Cambridge: Polity, [1985] 1987), p. 315.
105. Ibid., p. 315.
106. Jürgen Habermas, *The Theory of Communicative Action*, vol. 1, trans. Thomas McCarthy (Cambridge: Polity, [1981] 1984), p. 340.
107. Ibid., p. 287.
108. Ibid., p. 286.
109. Jürgen Habermas, *The Theory of Communicative Action*, vol. 2, trans. Thomas McCarthy (Cambridge: Polity, [1981] 1987), p. 305.
110. For a differently angled discussion of Habermas in connection with the concept of a seventeenth-century public sphere, see John Staines, 'Compassion in the Public Sphere of Milton and King Charles', in *Reading the Early Modern Passions*, ed. Gail Kern Paster, Katherine Rowe and Mary Floyd-Wilson (Philadelphia: University of Pennsylvania Press, 2004), pp. 92–7.
111. Thomas Wright, *The Passions of the Minde* (London: V.S. for W.B., 1601), p. 104.
112. As G. K. Hunter suggests, the dependence of truth and knowledge upon 'the rhetorical technique' of 'argumentum in utramque partem' was common to both Renaissance drama and rhetoric: G. K. Hunter, 'Rhetoric and Renaissance Drama', in *Renaissance Rhetoric*, ed. Peter Mack (Basingstoke: Macmillan, 1994), p. 112. For further discussion of Renaissance humanism and rhetoric, see Peter Mack, 'Humanist Rhetoric and Dialectic', in *The Cambridge Companion to Renaissance Humanism*, ed. Kraye, pp. 82–99; John Monfasani, 'Humanism and Rhetoric', in *Renaissance Humanism*, ed. Rabil, vol. 3, pp. 171–235.
113. Toulmin, *Cosmopolis*, p. 29.
114. Wilson, *Arte of Rhetorique*, p. B.ii.
115. Taylor, *Sources of the Self*, p. 175.
116. Stephen Greenblatt, *Renaissance Self-Fashioning* (Chicago: University of Chicago Press, 1980), p. 162.

Chapter 1 Questioning the Human: *Hamlet*

1. Dates of plays follow the dates given in *The Oxford Shakespeare*, 2nd edn, ed. Stanley Wells et al. (Oxford: Clarendon, [1986] 2005).
2. Shakespeare, *Hamlet*, ibid., IV, v, 175–84. All subsequent references in the text are to this edition.
3. Jürgen Habermas, *The Theory of Communicative Action*, vol. 1, trans. Thomas McCarthy (Cambridge: Polity, [1981] 1984), p. 47.
4. The words 'nature' and 'natural' have a range of meanings and associations in the sixteenth and seventeenth centuries, and the *Oxford English*

Dictionary implicates Shakespeare in a number of these. For further discussion of concepts of nature in Shakespeare, see Gabriel Egan, *Green Shakespeare* (London: Routledge, 2006); Graham Bradshaw, *Shakespeare's Scepticism* (Brighton: Harvester, 1987); John F. Danby, *Shakespeare's Doctrine of Nature: A Study of King Lear* (London: Faber and Faber, 1949).

5. Richard van Oort, 'Shakespeare and the Idea of the Modern', *New Literary History*, 37 (2006), 319–39, 325.
6. Edward Berry considers the universality of rites of transition in *Shakespeare's Comic Rites* (Cambridge: Cambridge University Press, 1984), pp. 1–5. He also discusses the role of ritual in Elizabethan society, pp. 22–32.
7. C. L. Barber, *Shakespeare's Festive Comedy* (Princeton: Princeton University Press, 1959), p. 8. Naomi Conn Liebler offers a contrasting perspective on the function of ritual in Shakespearean tragedy. 'What is clarified', she writes, 'is not, as Barber thought, the "relation between man and nature" but that between human beings and their own creations, the values that inform and sustain a civilization': Naomi Conn Liebler, *Shakespeare's Festive Tragedy* (London: Routledge, 1995), p. 8.
8. Stephen Greenblatt, *Will in the World* (London: Pimlico, 2005), p. 320.
9. Ibid., pp. 320–1.
10. Ibid., p. 320.
11. Ronald Knowles, '*Hamlet* and Counter-Humanism', *Renaissance Quarterly*, 52 (1999), 1046–69, 1061.
12. For discussion of revenge/revenge tragedy in *Hamlet* and/or the Renaissance more generally, see: Robert N. Watson, 'Tragedies of Revenge and Ambition', in *The Cambridge Companion to Shakespearean Tragedy*, ed. Claire McEachern (Cambridge: Cambridge University Press, 2002), pp. 160–81; *New Casebooks: Revenge Tragedy*, ed. Stevie Simkin (Basingstoke: Palgrave, 2001); John Kerrigan, *Revenge Tragedy* (Oxford: Oxford University Press, 1996), pp. 170–92; Harry Keyishian, *The Shapes of Revenge* (New Jersey: Humanities, 1995); Roland Mushat Frye, *The Renaissance Hamlet* (Princeton: Princeton University Press, 1984), pp. 22–37; Eleanor Prosser, *Hamlet and Revenge*, 2nd edn (Stanford: Stanford University Press, [1967] 1971); Fredson Bowers, *Elizabethan Revenge Tragedy, 1587–1642* (Princeton: Princeton University Press, 1940).
13. Sharon O'Dair, 'On the Value of Being a Cartoon, in Literature and Life', in *Harold Bloom's Shakespeare*, ed. Christy Desmet and Robert Sawyer (New York: Palgrave, 2001), p. 95.
14. On the Protestant associations of Wittenberg, see Shakespeare, *Hamlet*, The Arden Shakespeare, ed. Harold Jenkins (London: Methuen, 1982), p. 436.
15. The quotation is from the King James Bible.
16. Ewan Fernie, *Shame in Shakespeare* (London: Routledge, 2002), p. 121.
17. Charles Taylor, *Sources of the Self* (Cambridge: Cambridge University Press, 1989), p. 186.
18. Amanda Anderson, *The Way We Argue Now* (Princeton: Princeton University Press, 2006), p. 3.
19. F. R. Leavis, *Education and the University*, 2nd edn (Cambridge: Cambridge University Press, [1943] 1979), p. 77.

20. Andrew Hadfield, *The English Renaissance, 1500–1620* (Oxford: Blackwell, 2001), p. 240.
21. William J. Bouwsma, 'The Renaissance Discovery of Human Creativity', in *Humanity and Divinity in Renaissance and Reformation*, ed. John W. O'Malley, Thomas M. Izbicki and Gerald Christianson (Leiden: E. J. Brill, 1993), p. 32.
22. Peter Stallybrass, ' "Well Grubbed, Old Mole": Marx, *Hamlet*, and the (Un)fixing of Representation', in *Marxist Shakespeares*, ed. Jean E. Howard and Scott Cutler Shershow (Routledge: London, 2001), p. 27.

Chapter 2 Emptying the Human: *Othello*

1. Shakespeare, *Othello*, in *The Oxford Shakespeare*, 2nd edn, ed. Stanley Wells et al. (Oxford: Clarendon [1986] 2005), I, iii, 101. All subsequent references in the text are to this edition.
2. Alain Finkielkraut, *In the Name of Humanity: Reflections on the Twentieth Century* (London: Pimlico, [1996] 2001), p. 90.
3. In his introduction to the Arden edition of *Othello*, M. R. Ridley unfortunately promotes Eurocentric humanist stereotypes in the midst of ostensibly dismissing them: 'There are more races than one in Africa, and that a man is black in colour is no reason why he should, even to European eyes, look sub-human. One of the finest heads I have ever seen on any human being was that of a negro conductor on an American Pullman car': *Othello*, The Arden Shakespeare, ed. M. R. Ridley (London: Methuen, 1958), p. li.
4. Shakespeare, *King Lear*, in *The Oxford Shakespeare*, IV, v, 121–2. Both quarto and folio versions of *King Lear* are reproduced in *The Oxford Shakespeare*. I have used the folio text.
5. Jean Baudrillard, *Symbolic Exchange and Death*, trans. Iain Hamilton Grant (London: Sage, [1976] 1993), p. 125.
6. Erica Fudge, Ruth Gilbert and Susan Wiseman, 'Introduction: The Dislocation of the Human', in *At the Borders of the Human: Beasts, Bodies and Natural Philosophy in the Early Modern Period*, ed. Erica Fudge, Ruth Gilbert and Susan Wiseman (Basingstoke: Macmillan, 1999), p. 2.
7. Ibid., p. 1.
8. Ibid., p. 2.
9. Ania Loomba, 'Outsiders in Shakespeare's England', in *The Cambridge Companion to Shakespeare*, ed. Margreta de Grazia and Stanley Wells (Cambridge: Cambridge University Press, 2001), p. 162.
10. Jonathan Burton, ' "A Most Wily Bird": Leo Africanus, *Othello* and the Trafficking in Difference', in *Post-Colonial Shakespeares*, ed. Ania Loomba and Martin Orkin (Routledge: London, 1998), pp. 59–60. For further discussion of representations of racial difference in *Othello* and the Renaissance more generally, see Ania Loomba, '*Othello* and the Racial Question', in her *Shakespeare, Race, and Colonialism* (Oxford: Oxford University Press, 2002), pp. 91–111; Arthur L. Little, ' "An Essence That's Not Seen": The Primal Scene of Racism in *Othello*', *Shakespeare Quarterly*, 44 (1993), 304–24; Emily C. Bartels, 'Making More of

the Moor: Aaron, Othello, and Renaissance Refashionings of Race', *Shakespeare Quarterly*, 41 (1990), 433–54; Michael Neill, 'Unproper Beds: Race, Adultery, and the Hideous in *Othello*', *Shakespeare Quarterly*, 40 (1989), 379–412; Ania Loomba, *Gender, Race, Renaissance Drama* (Manchester: Manchester University Press, 1989).

11. Loomba and Orkin, 'Introduction: Shakespeare and the Post-Colonial Question', in *Post-Colonial Shakespeares*, ed. Loomba and Orkin, p. 7.
12. Frantz Fanon, *Black Skins, White Masks* (London: Pluto, [1952] 1986), p. 217.
13. Simon Robson, *The Choise of Change* (London: Roger Warde, 1585), title page; Robert Cawdray, *A Treasvrie or Store-Hovse of Similies* (London: Thomas Creede, 1600), title page.
14. Lorna Hutson, *Thomas Nashe in Context* (Oxford: Clarendon, 1989), p. 46.
15. Richard Halpern, *The Poetics of Primitive Accumulation* (Ithaca: Cornell University Press, 1991), p. 49.
16. Ibid., pp. 49–50.
17. These contrasting perspectives on the rhetorical culture of the Renaissance correspond to the distinctions outlined in the Introduction. For further discussion of the Renaissance commonplace tradition and its connection to rhetorical theory and practice, see Ann Moss, *Printed Commonplace-Books and the Structuring of Renaissance Thought* (Oxford: Clarendon, 1996); Mary Thomas Crane, 'Finding a Place: The Humanist Logic of Gathering and Framing', in her *Sayings, Self, and Society in Sixteenth Century England* (Princeton, NJ: Princeton University Press, 1993), pp. 12–38; Joan Marie Lechner, *Renaissance Concepts of the Commonplaces* (New York: Pageant, 1962); Walter J. Ong, *Ramus, Method, and the Decay of Dialogue* (Cambridge, MA: Harvard University Press, 1958).
18. Habermas, *Theory of Communicative Action*, vol. 1, p. 340.
19. For further discussion of Iago as improviser, see Stephen Greenblatt, *Renaissance Self-Fashioning* (Chicago: University of Chicago Press, 1980), pp. 232–7.
20. Richard Strier, 'Against the Rule of Reason: Praise of Passion from Petrarch to Luther to Shakespeare to Herbert', in *Reading the Early Modern Passions*, ed. Gail Kern Paster, Katherine Rowe and Mary Floyd-Wilson (Philadelphia: University of Pennsylvania Press, 2004), p. 23.
21. Ibid., p. 25.
22. Hugh Grady, *Shakespeare's Universal Wolf* (Oxford: Clarendon, 1996), p. 96.
23. 'Let me make clear', Grady writes, 'that my critique of "anti-humanism" implies no defense of the idea of an eternal human nature': ibid., p. 9.
24. For discussion of the 'kinship in ambiguity', as he calls it (p. 35), between such villains as Aaron (in *Titus Andronicus*), Richard III, Don John (in *Much Ado about Nothing*) and Iago, see Bernard Spivack, *Shakespeare and the Allegory of Evil* (New York: Columbia University Press, 1958).
25. Kiernan Ryan, *Shakespeare*, 3rd edn (Basingstoke: Palgrave, [1989] 2002), p. 86.
26. Samuel Taylor Coleridge, *Shakespearean Criticism*, 2nd edn, vol 1, ed. Thomas Middleton Raysor (New York: E. P. Dutton, [1930] 1960), p. 44.

For further discussion of Iago's motivation, along similar lines to my own, see Ewan Fernie, *Shame in Shakespeare* (London: Routledge, 2002), pp. 140–5. See also Spivack, *Shakespeare and the Allegory of Evil*, pp. 7–16.

27. 'Love lyrics', writes Marotti, 'could express figuratively the realities of suit, service and recompense with which ambitious men were insistently concerned as well as the frustrations and disappointments experienced in socially competitive environments': Arthur F. Marotti, ' "Love Is Not Love": Elizabethan Sonnet Sequences and the Social Order', *English Literary History*, 49 (1982), 396–428, 398.
28. Walter Cohen, '*Othello*', in *The Norton Shakespeare*, ed. Stephen Greenblatt et al. (New York: Norton, 1997), p. 2095.
29. Ryan, *Shakespeare*, p. 83.
30. Dominique Janicaud, *On the Human Condition*, trans. Eileen Brennan (London: Routledge, [2002] 2005), p. 22. In her conclusion, Janicaud calls for a '*cautious humanism*, warning against the inhuman or the subhuman, and an *opening up to possible* superhumans (or everything other than the "all too human": disturbing, strange, radically creative) that lie dormant within us. On the one hand, the *defence* of the human against the inhuman, on the other, the *illustration* of what surpasses the human in man': p. 58.

Chapter 3 Ironising the Human: *The Merchant of Venice*

1. Shakespeare, *The Merchant of Venice*, in *The Oxford Shakespeare*, 2nd edn, ed. Stanley Wells et al. (Oxford: Clarendon, [1986] 2005), V, i, 54–65. All subsequent references in the text are to this edition.
2. Lawrence Danson, *The Harmonies of The Merchant of Venice* (New Haven: Yale University Press, 1978), pp. 4–11.
3. For a clear identification of irony as Zeitgeist, see the quotation in my Introduction from Roger Rosenblatt's article in *Time* magazine.
4. Catherine Belsey, 'Love in Venice', *Shakespeare Survey*, 44 (1991), 41–53, 42.
5. 'Ironists', writes Rorty, 'do not take the point of discursive thought to be *knowing*, in any sense that can be explicated by notions like "reality", "real essence", "objective point of view," and "the correspondence of language and reality" ': Richard Rorty, *Contingency, Irony, and Solidarity* (Cambridge: Cambridge University Press, 1989), p. 75.
6. Hélène Cixous et al., 'Conversations with Hélène Cixous and Members of the Centre d'Etudes Féminines', in *Writing Differences: Readings from the Seminar of Hélène Cixous*, ed. Susan Sellers (New York: St. Martin's, 1988), p. 147.
7. Valentine Cunningham, *Reading after Theory* (Oxford: Blackwell, 2002), p. 148.
8. See Desiderius Erasmus, *Praise of Folly and Letter to Martin Dorp*, trans. Betty Radice (Harmondsworth: Penguin, [1509 and 1515] 1971), pp. 188–208, for the account of Christian folly. Self-love is treated on pp. 131–5. Folly's criticisms of scholastic overspecialisation are made on p. 156 (and discussed in my Introduction).

9. C. L. Barber, *Shakespeare's Festive Comedy* (Princeton: Princeton University Press, 1959), p. 187.
10. Ibid., p. 187.
11. Michael Ferber, 'The Ideology of *The Merchant of Venice*', *English Literary Renaissance*, 20 (1990), 431–64, 431.
12. Rorty, *Contingency, Irony, and Solidarity*, p. 73.
13. Ibid., p. 73.
14. Ferber, 'The Ideology of *The Merchant of Venice*', 461, 463.
15. Ibid., 463–4.
16. Ibid., 464.
17. Barber, *Shakespeare's Festive Comedy*, p. 180.
18. Ibid., pp. 188–9.
19. Ibid., p. 189.
20. Ibid., p. 188.
21. *Gemeinschaft* is usually translated as 'community', and *Gesellschaft* as 'society' or 'civil society'. 'Community', writes Tönnies, 'means genuine, enduring life together, whereas Society is a transient and superficial thing. Thus *Gemeinschaft* must be understood as a living organism in its own right, while *Gesellschaft* is a mechanical aggregate and artefact': Ferdinand Tönnies, *Community and Civil Society*, trans. Jose Harris and Margaret Hollis (Cambridge: Cambridge University Press, [1887] 2001), p. 19.
22. Eva Hoffman, *Lost in Translation* (London: Vintage, [1989] 1998), p. 5.
23. Ibid., p. 5.
24. Lauren Berlant, 'Critical Inquiry, Affirmative Culture', *Critical Inquiry*, 30 (2004), 445–51, 448.
25. Alan Sinfield, 'How to Read *The Merchant of Venice* without Being Heterosexist', in *Alternative Shakespeares*, vol. 2, ed. Terence Hawkes (London: Routledge, 1996), p. 136.
26. Barber, *Shakespeare's Festive Comedy*, pp. 166–7.
27. Curtis Perry, 'Commerce, Community, and Nostalgia in *The Comedy of Errors*', in *Money and the Age of Shakespeare: Essays in New Economic Criticism*, ed. Lynda Woodbridge (Basingstoke: Palgrave, 2003), p. 40.
28. Eric Spencer, 'Taking Excess, Exceeding Account: Aristotle Meets *The Merchant of Venice*', in *Money and the Age of Shakespeare*, ed. Woodbridge, p. 150.
29. For discussion of the play's (and period's) representations of Jews, together with the anti-Semitism and/or implied criticism of anti-Semitism in the play, see Ania Loomba, 'Religion, Money, and Race', in her *Shakespeare, Race and Colonialism* (Oxford: Oxford University Press, 2002), pp. 135–60; Peter Berek, 'The Jew as Renaissance Man', *Renaissance Quarterly*, 51 (1998), 128–62; James Shapiro, *Shakespeare and the Jews* (New York: Columbia University Press, 1996); Thomas Moison, ' "Which Is the Merchant Here? and Which the Jew"?: Subversion and Recuperation in *The Merchant of Venice*', in *Shakespeare Reproduced: The Text in History and Ideology*, ed. Jean E. Howard and Marion F. O'Connor (New York: Routledge, 1987), pp. 188–206; Walter Cohen, '*The Merchant of Venice* and the Possibilities of Historical Criticism', *English Literary History*, 49 (1982), 765–89.

30. Barber, *Shakespeare's Festive Comedy*, p. 179.
31. René Girard, *A Theater of Envy: William Shakespeare*, 2nd edn (Leominster: Gracewing, [1991] 2000), p. 249.
32. Ibid., p. 249.
33. Edward Berry, 'Laughing at "Others" ', in *The Cambridge Companion to Shakespearean Comedy*, ed. Alexander Leggatt (Cambridge: Cambridge University Press, 2002), p. 131.
34. Ibid., pp. 137–8.
35. Katharine Eisaman Maus, '*The Merchant of Venice*', in *The Norton Shakespeare*, ed. Stephen Greenblatt et al. (New York: Norton, 1997), pp. 1085–6.
36. Tom McAlindon makes a comparable point in an article on *King Lear*. 'We may believe', he writes, 'that ideas, discourses, socio-economic forces, or power are the primary determinants of what people say and do; but this text [*Lear*] intimates that the clue to thought and action, and ultimately to social change and human history, lies in the heart': Tom McAlindon, 'Tragedy, *King Lear*, and the Politics of the Heart', *Shakespeare Survey*, 44 (1991), 85–90, 88.
37. Hugh Grady, *Shakespeare's Universal Wolf* (Oxford: Clarendon, 1996), p. 19.
38. Richard Halpern, *Shakespeare among the Moderns* (Ithaca: Cornell University Press, 1997), p. 213.
39. Danson, *The Harmonies of The Merchant of Venice*, p. 8.
40. Girard, *A Theater of Envy*, p. 253.

Chapter 4 Historicising the Human, Humanising the Historical: *I Henry IV*

1. Carla Mazzio and Douglas Trevor, 'Dreams of History: An Introduction', in *Historicism, Psychoanalysis and Early Modern Culture*, ed. Carla Mazzio and Douglas Trevor (New York and London: Routledge, 2000), p. 1.
2. For discussion of these various historicisms, see *Presentist Shakespeares*, ed. Hugh Grady and Terence Hawkes (London: Routledge, 2006); *Money and the Age of Shakespeare: Essays in New Economic Criticism*, ed. Lynda Woodbridge (Basingstoke: Palgrave, 2003); Terence Hawkes, *Shakespeare in the Present* (London: Routledge, 2002); *Practicing New Historicism*, ed. Catherine Gallagher and Stephen Greenblatt (Chicago: University of Chicago Press, 2000); *Historicism, Psychoanalysis and Early Modern Culture*, ed. Mazzio and Trevor; James Cunningham, *Shakespeare's Tragedies and Modern Critical Theory* (Madison: Fairleigh Dickinson University Press, 1997), chapters 2 and 3; Lisa Jardine, *Reading Shakespeare Historically* (London: Routledge, 1996); Albert Cook, 'Historiography and/or Historicism: Context and Theoretical (De)-Integration of Renaissance Drama', *Centennial Review*, 40 (1996), 31–47; Kathleen E. McLuskie, ' "Old Mouse-Eaten Records": The Anxiety of History', *English Literary Renaissance*, 25 (1995), 415–31; Katharine E. Maus, 'Renaissance Studies Today', *English Literary Renaissance*, 25 (1995), 402–14; Lisa

Jardine, 'Strains of Renaissance Reading', *English Literary Renaissance*, 25 (1995), 289–306; *The New Historicism*, ed. H. Aram Veeser (New York: Routledge, 1994); *New Historicism and Renaissance Drama*, ed. Richard Wilson and Richard Dutton (London: Longman, 1992); *The Matter of Difference: Materialist Feminist Criticism of Shakespeare*, ed. Valerie Wayne (New York: Harvester Wheatsheaf, 1991); *Uses of History: Marxism, Postmodernism and the Renaissance*, ed. Francis Barker, Peter Hulme and Margaret Iversen (Manchester: Manchester University Press, 1991); David Simpson, 'Literary Criticism and the Return to "History" ', *Critical Inquiry*, 14 (1988), 721–47; Richard Strier et al., 'Historicism, New and Old: Excerpts from a Panel Discussion', in *'The Muses Common-Weale': Poetry and Politics in the Seventeenth Century*, ed. Claude J. Summers and Ted-Larry Pebworth (Columbia: University of Missouri Press, 1988), pp. 207–17; Edward Pechter, 'The New Historicism and Its Discontents: Politicizing Renaissance Drama', *PMLA*, 102 (1987), 292–303; Jean E. Howard, 'The New Historicism in Renaissance Studies', *English Literary Renaissance*, 16 (1986), 13–43.

3. Stephen Greenblatt, 'Resonance and Wonder', in his *Learning to Curse: Essays in Early Modern Culture* (New York: Routledge, 1990), p. 165. For an interesting discussion of the use of anecdotes in new historicism, see John Lee, *Shakespeare's Hamlet and the Controversies of the Self* (Oxford: Clarendon, 2000), pp. 67–9.
4. Margreta de Grazia, 'The Ideology of Superfluous Things: *King Lear* as Period Piece', in *Subject and Object in Renaissance Culture*, ed. Margreta de Grazia, Maureen Quilligan and Peter Stallybrass (Cambridge: Cambridge University Press, 1996), p. 19.
5. Veeser, in *The New Historicism*, p. 2.
6. Aristotle, *The Politics*, rev. edn, trans. T. A. Sinclair (London: Penguin, 1981), p. 198, p. 59.
7. Ibid., p. 61.
8. Michael Ferber, 'The Ideology of *The Merchant of Venice*', *English Literary Renaissance*, 20 (1990), 431–64, 463.
9. Pechter, 'The New Historicism and Its Discontents', 299.
10. See Chapter 3.
11. David Scott Kastan, 'Shakespeare and English History', in *The Cambridge Companion to Shakespeare*, ed. Margreta de Grazia and Stanley Wells (Cambridge: Cambridge University Press, 2001), p. 167.
12. Raphael Samuel, *Theatres of Memory*, vol. 1 (London: Verso, 1994), p. 198.
13. Fredric Jameson, 'Marxism and Historicism' [1979], in his *The Ideologies of Theory, Essays, 1971–1986,* vol. 2*: The Syntax of History* (London: Routledge, 1988), p. 175.
14. Ibid., p. 157.
15. Paul Hamilton, *Historicism* (London: Routledge, 1996), p. 41.
16. William Bouwsma, *A Usable Past* (Berkeley: University of California Press, 1990), p. 2.
17. David Scott Kastan, *Shakespeare after Theory* (New York: Routledge, 1999), p. 16.
18. Ibid., p. 16.
19. Ewan Fernie, *Shame in Shakespeare* (London: Routledge, 2002), p. 4.

20. Philip Sidney, *A Defence of Poetry*, ed. Jan Van Dorsten (Oxford: Oxford University Press, [1595] 1966), pp. 31–2.
21. Ibid., pp. 36–7.
22. Ibid., p. 33.
23. Christophe Bode and Wolfgang Klooss, 'Introduction', in *Historicizing/Contemporizing Shakespeare*, ed. Christophe Bode and Wolfgang Klooss (Trier: Wissenschaftlicher, 2000), p. 15.
24. Fernie, *Shame in Shakespeare*, p. 23.
25. See, for example, Greenblatt, 'The Cultivation of Anxiety: King Lear and His Heirs', in his *Learning to Curse*, pp. 80–98.
26. Mark David Rasmussen's introduction to this volume is called 'New Formalisms?': *Renaissance Literature and Its Formal Engagements*, ed. Mark David Rasmussen (New York: Palgrave, 2002), pp. 1–14.
27. Heather Dubrow, 'The Politics of Aesthetics: Recuperating Formalism and the Country House Poem', in *Renaissance Literature and Its Formal Engagements*, ed. Rasmussen, p. 77.
28. Elizabeth Harris Sagaser, 'Flirting with Eternity: Teaching Form and Meter in a Renaissance Poetry Course', in *Renaissance Literature and its Formal Engagements*, ed. Rasmussen, p. 187.
29. Ibid., p. 199.
30. Sidney, *A Defence*, p. 32.
31. Hanan Yoran, 'Thomas More's *Richard III*: Probing the Limits of Humanism', *Renaissance Studies*, 15 (2001), 514–37, 524. Yoran's overall emphasis, however, is on 'humanist history' as the precursor of 'modern historiographic discipline' and notions of historical difference and distance: p. 525.
32. Ibid., p. 524.
33. Timothy Hampton, *Writing from History: The Rhetoric of Exemplarity in Renaissance Literature* (Ithaca: Cornell University Press, 1990), pp. 8–9.
34. Ferber, 'The Ideology of *The Merchant of Venice*', 464; Fernie, *Shame in Shakespeare*, p. 23; Terry Eagleton, *After Theory* (London: Allen Lane, 2003), p. 184. See Chapter 3 for further discussion of Ferber, and the Introduction for further discussion of Fernie and Eagleton.
35. Shakespeare, *I Henry IV*, in *The Oxford Shakespeare*, 2nd edn, ed. Stanley Wells et al. (Oxford: Clarendon, [1986] 2005), II, v, 485–6. All subsequent references in the text are to this edition.
36. A. P. Rossiter, *Angel with Horns*, ed. Graham Storey (London: Longman, [1961] 1989), p. 63. Expanding on Rossiter, Graham Bradshaw suggests that 'Hal's tragedy . . . is that he can become nothing other and nothing more than a King': Graham Bradshaw, *Misrepresentations: Shakespeare and the Materialists* (Ithaca: Cornell University Press, 1993), p. 122. For a differently focused discussion of Hal's humanity/inhumanity, see David Ruiter, 'Harry's (In)human Face', in *Spiritual Shakespeares*, ed. Ewan Fernie (London: Routledge, 2005), pp. 50–72.
37. Concepts of the 'only human' will be further discussed in Chapters 6 and 7.
38. Terry Eagleton, *The Ideology of the Aesthetic* (Oxford: Blackwell, 1990), p. 13.
39. François Laroque, 'Shakespeare's "Battle of Carnival and Lent": The Falstaff Scenes Reconsidered (*1 & 2 Henry IV*)', in *Shakespeare and Carnival: After Bakhtin*, ed. Ronald Knowles (Basingstoke: Macmillan, 1998), p. 94.

40. Ibid., p. 93.
41. Thomas Wright, *The Passions of the Minde* (London: V.S. for W.B., 1601), pp. 12–13.
42. On the system of debt and credit in the play, see Lars Engle, *Shakespearean Pragmatism: Market of His Time* (Chicago: University of Chicago Press, 1993), pp. 118–28.
43. 'The spirit indeed *is* willing, but the flesh *is* weak' (Matthew 26: 41), King James Bible.
44. Wright, *Passions*, p. 109.
45. 'Carnival', writes Michael Bristol, 'is a travesty; costumes, insignia of rank and identity, and all other symbolic manifestations are mimicked or misappropriated for purposes of aggressive mockery and laughter': Michael Bristol, *Carnival and Theater* (London: Methuen, 1985), p. 63.
46. Harold Bloom also argues for a kind of morality, described as 'pragmatic courage', in Falstaff: Harold Bloom, *Shakespeare: The Invention of the Human* (London: Fourth Estate, [1998] 1999), p. 292.
47. Gail Kern Paster, *Humoring the Body* (Chicago: University of Chicago Press, 2004), p. 195.
48. For a discussion of Hal's role-playing, seen in the context of the protocolonialist collector mentality of the Renaissance, see Steven Mullaney, 'Strange Things, Gross Terms, Curious Customs: The Rehearsal of Cultures in the Late Renaissance', in *Representing the English Renaissance*, ed. Stephen Greenblatt (Berkeley: University of California Press, [1983] 1988), pp. 65–92.
49. Samuel Taylor Coleridge, *Biographia Literaria*, in *The Oxford Authors: Samuel Taylor Coleridge*, ed. H. J. Jackson (Oxford: Oxford University Press, 1985), p. 320.
50. Wesley Morris, 'Of Wisdom and Competence', in *The Revenge of the Aesthetic*, ed. Michael P. Clark (Berkeley: University of California Press, 2000), p. 151.
51. Bloom, *Shakespeare*, p. 309.
52. Eagleton, *The Ideology of the Aesthetic*, p. 13.
53. Ibid., p. 23.
54. Douglas Bruster, *Drama and the Market in the Age of Shakespeare* (Cambridge: Cambridge University Press, 1992), p. 38.
55. Charles Taylor, *Sources of the Self* (Cambridge: Cambridge University Press, 1989), p. 292.

Chapter 5 Ethics: *Macbeth*

1. Adrian Poole, 'A. C. Bradley's Shakespearean Tragedy', *Essays in Criticism*, 55 (2005), 58–70, 70.
2. Dominic Rainsford and Tim Woods, 'Introduction: Ethics and Intellectuals', in *Critical Ethics*, ed. Dominic Rainsford and Tim Woods (Basingstoke: Macmillan, 1999), p. 15. Further examples of the resurgence of interest in ethical criticism include: *Critical Quarterly*, 47, special issue: Against Transgression (2005); Brian Stock, 'Ethics and the Humanities: Some Lessons of Historical Experience', *New Literary History*, 36 (2005),

1–17; *Renegotiating Ethics in Literature, Philosophy, and Theory*, ed. Jane Adamson, Richard Freadman and David Parker (Cambridge: Cambridge University Press, 1998); *The Ethics in Literature*, ed. Andrew Hadfield, Dominic Rainsford and Tim Woods (Basingstoke: Macmillan, 1999); Robert Eaglestone, *Ethical Criticism: Reading after Levinas* (Edinburgh: Edinburgh University Press, 1997); Martha Nussbaum, *Love's Knowledge* (Oxford: Oxford University Press, 1990); Tobin Siebers, *The Ethics of Criticism* (Ithaca: Cornell University Press, 1988).

3. Gail Kern Paster, *Humoring the Body* (Chicago: University of Chicago Press, 2004), p. 9 and *passim*.
4. Ibid., p. 9.
5 Habermas's characterisation of mythical thought is discussed in Chapter 1.
6. For further discussion of the importance of the emotions in Shakespeare and/or the Renaissance more generally, see Richard Strier, 'Against the Rule of Reason: Praise of Passion from Petrarch to Luther to Shakespeare to Herbert', in *Reading the Early Modern Passions*, ed. Gail Kern Paster, Katherine Rowe and Mary Floyd-Wilson (Philadelphia: University of Pennsylvania Press, 2004), pp. 23–42 (previously referred to in Chapter 2); Heather James, 'Dido's Ear: Tragedy and the Politics of Response', *Shakespeare Quarterly*, 52 (2001), 360–82; Tom McAlindon, 'Tragedy, *King Lear*, and the Politics of the Heart', *Shakespeare Survey*, 44 (1991), 85–90.
7. Thomas Wright, *The Passions of the Minde* (London: V.S. for W.B., 1601), pp. 22–3.
8. Shakespeare, *Macbeth*, in *The Oxford Shakespeare*, 2nd edn, ed. Stanley Wells et al. (Oxford: Clarendon, [1986] 2005), II, iii, 113–14. All subsequent references in the text are to this edition.
9. Katherine Rowe, 'Humoral Knowledge and Liberal Cognition in Davenant's *Macbeth*', in *Reading the Early Modern Passions*, ed. Paster et al., p. 176.
10. Terry Eagleton, *Sweet Violence: The Idea of the Tragic* (Oxford: Blackwell, 2003), p. 168.
11. Adrian Poole writes that 'comfort was still a strong word in Shakespeare's time, though like many strong words it has suffered shrinkage. It should banish fear and ground hope': Adrian Poole, *Tragedy and the Greek Example* (Oxford: Blackwell, 1997), p. 52.
12. Ashley Tauchert, 'Among the Dark Satanic Wheels: Transgressing Transgression', *Critical Quarterly*, 47 (2005), 1–11, 4.
13. Georges Bataille, *Eroticism*, trans. Mary Dalwood (London: Marion Boyars, [1957] 1987), pp. 38–9.
14. Friedrich Nietzsche, *Twilight of the Idols and The Antichrist*, trans. R. J. Hollingdale (Harmondsworth: Penguin, 1968), p. 73.
15. Tauchert, 'Among the Dark Satanic Wheels', 3.
16. Friedrich Nietzsche, *Beyond Good and Evil*, trans. R. J. Hollingdale (Harmondsworth: Penguin, 1973), p. 138.
17. In *Discipline and Punish*, for example, morality is treated as an index of changes in regimens of power, the assumption being that morality is not an autonomous discourse and not of interest in and for itself: Michel Foucault, *Discipline and Punish: The Birth of the Prison*, trans. Alan Sheridan (Harmondsworth: Penguin, [1975] 1982).
18. Nietzsche, *Beyond Good and Evil*, pp. 36, 35.

19. An example of the use of Foucault's scheme is Natasha Korda, ' "Judicious oeillades": Supervising Marital Property in *The Merry Wives of Windsor*', in *Marxist Shakespeares*, ed. Jean E. Howard and Scott Cutler Shershow (London: Routledge, 2001), pp. 82–103. For criticism of new historicism's methods and preoccupations, see William Kerrigan, 'The Case for Bardolatry', in *Harold Bloom's Shakespeare*, ed. Christy Desmet and Robert Sawyer (New York: Palgrave, 2001), pp. 33–42.
20. Ewan Fernie, 'Introduction', in *Spiritual Shakespeares*, ed. Ewan Fernie (London: Routledge, 2005), p. 5.
21. Ibid., p. 6.
22. Rowe, 'Humoral Knowledge and Liberal Cognition', p. 183.
23. Robert Watson, 'Tragedies of Revenge and Ambition', in *The Cambridge Companion to Shakespearean Tragedy*, ed. Claire McEachern (Cambridge: Cambridge University Press, 2002), p. 161.
24. For his account of language as a 'two-sided psychological entity', see Ferdinand de Saussure, *Course in General Linguistics*, trans. Roy Harris (London: Duckworth, [1972] 1983), p. 66.
25. See Harry Levin, *Christopher Marlowe: The Overreacher* (London: Faber and Faber, [1952] 1965).
26. Pico is discussed in the Introduction.
27. Friedrich Nietzsche, *Thus Spake Zarathustra*, trans. R. J. Hollingdale (Harmondsworth: Penguin, [1883] 1961), p. 42.
28. Stephen Greenblatt, *Will in the World* (London: Pimlico, 2005), p. 140. Greenblatt's comment is part of an argument about Lady Macbeth's 'ability to follow the twists and turns of her husband's innermost character, to take her spouse in'.
29. Jonathan Dollimore, 'Afterword', in *Spiritual Shakespeares*, ed. Fernie, p. 217.
30. Ibid., p. 217.

Chapter 6 Only Human: *Coriolanus*

1. Jürgen Habermas, *The Philosophical Discourse of Modernity*, trans. Frederick Lawrence (Cambridge: Polity, [1985] 1987), p. 315.
2. Sigmund Freud, *The Interpretation of Dreams*, trans. James Strachey (London: Penguin, 1991), p. 367.
3. Julia Kristeva, *Black Sun: Depression and Melancholia*, trans. Leon S. Roudiez (New York: Columbia University Press, 1989), p. 43.
4. Nancy Chodorow, *The Reproduction of Mothering: Psychoanalysis and the Sociology of Gender* (Berkeley: University of California Press, 1978), p. 93.
5. For an interesting discussion of the tension between community and narcissism in the play, which also connects narcissism with scepticism, see Stanley Cavell, *Disowning Knowledge in Six Plays of Shakespeare* (New York: Cambridge University Press, 1987), pp. 143–77.
6. Shakespeare, *Coriolanus*, in *The Oxford Shakespeare*, 2nd edn, ed. Stanley Wells et al. (Oxford: Clarendon, [1986] 2005), V, iii, 35–7. All subsequent references in the text are to this edition.

7. Burton Hatlen, 'The "Noble Thing" and the "Boy of Tears": Coriolanus and the Embarrassments of Identity', *English Literary Renaissance*, 27 (1997), 393–420, 406–7.
8. Janet Adelman, *Suffocating Mothers: Fantasies of Maternal Origin in Shakespeare's Plays, Hamlet to The Tempest* (New York: Routledge, 1992), pp. 4–5.
9. Ibid., pp. 4, 6.
10. Ibid., p. 7.
11. Hatlen, 'The "Noble Thing" and the "Boy of Tears" ', 401.
12. Ewan Fernie, *Shame in Shakespeare* (London: Routledge, 2002), p. 213.
13. Interpretations of the play which imply that Coriolanus is complex because unwilling or unable to acknowledge what he lacks as a human being are contested by Cynthia Marshall, who adopts the more resolutely constructionist perspective that the 'advent of complexity is a theatrical effect': Cynthia Marshall, 'Wound-man: Coriolanus, Gender, and the Theatrical Construction of Identity', in *Feminist Readings of Early Modern Culture: Emerging Subjects*, ed. Valerie Traub, M. Lindsay Kaplan and Dympna Callaghan (Cambridge: Cambridge University Press, 1996), p. 104.
14. Katharine Eisaman Maus, '*Coriolanus*', in *The Norton Shakespeare*, ed. Stephen Greenblatt et al. (New York: Norton, 1997), p. 2789.
15. Gail Kern Paster, *Humoring the Body* (Chicago: University of Chicago Press, 2004), p. 195.
16. Adelman, *Suffocating Mothers*, p. 150.
17. The issue of the pathology which this normative perspective implies is discussed in more detail in Chapter 9.
18. Stephen Greenblatt, *Will in the World* (London: Pimlico, 2005), p. 388.
19. Paster, *Humoring the Body*, p. 9 and *passim*.
20. Martha Nussbaum, *Upheavals of Thought: The Intelligence of the Emotions* (Cambridge: Cambridge University Press, 2001), p. 473.
21. Ibid., p. 272.
22. Like other psychoanalytically oriented critics, Madelon Sprengnether locates a 'preoedipal plot' in the play, in which 'the hero both desires and fears the annihilation of his identity that intimacy with a woman either threatens or requires': Madelon Sprengnether, 'Annihilating Intimacy in *Coriolanus*', in *Women in the Middle Ages and the Renaissance*, ed. Mary Beth Rose (Syracuse: Syracuse University Press, 1986), p. 89.
23. Nussbaum, *Upheavals of Thought*, p. 192.
24. Isobel Armstrong, *The Radical Aesthetic* (Oxford: Blackwell, 2000), p. 138.
25. Gail Kern Paster, Katherine Rowe and Mary Floyd-Wilson, 'Introduction', in *Reading the Early Modern Passions*, ed. Gail Kern Paster, Katherine Rowe and Mary Floyd-Wilson (Philadelphia: University of Pennsylvania Press, 2004), p. 10.

Chapter 7 Humility: *Love's Labour's Lost*

1. The *locus classicus* for the notion that comedy presents 'base' as opposed to 'elevated' versions of reality is Aristotle, comedy according to Aristotle

being 'an imitation of persons who are inferior': Aristotle, *Poetics*, trans. Gerald F. Else (Ann Arbor: University of Michigan Press, 1967), p. 23.
2. Michael Bristol, *Carnival and Theater* (New York: Methuen, 1985), p. 65.
3. Ibid., p. 67.
4. Simon Critchley, *On Humour* (London: Routledge, 2002), p. 102.
5. Shakespeare, *Love's Labour's Lost*, in *The Oxford Shakespeare*, 2nd edn, ed. Stanley Wells et al. (Oxford: Clarendon, [1986] 2005), I, i, 175. All subsequent references in the text are to this edition.
6. Lynne Magnusson, 'Language and Comedy', in *The Cambridge Companion to Shakespearean Comedy*, ed. Alexander Leggatt (Cambridge: Cambridge University Press, 2002), p. 157.
7. For an extended discussion of blushing, including its relevance to gender issues, see Brian Cummings, 'Animal Passions and Human Sciences: Shame, Blushing and Nakedness in Early Modern Europe and the New World', in *At the Borders of the Human*, ed. Erica Fudge, Ruth Gilbert and Susan Wiseman (Basingstoke: Macmillan, 1999), pp. 28–32.
8. C. L. Barber, *Shakespeare's Festive Comedy* (Princeton: Princeton University Press, 1959), p. 92.
9. Desiderius Erasmus, *Praise of Folly and Letter to Martin Dorp*, trans. Betty Radice (Harmondsworth: Penguin, [1509 and 1515] 1971). Christian folly, for example, is wise folly: pp. 188–208; scholastic obscurantism is foolish folly: p. 156; and self-love is a combination of both: pp. 131–5 and *passim*. Folly in Erasmus's text is also discussed in Chapter 3.
10. Shakespeare, *As You Like It*, in *The Oxford Shakespeare*, V, i, 30–1.
11. Terry Eagleton, *The Ideology of the Aesthetic* (Oxford: Blackwell, 1990), p. 13.
12. See, for example, Northrop Frye, *Anatomy of Criticism: Four Essays* (Princeton: Princeton University Press, 1957), pp. 163–86, and *A Natural Perspective: The Development of Shakespearean Comedy and Romance* (New York: Columbia University Press, 1965); Barber, *Shakespeare's Festive Comedy*; Edward Berry, *Shakespeare's Comic Rites* (Cambridge: Cambridge University Press, 1984). Frye's theory of archetypes is discussed in Chapter 9.
13. The public as well as ontological significance of love for Renaissance writers in general is attested by William Kerrigan, who writes (of John Donne) that 'he lived at a time when love could be said to be the dominant preoccupation of a major living philosophy, Neoplatonism, and not exactly peripheral in the university tradition'. He continues: 'in no subsequent period in the history of English verse is love poetry a central ambition': William Kerrigan, 'What Was Donne Doing?', *South Central Review*, 4 (1987), 2–15, 6.

Chapter 8 Love: *As You Like It*

1. Catherine Belsey, *The Subject of Tragedy* (London: Methuen, 1985), pp. 81–2.
2. Jonathan Dollimore, *Radical Tragedy*, 3rd edn (Basingstoke: Palgrave, [1984] 2004), p. 253.

3. Francis Barker, *The Tremulous Private Body* (London: Methuen, 1984), p. 15.
4. Belsey is the partial exception, as she does in *The Subject of Tragedy* discuss the struggle of women to establish themselves as liberal humanist subjects (pp. 129–221). However, the kind of humanism she examines (liberal humanism) is still conceived as a dominant ideology.
5. Shakespeare, *As You Like It*, in *The Oxford Shakespeare*, 2nd edn, ed. Stanley Wells et al. (Oxford: Clarendon, [1986] 2005), II, iii, 57–8. All subsequent references in the text are to this edition.
6. William Kerrigan makes the similar point that the 'new self-interestedness with which men move upward in hierarchies, forgetting the antique bonds of service, as represented here by Adam' is 'old news' as far as its repeated representation in Shakespeare's plays is concerned: William Kerrigan, 'Female Friends and Fraternal Enemies in *As You Like It*', in *Desire in the Renaissance*, ed. Valeria Finucci and Regina Schwartz (Princeton: Princeton University Press, 1994), p. 185.
7. Louis Montrose contextualises Oliver's behaviour by linking it to 'the gentry's drive to aggrandize and perpetuate their estates', a drive which led them 'to a ruthless application of primogeniture': Louis Adrian Montrose, '"The Place of a Brother" in *As You Like It*: Social Process and Comic Form', *Shakespeare Quarterly*, 32 (1981), 28–54, 32.
8. Zygmunt Bauman, *Liquid Love* (Cambridge: Polity, 2003), p. vii.
9. Ibid., p. 28.
10. Jean Howard, '*As You Like It*', in *The Norton Shakespeare*, ed. Stephen Greenblatt et al. (New York: Norton, 1997), p. 1596.
11. For further discussion of the mobility of desire in the play, see Mario Digangi, *The Homoerotics of Early Modern Drama* (Cambridge: Cambridge University Press, 1997), pp. 50–63; Peter Stallybrass, 'Transvestism and the "Body Beneath": Speculating on the Boy Actor', in *Erotic Politics*, ed. Susan Zimmerman (New York: Routledge, 1992), pp. 64–83; Valerie Traub, *Desire and Anxiety: Circulations of Sexuality in Shakespearean Drama* (London: Routledge, 1992), pp. 117–44.
12. Digangi, *The Homoerotics of Early Modern Drama*, p. 55.
13. Roland Barthes, *A Lover's Discourse*, trans. Richard Howard (London: Penguin, [1977] 1990), p. 3.
14. Ibid., p. 6.
15. Catherine Belsey, *Desire: Love Stories in Western Culture* (Oxford: Blackwell, 1994), p. 209.
16. Catherine Bates, 'Love and Courtship', in *The Cambridge Companion to Shakespearean Comedy*, ed. Alexander Leggatt (Cambridge: Cambridge University Press, 2002), p. 105.

Chapter 9 Hope: *The Winter's Tale*

1. Samuel Beckett, *Endgame* (London: Faber and Faber, [1958] 1964), p. 16.
2. Ibid., pp. 17, 26.
3. Ibid., p. 26.

4. Zygmunt Bauman, *Liquid Love* (Cambridge: Polity, 2003), p. xiii and *passim.*
5. Northrop Frye, *Anatomy of Criticism: Four Essays* (Princeton: Princeton University Press, 1957), pp. 183–5, 187.
6. Ibid., p. 186.
7. Ibid., p. 186.
8. Fredric Jameson, *The Political Unconscious* (London: Methuen, 1981), pp. 112–13.
9. Frye, *Anatomy of Criticism*, pp. 187–8.
10. Robin Headlam Wells, *Shakespeare's Humanism* (Cambridge: Cambridge University Press, 2005), p. 106. See the Introduction for further discussion of Headlam Wells's book.
11. Gail Kern Paster, *Humoring the Body* (Chicago: University of Chicago Press, 2004), p. 9 and *passim.*
12. Beckett, *Endgame*, p. 27.
13. Shakespeare, *The Winter's Tale*, in *The Oxford Shakespeare*, 2nd edn, ed. Stanley Wells et al. (Oxford: Clarendon, [1986] 2005), II, iii, 116–21. All subsequent references in the text are to this edition.
14. 'Affection' is often paraphrased by editors as 'passion'. See, as examples, *The Norton Shakespeare*, ed. Stephen Greenblatt et al. (New York: Norton, 1997), p. 2888, and William Shakespeare, *The Winter's Tale*, ed. Frank Kermode (New York: Signet, 1963), p. 46. However, the use of the word in this context has caused considerable editorial difficulties. For a discussion of some of these, see Catherine Belsey, *Shakespeare and the Loss of Eden* (Basingstoke: Macmillan, 1999), pp. 105–7.
15. Belsey, *Shakespeare and the Loss of Eden*, p. 103.
16. Ibid., p. 107.
17. Headlam Wells also discusses Belsey's Lacanian reading of the play, but in more strongly critical terms: Headlam Wells, *Shakespeare's Humanism*, pp. 93–4.
18. Northrop Frye, *A Natural Perspective: The Development of Shakespearean Comedy and Romance* (New York: Columbia University Press, 1965), p. 104.
19. *The Winter's Tale*, ed. Kermode, p. xxxi.
20. Belsey, *Shakespeare and the Loss of Eden*, p. 126.
21. Janet Adelman, *Suffocating Mothers: Fantasies of Maternal Origin in Shakespeare's Plays, Hamlet to The Tempest* (New York: Routledge, 1992), p. 231.
22. Ibid., p. 231.
23. Ibid., p. 229.
24. Michael Ferber, 'The Ideology of *The Merchant of Venice*', *English Literary Renaissance*, 20 (1990), 431–64, 464.
25. Richard Wilson, 'Making Men of Monsters: Shakespeare in the Company of Strangers', *Shakespeare*, 1 (2005), 8–28, 20.
26. Shakespeare, *A Midsummer Night's Dream*, in *The Oxford Shakespeare*, V, i, 7–22.
27. See the contrasting models of artistic creation discussed in Chapter 1 in the context of Hamlet's anxiety about the subjective creation, as opposed to objective existence, of meaning in the world.

28. For a differently focused discussion of art and nature in the play, see Headlam Wells, *Shakespeare's Humanism*, pp. 90–3.
29. Anthony Gash, 'Carnival and the Sacred', in *Shakespeare and Carnival*, ed. Ronald Knowles (Basingstoke: Macmillan, 1998), p. 190.
30. Belsey, *Shakespeare and the Loss of Eden*, p. 127.

Conclusion

1. Shakespeare, *The Tempest*, in *The Oxford Shakespeare*, 2nd edn, ed. Stanley Wells et al. (Oxford: Clarendon [1986] 2005), II, i, 154–62. The subsequent reference is to this edition.
2. 'In Utopia they have a six-hour working day – three hours in the morning, then lunch – then a two-hour break – then three more hours in the afternoon, followed by supper': Thomas More, *Utopia*, trans. Paul Turner (Harmondsworth: Penguin, [1516] 1965), pp.70–1.
3. Shakespeare, *King Lear*, in *The Oxford Shakespeare*, IV, v, 147–50.

Bibliography

Primary Sources

Cawdray, Robert, *A Treasvrie or Store-Hovse of Similies* (London: Thomas Creede, 1600).

Erasmus, Desiderius, *Praise of Folly and Letter to Martin Dorp*, trans. Betty Radice (Harmondsworth: Penguin, [1509 and 1515] 1971).

Mirandola, Pico della, *On the Dignity of Man and Other Works*, trans. Charles Glenn Wallis et al. (Indianapolis: Bobbs-Merrill Educational, [*c.*1486] 1965).

More, Thomas, *Utopia*, trans. Paul Turner (Penguin: Harmondsworth, [1516] 1965).

Robson, Simon, *The Choise of Change* (London: Roger Warde, 1585).

Shakespeare, William, *The Oxford Shakespeare: The Complete Works*, 2nd edn, ed. Stanley Wells et al. (Oxford: Clarendon, [1986] 2005).

Sidney, Philip, *A Defence of Poetry*, ed. Jan Van Dorsten (Oxford: Oxford University Press, [1595] 1966).

Wilson, Thomas, *The Arte of Rhetorique, 1553. And Now Newly Set forth Againe, with a Prologue to the Reader, 1567* (London: George Robinson, [1553] 1585).

Wright, Thomas, *The Passions of the Minde* (London: V.S. for W.B., 1601).

Histories of English

Baldick, Chris, *Criticism and Literary Theory: 1890 to the Present* (London: Longman, 1996).

——, *The Social Mission of English Criticism* (Oxford: Clarendon, 1983).

Clark, Timothy, 'Literary Force, Institutional Values', in *The Question of Literature*, ed. Elizabeth Beaumont Bissell (Manchester: Manchester University Press, 2002), pp. 91–104.

Court, Franklin, E., *Institutionalizing English Literature: The Culture and Politics of Literary Studies, 1750–1900* (Stanford, CA: Stanford University Press, 1992).

Doyle, Brian, *English and Englishness* (London: Routledge, 1989).

Eagleton, Terry, *The Function of Criticism* (London: Verso, 1984).
Graff, Gerald, *Professing Literature* (Chicago: University of Chicago Press, 1987).
Gross, John, *The Rise and Fall of the Man of Letters* (London: Weidenfeld and Nicolson, 1969).
Guillory, John, 'Literary Study and the Modern System of the Disciplines', in *Disciplinarity at the Fin de Siècle*, ed. Amanda Anderson and Joseph Valente (Princeton: Princeton University Press, 2002), pp. 19–43.
——, *Cultural Capital* (Chicago: University of Chicago Press, 1993).
Hunter, Ian, *Culture and Government: The Emergence of Literary Education* (Basingstoke: Macmillan, 1988).
Mulhern, Francis, *The Moment of 'Scrutiny'* (London: New Left, 1979).
Palmer, D. J., *The Rise of English Studies* (London: Oxford University Press, 1965).
Viswanathan, Gauri, 'Subjecting English and the Question of Representation', in *Disciplinarity at the Fin de Siècle*, ed. Amanda Anderson and Joseph Valente (Princeton: Princeton University Press, 2002), pp. 177–95.
——, *Masks of Conquest: Literary Study and British Rule in India* (London: Faber and Faber [1989], 1990).
Warner, Michael, 'Professionalization and the Rewards of Literature', *Criticism*, 26 (1985), 1–28.

Literature; Aesthetics

Adorno, Theodor, 'Reconciliation under Duress' [1961], in *Aesthetics and Politics*, ed. Ernst Bloch et al. (London: Verso, [1977] 1980), pp. 151–76.
Armstrong, Isobel, *The Radical Aesthetic* (Oxford: Blackwell, 2000).
Arnold, Matthew, *Essays in Criticism: First and Second Series* (London: Dent, 1964).
Bissell, Elizabeth Beaumont (ed.), *The Question of Literature* (Manchester: Manchester University Press, 2002).
Bloch, Ernst, et al. (eds), *Aesthetics and Politics* (London: Verso, [1977] 1980).
Carey, John, *What Good Are the Arts?* (London: Faber and Faber, 2005).
Clark, Michael P. (ed.), *The Revenge of the Aesthetic* (Berkeley: University of California Press, 2000).
Cunningham, Valentine, *Reading after Theory* (Oxford: Blackwell, 2002).
Docherty, Thomas, 'Aesthetic Education and the Demise of Experience', in *The New Aestheticism*, ed. John Joughin (Manchester: Manchester University Press, 2003), pp. 23–35.
Dubrow, Heather, 'The Politics of Aesthetics: Recuperating Formalism and the Country House Poem', in *Renaissance Literature and Its Formal Engagements*, ed. Mark David Rasmussen (New York: Palgrave, 2002), pp. 67–88.
Eaglestone, Robert, 'Critical Knowledge, Scientific Knowledge and the Truth of Literature', in *The New Aestheticism*, ed. John Joughin (Manchester: Manchester University Press, 2003), pp. 151–66.
Eagleton, Terry, *After Theory* (London: Allen Lane, 2003).

——, *The Ideology of the Aesthetic* (Oxford: Blackwell, 1990).
Engell, James, and David Perkins (eds), *Teaching Literature: What Is Needed Now* (Cambridge, MA: Harvard University Press, 1988).
Greenblatt, Stephen, 'Resonance and Wonder', in his *Learning to Curse: Essays in Early Modern Culture* (New York: Routledge, 1990), pp. 161–83.
Hunter, Ian, 'Aesthetics and Cultural Studies', in *Cultural Studies*, ed. Lawrence Grossberg et al. (New York: Routledge, 1992), pp. 347–72.
Joughin, John (ed.), *The New Aestheticism* (Manchester: Manchester University Press, 2003).
Leavis, F. R., *Education and the University*, 2nd edn (Cambridge: Cambridge University Press, [1943] 1979).
Matz, Robert, *Defending Literature in Early Modern England* (Cambridge: Cambridge University Press, 2000).
Morris, Wesley, 'Of Wisdom and Competence', in *The Revenge of the Aesthetic*, ed. Michael P. Clark (Berkeley: University of California Press, 2000), pp. 136–56.
Mousley, Andy, 'Renaissance Literary Studies after Theory: Aesthetics, History and the Human', *Literature Compass*, 1 (2004), www.literature-compass.com.
——, 'Humanising Contemporary Theory, Re-Humanising Literature', *Working Papers on the Web: The Value of Literature*, 2 (2000), http:// extra.shu.ac.uk/wpw/value/.
Nehamas, Alexander, *The Art of Living: Socratic Reflections from Plato to Foucault* (Berkeley: University of California Press, 2000).
Rasmussen, Mark David (ed.), *Renaissance Literature and Its Formal Engagements* (New York: Palgrave, 2002).
Robson, Mark, 'Defending Poetry, or, Is There an Early Modern Aesthetic?', in *The New Aestheticism*, ed. John Joughin (Manchester: Manchester University Press), pp. 119–30.
Sagaser, Elizabeth Harris, 'Flirting with Eternity: Teaching Form and Meter in a Renaissance Poetry Course', in *Renaissance Literature and Its Formal Engagements*, ed. Mark David Rasmussen (New York: Palgrave, 2002), pp. 185–206.
Watson, Robert N., 'Teaching "Shakespeare": Theory versus Practice', in *Teaching Literature: What Is Needed Now*, ed. James Engell and David Perkins (Cambridge, MA: Harvard University Press, 1988), pp. 121–50.

Ethical Criticism

Adamson, Jane, 'Against Tidiness: Literature and/versus Moral Philosophy', in *Renegotiating Ethics in Literature, Philosophy, and Theory*, ed. Jane Adamson et al. (Cambridge: Cambridge University Press, 1998), pp. 84–110.
—— et al. (eds), *Renegotiating Ethics in Literature, Philosophy, and Theory* (Cambridge: Cambridge University Press, 1998).
Critical Quarterly, 47, special issue: Against Transgression (2005).
Eaglestone, Roger, *Ethical Criticism: Reading after Levinas* (Edinburgh: Edinburgh University Press, 1997).

Gaita, Raimond, 'Common Understanding and Individual Voices', in *Renegotiating Ethics in Literature, Philosophy, and Theory*, ed. Jane Adamson, Richard Freadman and David Parker (Cambridge: Cambridge University Press, 1998), pp. 269–88.

Goldberg, S. L., *Agents and Lives: Moral Thinking in Literature* (Cambridge: Cambridge University Press, 1993).

Hadfield, Andrew, et al. (eds), *The Ethics in Literature* (Basingstoke: Macmillan, 1999).

Haines, Simon, 'Deepening the Self: The Language of Ethics and the Language of Literature', in *Renegotiating Ethics in Literature, Philosophy, and Theory*, ed. Jane Adamson et al. (Cambridge: Cambridge University Press, 1998), pp. 21–38.

Nussbaum, Martha, *Love's Knowledge* (Oxford: Oxford University Press, 1990).

Parker, David, 'Ethics, Value and the Politics of Recognition', in *Critical Ethics*, ed. Dominic Rainsford and Tim Woods (Basingstoke: Macmillan, 1999), pp. 152–68.

Rainsford, Dominic, and Tim Woods (eds), *Critical Ethics* (Basingstoke: Macmillan, 1999).

Siebers, Tobin, *The Ethics of Criticism* (Ithaca: Cornell University Press, 1988).

Stock, Brian, 'Ethics and the Humanities: Some Lessons of Historical Experience', *New Literary History*, 36 (2005), 1–17.

Tauchert, Ashley, 'Among the Dark Satanic Wheels: Transgressing Transgression', *Critical Quarterly*, 47 (2005), 1–11.

Historicisms; Historiography

Barker, Francis, et al. (eds), *Uses of History: Marxism, Postmodernism and the Renaissance* (Manchester: Manchester University Press, 1991).

Bode, Christophe, and Wolfgang Klooss (eds), *Historicizing/Contemporizing Shakespeare* (Trier: Wissenschaftlicher, 2000).

Cook, Albert, 'Historiography and/or Historicism: Context and Theoretical (De)-Integration of Renaissance Drama', *Centennial Review*, 40 (1996), 31–47.

Gallagher, Catherine, and Stephen Greenblatt (eds), *Practicing New Historicism* (Chicago: University of Chicago Press, 2000).

Grady, Hugh, and Terence Hawkes (eds), *Presentist Shakespeares* (London: Routledge, 2006).

Grazia, Margreta de, 'The Ideology of Superfluous Things: *King Lear* as Period Piece', in *Subject and Object in Renaissance Culture*, ed. Margreta de Grazia et al. (Cambridge: Cambridge University Press, 1996), pp. 17–42.

Hamilton, Paul, *Historicism* (London: Routledge, 1996).

Hampton, Timothy, *Writing from History: The Rhetoric of Exemplarity in Renaissance Literature* (Ithaca: Cornell University Press, 1990).

Hawkes, Terence, *Shakespeare in the Present* (London: Routledge, 2002).

Howard, Jean E., 'The New Historicism in Renaissance Studies', *English Literary Renaissance*, 16 (1986), 13–43.

Jameson, Fredric, *The Ideologies of Theory: Essays, 1971–1986*, vol. 2: *The Syntax of History* (London: Routledge, 1988).
Jardine, Lisa, *Reading Shakespeare Historically* (London and New York: Routledge, 1996).
——, 'Strains of Renaissance Reading', *English Literary Renaissance*, 25 (1995), 289–306.
Kastan, David Scott, *Shakespeare after Theory* (New York: Routledge, 1999).
Knowles, Ronald, *Shakespeare's Arguments with History* (Basingstoke: Palgrave, 2002).
Lehan, Richard, 'The Theoretical Limits of the New Historicism', *New Literary History*, 21 (1990), 533–53.
Maus, Katharine E., 'Renaissance Studies Today', *English Literary Renaissance*, 25 (1995), 402–14.
Mazzio, Carla, and Douglas Trevor (eds), *Historicism, Psychoanalysis and Early Modern Culture* (New York: Routledge, 2000).
McLuskie, Kathleen E., '"Old Mouse-Eaten Records": The Anxiety of History', *English Literary Renaissance*, 25 (1995), 415–31.
Pechter, Edward, 'The New Historicism and Its Discontents: Politicizing Renaissance Drama', *PMLA*, 102 (1987), 292–303.
Samuel, Raphael, *Theatres of Memory*, vol. 1 (London: Verso, 1994).
Simpson, David, 'Literary Criticism and the Return to "History"', *Critical Inquiry*, 14 (1988), 721–47.
Strier, Richard, et al., 'Historicism, New and Old: Excerpts from a Panel Discussion', in *'The Muses Common-Weale': Poetry and Politics in the Seventeenth Century*, ed. Claude J. Summers and Ted-Larry Pebworth (Columbia: University of Missouri Press, 1988), pp. 207–17.
Veeser, H. Aram (ed.), *The New Historicism* (New York: Routledge, 1994).
Wayne, Valerie (ed.), *The Matter of Difference: Materialist Feminist Criticism of Shakespeare* (New York: Harvester Wheatsheaf, 1991).
Wilson, Richard and Richard Dutton (eds), *New Historicism and Renaissance Drama* (London: Longman, 1992).
Woodbridge, Lynda (ed.), *Money and the Age of Shakespeare: Essays in New Economic Criticism* (Basingstoke: Palgrave, 2003).

Humanism; Anti-Humanism; Post-Humanism

Allen, Norm R. (ed.), *African-American Humanism: An Anthology* (Buffalo, NY: Prometheus, 1991).
Arac, Jonathan (ed.), *After Foucault: Humanistic Knowledge, Postmodern Challenges* (New Brunswick: Rutgers University Press, 1988).
Arendt, Hannah, *The Human Condition* (Chicago: University of Chicago Press, [1958] 1998).
Arkoun, Mohammed, 'From Islamic Humanism to the Ideology of Liberation', in *Humanism toward the Third Millennium*, ed. Fons Elders (Amsterdam: VUB Press, 1993), pp. 13–21.
Badmington, Neil (ed.), *Post-Humanism* (London: Palgrave, 2000).
Belsey, Catherine, *Critical Practice* (London: Methuen, 1980).

Blackham, H. J, *Humanism* (Harmondsworth: Penguin, 1968).
—— et al., *Objections to Humanism* (London: Penguin, [1963] 1965).
Blair, Brook Montgomery, 'Post-metaphysical and Radical Humanist Thought in the Writings of Machiavelli and Nietzsche', *History of European Ideas*, 27 (2001), 199–238.
Bookchin, Murray, *Re-enchanting Humanity: A Defense of the Human Spirit against Antihumanism, Misanthropy, Mysticism, and Primitivism* (London: Cassell, 1995).
Brewster, Scott, et al. (eds), *Inhuman Reflections: Rethinking the Limits of the Human* (Manchester: Manchester University Press, 2000).
Bullock, Alan, *The Humanist Tradition in the West* (New York: Thames & Hudson, 1985).
Carroll, John, *Humanism: The Wreck of Western Culture* (London: Fontana, 1993).
Chambers, Iain, *Culture after Humanism: History, Culture, Subjectivity* (London: Routledge, 2001).
Chomsky, Noam, *The New Military Humanism: Letters from Kosovo* (London: Pluto, 1999).
Comparative Criticism, 23, special issue: Humanist Traditions in the Twentieth Century (2001).
Davies, Tony, *Humanism* (London: Routledge, 1997).
Diogenes, 52, special issue: Emerging Humanisms (2005).
Douzinas, Costas, 'Human Rights, Humanism and Desire', *Angelaki*, 6 (2001), 183–206.
Ehrenfeld, David, *The Arrogance of Humanism* (New York: Oxford University Press, 1981).
Elders, Fons (ed.), *Humanism toward the Third Millennium* (Amsterdam: VUB Press, 1993).
Finkielkraut, Alain, *In the Name of Humanity* (London: Pimlico, [1996] 2001).
Fraser, Nancy, 'Foucault's Body-Language: A Post-Humanist Political Rhetoric', *Salmagundi*, 61 (1983), 61–3.
Fukuyama, Francis, *Our Posthuman Future: Consequences of the Biotechnology Revolution* (London: Profile, 2002).
Glover, Jonathan, *Humanity: A Moral History of the Twentieth Century* (London: Jonathan Cape, 1999).
Goicoechea, David, et al. (eds), *The Question of Humanism* (Buffalo, NY: Prometheus, 1991).
Good, Graham, *Humanism Betrayed: Theory, Ideology and Culture in the Contemporary Universe* (Montreal: McGill-Queen's University Press, 2001).
Goodman, Lenn E., *Islamic Humanism* (Oxford: Oxford University Press, 2003).
Gray, John, *Straw Dogs: Thoughts on Humans and Other Animals* (London: Granta, 2002).
Grayling, A. C., *The Meaning of Things: Applying Philosophy to Life* (London: Weidenfeld & Nicolson, 2001).
Halliwell, Martin, and Andy Mousley, *Critical Humanisms: Humanist/Anti-Humanist Dialogues* (Edinburgh: Edinburgh University Press, 2003).
Harpham, Geoffrey Galt, 'Beneath and beyond the "Crisis in the Humanities"', *New Literary History*, 36 (2005), 21–36.

Hoeveler, J. David, Jr, *The New Humanism: A Critique of Modern America, 1900–1940* (Charlottesville, VA: University of Virginia Press, 1977).
Huxley, Julian, *Essays of a Humanist* (London: Penguin, 1964).
Janicaud, Dominique, *On the Human Condition*, trans. Eileen Brennan (London: Routledge, [2002] 2005).
Johnson, Pauline, *Feminism as Radical Humanism* (Boulder, CO: Westview, 1994).
Kurtz, Paul, *Skepticism and Humanism: The New Paradigm* (New Brunswick: Transaction, 2001).
——, *Forbidden Fruit: The Ethics of Humanism* (Buffalo, NY: Prometheus, 1988).
Levinas, Emmanuel, *Humanisme de l'autre homme* (Montpellier: Fata Morgana, 1972).
Lyotard, Jean-François, *The Inhuman: Reflections on Time*, trans. Geoffrey Bennington and Rachel Bowlby (Cambridge: Polity, [1988] 1991).
Maritain, Jacques, *Integral Humanism, Freedom in the Modern World, and A Letter on Independence*, trans. Otto Bird (Notre Dame, IN: University of Notre Dame Press, 1996).
Mousley, Andy, 'Humanism', *The Literary Encyclopedia*, 2001, http://www.litencyc.com.
——,'Post-Theory, Literature, Marxism', *Keywords*, 3 (2000), 59–73.
Norman, Richard, *Humanism* (London: Routledge, 2004).
Nussbaum, Martha C., *Cultivating Humanity: A Classical Defense of Reform in Liberal Education* (Cambridge, MA: Harvard University Press, 1997).
——, 'Human Functioning and Social Justice: In Defense of Aristotelian Essentialism', *Political Theory*, 20 (1992), 202–46.
Ohmann, Richard, *Politics of Letters* (Middletown, CT: Wesleyan University Press, 1987).
Pinn, Anthony B. (ed.), *By These Hands: A Documentary History of African American Humanism* (New York: New York University Press, 2001).
Plowright, Bernard, *Humanism: Pagan or Christian?* (London: Independent, 1932).
Praharaj, D. M., *Humanism in Contemporary Indian Philosophical Perspectives* (Meerut: Anu, 1995).
Rieff, David, *A Bed for the Night: Humanitarianism in Crisis* (New York: Simon & Schuster, 2002).
Said, Edward, *Humanism and Democratic Criticism* (New York: Columbia University Press, 2004).
Sartre, Jean-Paul, *Existentialism and Humanism*, trans. Philip Mairet (London: Methuen, [1946] 1948).
Scholes, Robert, 'Presidential Address 2004: The Humanities in a Posthumanist World', *PMLA*, 120 (2005), 724–33.
Seidman, Barry. F., and Neil J. Murphy (eds), *Toward a New Political Humanism* (New York: Prometheus, 2004).
Soper, Kate, *What is Nature? Culture, Politics and the Non-Human* (Oxford: Blackwell, 1995).
——, 'Feminism, Humanism and Postmodernism', *Radical Philosophy*, 55 (1990), 11–17.
——, *Humanism and Anti-Humanism* (London: Hutchinson, 1986).

Spanos, William V., *The End of Education: Toward Posthumanism* (Minneapolis, MN: University of Minnesota Press, 1993).
Todorov, Tzvetan, *Imperfect Garden: The Legacy of Humanism* (Princeton, NJ: Princeton University Press, 2002).
——, *On Human Diversity*, trans. Catherine Porter (Cambridge, MA: Harvard University Press, 1993).
Waldby, Catherine, *The Visible Human Project: Informatic Bodies and Posthuman Medicine* (London: Routledge, 2000).
Wallace, Jeff, *D. H. Lawrence, Science and the Posthuman* (Basingstoke: Palgrave, 2005).
Young, Iris Marion, 'Humanism, Gynocentrism, and Feminist Politics', *Women's Studies International Forum*, 8 (1985), 173–85.
Zeldin, Theodore, *An Intimate History of Humanity* (London: Vintage, 1998).

Renaissance Humanism; Shakespeare and Humanism

Andic, Martin, 'What Is Renaissance Humanism?', in *The Question of Humanism*, ed. David Goicoechea et al. (Buffalo, NY: Prometheus, 1991), pp. 83–98.
Barker, Francis, *The Tremulous Private Body* (London: Methuen, 1984).
Belsey, Catherine, *The Subject of Tragedy* (London: Methuen, 1985).
Berek, Peter, 'The Jew as Renaissance Man', *Renaissance Quarterly*, 51 (1998), 128–62.
Blair, Brook Montgomery, 'Post-metaphysical and Radical Humanist Thought in the Writings of Machiavelli and Nietzsche', *History of European Ideas*, 27 (2001), 199–238.
Bloom, Harold, *Shakespeare: The Invention of the Human* (London: Fourth Estate, [1998] 1999).
Bouwsma, William J., 'The Renaissance Discovery of Human Creativity', in *Humanity and Divinity in Renaissance and Reformation*, ed. John W. O'Malley et al. (Leiden: E. J. Brill, 1993), pp. 17–34.
——, 'Two Faces of Humanism: Stoicism and Augustinianism in Renaissance Thought' [1975], in his *A Usable Past* (Berkeley: University of California Press, 1990), pp. 19–73.
Burckhardt, Jacob, *The Civilization of the Renaissance in Italy*, trans. S. G. C. Middlemore (London: Phaidon, [1860] 1950).
Burrow, Colin, 'Shakespeare and Humanistic Culture' in *Shakespeare and the Classics*, ed. Charles Martindale and A. B. Taylor (Cambridge: Cambridge University Press, 2004), pp. 9–27.
Bushnell, Rebecca W., *A Culture of Teaching: Early Modern Humanism in Theory and Practice* (Ithaca: Cornell University Press, 1996).
Cartwright, Kent, *Theatre and Humanism: English Drama in the Sixteenth Century* (Cambridge: Cambridge University Press, 1999).
Cassirer, Ernst, et al. (eds), *The Renaissance Philosophy of Man* (Chicago: University of Chicago Press, 1948).
Desmet, Christy, and Robert Sawyer (eds), *Harold Bloom's Shakespeare* (New York: Palgrave, 2001).

Dollimore, Jonathan, *Radical Tragedy*, 3rd edn (Basingstoke: Palgrave, [1984] 2004).
Fudge, Erica, et al. (eds), *At the Borders of the Human* (Basingstoke: Macmillan, 1999).
Giustiniani, V. R., '*Homo*, *Humanus*, and the Meanings of "Humanism"', *Journal of the History of Ideas*, 46 (1985), 167–95.
Grafton, Anthony and Lisa Jardine, *From Humanism to the Humanities: Education and the Liberal Arts in Fifteenth- and Sixteenth-Century Europe* (London: Duckworth, 1986).
Hankins, James, 'Two Twentieth-Century Interpreters of Renaissance Humanism: Eugenio Garin and Paul Oskar Kristeller', *Comparative Criticism*, 23, special issue: Humanist Traditions in the Twentieth Century, (2001), 3–19.
—— (ed.), *Renaissance Civic Humanism: Reappraisals and Reflections* (Cambridge: Cambridge University Press, 2000).
Knowles, Ronald, '*Hamlet* and Counter-Humanism', *Renaissance Quarterly*, 52 (1999), 1046–69.
Kraye, Jill (ed.), *The Cambridge Companion to Renaissance Humanism* (Cambridge: Cambridge University Press, 1996).
Kraye, Jill, and M. W. F. Stone (eds), *Humanism and Early Modern Philosophy* (London: Routledge, 2000).
Martindale, Charles, and A. B. Taylor (eds), *Shakespeare and the Classics* (Cambridge: Cambridge University Press, 2004).
O'Dair, Sharon, 'On the Value of Being a Cartoon, in Literature and Life', in *Harold Bloom's Shakespeare*, ed. Christy Desmet and Robert Sawyer (New York: Palgrave, 2001), pp. 81–96.
O'Malley, John W., et al. (eds), *Humanity and Divinity in Renaissance and Reformation* (Leiden: E. J. Brill, 1993).
Peltonen, Markku, *Classical Humanism and Republicanism in English Political Thought* (Cambridge: Cambridge University Press, 1995).
Pincombe, Mike, *Elizabethan Humanism* (London: Longman, 2001).
——, 'Some Sixteenth-Century Records of the Words *Humanist* and *Humanitian*', *Review of English Studies*, 44 (1993), 1–15.
Rabil, Albert, Jr (ed.), *Renaissance Humanism: Foundations, Forms and Legacy*, 3 vols (Philadelphia: University of Pennsylvania Press, 1988).
Ruiter, David, 'Harry's (In)human Face', in *Spiritual Shakespeares*, ed. Ewan Fernie (London: Routledge, 2005), pp. 50–72.
Schiffman, Zachary (ed.), *Humanism and the Renaissance* (Boston: Houghton Mifflin, 2002).
Wells, Robin Headlam, *Shakespeare's Humanism* (Cambridge: Cambridge University Press, 2005).
Wolfe, Jessica, *Humanism, Machinery, and Renaissance Literature* (Cambridge: Cambridge University Press, 2004).
Woolfson, Jonathan (ed.), *Reassessing Tudor Humanism* (Basingstoke: Palgrave, 2002).
Yoran, Hanan, 'Thomas More's *Richard III*: Probing the Limits of Humanism', *Renaissance Studies*, 15 (2001), 514–37.

Modernity; Shakespeare and Modernity

Adorno, Theodor, and Max Horkheimer, *Dialectic of Enlightenment*, trans. John Cumming (London: Verso, [1944] 1979).
Anderson, Amanda, *The Way We Argue Now* (Princeton: Princeton University Press, 2006).
Bauman, Zygmunt, *Liquid Love* (Cambridge: Polity, 2003).
Bentley, Jerry H., 'Renaissance Culture and Western Pragmatism', in *Humanity and Divinity in Renaissance and Reformation*, ed. John W. O'Malley et al. (Leiden: E. J. Brill, 1993), pp. 35–52.
Bruster, Douglas, *Drama and the Market in the Age of Shakespeare* (Cambridge: Cambridge University Press, 1992).
Engle, Lars, '*Measure for Measure* and Modernity: The Problem of the Sceptic's Authority', in *Shakespeare and Modernity*, ed. Hugh Grady (London: Routledge, 2000), pp. 85–104.
Grady, Hugh, (ed.), *Shakespeare and Modernity* (London: Routledge, 2000).
Grady, Hugh, *Shakespeare's Universal Wolf* (Oxford: Clarendon, 1996).
Greenblatt, Stephen, *Renaissance Self-Fashioning* (Chicago: University of Chicago Press, 1980).
Habermas, Jürgen, *The Philosophical Discourse of Modernity*, trans. Frederick Lawrence (Cambridge: Polity, [1985] 1987).
——, *The Theory of Communicative Action*, vol. 1, trans. Thomas McCarthy (Cambridge: Polity, [1981] 1984).
——, *The Theory of Communicative Action*, vol. 2, trans. Thomas McCarthy (Cambridge: Polity, [1981] 1987).
Halpern, Richard, *Shakespeare among the Moderns* (Ithaca: Cornell University Press, 1997).
Leinwand, Theodore B., *Theatre, Finance and Society in Early Modern England* (Cambridge: Cambridge University Press, 1999).
Oort, Richard van, 'Shakespeare and the Idea of the Modern', *New Literary History*, 37 (2006), 319–39.
Perry, Curtis, 'Commerce, Community, and Nostalgia in *The Comedy of Errors*', in *Money and the Age of Shakespeare: Essays in New Economic Criticism*, ed. Lynda Woodbridge (Basingstoke: Palgrave, 2003), pp. 39–51.
Rorty, Richard, *Contingency, Irony, and Solidarity* (Cambridge: Cambridge University Press, 1989).
Taylor, Charles, *Sources of the Self* (Cambridge: Cambridge University Press, 1989).
Tönnies, Ferdinand, *Community and Civil Society*, trans. Jose Harris and Margaret Hollis (Cambridge: Cambridge University Press, [1887] 2001).
Toulmin, Stephen, *Cosmopolis: The Hidden Agenda of Modernity* (Chicago: University of Chicago Press, 1990).
Weber, Max, *General Economic History*, trans. Frank H. Knight (London: George Allen and Unwin, 1927).

Emotion; Shakespeare and Emotion

Belsey, Catherine, *Desire: Love Stories in Western Culture* (Oxford: Blackwell, 1994).

Cummings, Brian, 'Animal Passions and Human Sciences: Shame, Blushing and Nakedness in Early Modern Europe and the New World', in *At the Borders of the Human*, ed. Erica Fudge et al. (Basingstoke: Macmillan, 1999), pp. 27–50.

Damasio, Antonio, *The Feeling of What Happens* (London: Vintage, 2000).

Greenblatt, Stephen, 'The Cultivation of Anxiety: King Lear and His Heirs', in his *Learning to Curse: Essays in Early Modern Culture* (New York: Routledge, 1990), pp. 80–98.

James, Heather, 'Dido's Ear: Tragedy and the Politics of Response', *Shakespeare Quarterly*, 52 (2001), 360–82.

McAlindon, Tom, 'Tragedy, *King Lear*, and the Politics of the Heart', *Shakespeare Survey*, 44 (1991), 85–90.

Nussbaum, Martha, *Upheavals of Thought: The Intelligence of the Emotions* (Cambridge: University Press, 2001).

Paster, Gail Kern, *Humoring the Body* (Chicago: University of Chicago Press, 2004).

——, et al. (eds), *Reading the Early Modern Passions* (Philadelphia: University of Pennsylvania Press, 2004).

Sprengnether, Madelon, 'Annihilating Intimacy in *Coriolanus*', in *Women in the Middle Ages and the Renaissance*, ed. Mary Beth Rose (Syracuse: Syracuse University Press, 1986), pp. 89–111.

Strier, Richard, 'Against the Rule of Reason: Praise of Passion from Petrarch to Luther to Shakespeare to Herbert', in *Reading the Early Modern Passions*, ed. Gail Kern Paster et al. (Philadelphia: University of Pennsylvania Press, 2004), pp. 23–42.

Terada, Rei, *Feeling in Theory: Emotion after the 'Death of the Subject'* (Cambridge, MA: Harvard University Press).

Shakespeare

Adelman, Janet, *Suffocating Mothers: Fantasies of Maternal Origin in Shakespeare's Plays, Hamlet to The Tempest* (New York: Routledge, 1992).

Barber, C. L., *Shakespeare's Festive Comedy* (Princeton: Princeton University Press, 1959).

Bate, Jonathan, *The Genius of Shakespeare* (London: Picador, 1997).

Bates, Catherine, 'Love and Courtship', in *The Cambridge Companion to Shakespearean Comedy*, ed. Alexander Leggatt (Cambridge: Cambridge University Press, 2002), pp. 102–22.

Belsey, Catherine, *Shakespeare and the Loss of Eden* (Basingstoke: Macmillan, 1999).

Berry, Edward, 'Laughing at "Others"', in *The Cambridge Companion to Shakespearean Comedy*, ed. Alexander Leggatt (Cambridge: Cambridge University Press, 2002), pp. 123–38.

——, *Shakespeare's Comic Rites* (Cambridge: Cambridge University Press, 1984).

Boorman, S. C., *Human Conflict in Shakespeare* (London: Routledge and Kegan Paul, 1987).

Bradley, A. C., *Shakespearean Tragedy*, 3rd edn (Basingstoke: Macmillan, [1904] 1992).
Bradshaw, Graham, *Misrepresentations: Shakespeare and the Materialists* (Ithaca: Cornell University Press, 1993).
——, *Shakespeare's Scepticism* (Brighton: Harvester, 1987).
Cavell, Stanley, *Disowning Knowledge in Six Plays of Shakespeare* (New York: Cambridge University Press, 1987).
Danby, John F., *Shakespeare's Doctrine of Nature* (London: Faber and Faber, 1949).
Engle, Lars, *Shakespearean Pragmatism: Market of His Time* (Chicago: Chicago University Press, 1993).
Fernie, Ewan (ed.), *Spiritual Shakespeares* (London: Routledge, 2005).
Fernie, Ewan, *Shame in Shakespeare* (London: Routledge, 2002).
Frye, Northrop, *A Natural Perspective: The Development of Shakespearean Comedy and Romance* (New York: Columbia University Press, 1965).
Girard, René, *A Theater of Envy: William Shakespeare*, 2nd edn (Leominster: Gracewing, [1991] 2000).
Goddard, Harold, *The Meaning of Shakespeare*, 2 vols (Chicago: University of Chicago Press, [1951] 1960).
Greenblatt, Stephen, *Will in the World* (London: Pimlico, 2005).
Hawkes, Terence (ed.), *Alternative Shakespeares*, vol. 2 (London: Routledge, 1996).
Howard, Jean E., and Scott Cutler Shershow (eds), *Marxist Shakespeares* (London: Routledge, 2001).
Joughin, John (ed.), *Philosophical Shakespeares* (London: Routledge, 2000).
Knight, G. Wilson, *The Crown of Life* (London: Methuen, [1947] 1948).
——, *The Wheel of Fire* (London: Oxford University Press, 1930).
Knights, L. C., *'Hamlet' and Other Shakespearean Essays* (Cambridge: Cambridge University Press, 1979).
Knowles, Ronald (ed.), *Shakespeare and Carnival: After Bakhtin* (Basingstoke: Macmillan, 1998).
Liebler, Naomi Conn, *Shakespeare's Festive Tragedy* (London: Routledge, 1995).
Loomba, Ania, *Shakespeare, Race, and Colonialism* (Oxford: Oxford University Press, 2002).
——, 'Outsiders in Shakespeare's England', in *The Cambridge Companion to Shakespeare*, ed. Margreta de Grazia and Stanley Wells (Cambridge: Cambridge University Press, 2001), pp. 147–66.
—— and Martin Orkin (eds), *Post-Colonial Shakespeares* (Routledge: London, 1998).
Margolies, David, *Monsters of the Deep* (Manchester: Manchester University Press, 1992).
Rossiter, A. P., *Angel with Horns*, ed. Graham Storey (London: Longman, [1961] 1989).
Ryan, Kiernan, *Shakespeare*, 3rd edn (Basingstoke: Palgrave, [1989] 2002).
Traub, Valerie, *Desire and Anxiety: Circulations of Sexuality in Shakespearean Drama* (London: Routledge, 1992).
Watson, Robert N., 'Tragedies of Revenge and Ambition', in *The Cambridge Companion to Shakespearean Tragedy*, ed. Claire McEachern (Cambridge: Cambridge University Press, 2002), pp. 160–81.

Index

Chapter 2
original sin
misuse of K
the easy way + the hard way
de Rom - a spectacular example of how not to live
C15th new kind of study to improve one's soul